THE GREEN APPLE TREE

A Memory That Refused
to Stay Buried

GENE FACKLER

Copyright © 2025 by Gene Fackler
All rights reserved.

Paperback: 978-1-7374272-2-3
eBook: 978-1-7374272-3-0
Library of Congress Control Number: 2025910793

No part of this publication may be reproduced, stored in a retrieval system, or transmitted in any form or by any means—electronic, mechanical, photocopying, recording, or otherwise—without the prior written permission of the copyright owner, except for brief quotations used in reviews or scholarly works.

This book is a work of fiction/nonfiction. Names, characters, places, and incidents are either the product of the author's imagination or used fictitiously. Any resemblance to actual persons, living or dead, events, or locales is purely coincidental.

This book is 100% the intellectual property of the author.

All publishing rights and ownership of the content remain solely with the author.

Design and Interior formatting services provided by:
Sweetspire Literature Management

To Judith and Helen, Chelsea angels

TABLE OF CONTENTS

Summer 1986 1

    Introduction 3

Late Spring 1963 9

    Chapter 1 11
    Chapter 2 36
    Chapter 3 60
    Chapter 4 85
    Chapter 5 115
    Chapter 6 137
    Chapter 7 176
    Chapter 8 205
    Chapter 9 249
    Chapter 10 288

    Epilogue 321

Summer 1986

INTRODUCTION

The glass door hissed shut, and the cold air and darkness pulled him in like a selfish lover. He stepped blindly through the short, contrived foyer, navigating by sliding the knuckles of his right hand along the paneling. At the end, he pushed aside the weighted curtain and stepped through, then waited for his eyes to adjust to the dim light.

Slowly, a bar emerged in the collage of fractured neon. Forms shifting in the glow would turn and reveal faces that would spin away just as he was beginning to comprehend them. A winding path through the mismatched tables and chairs finally presented itself, and he headed for the end of the bar along the far wall, away from the clattering pool balls and the hillbilly whine of the jukebox. He pulled out the next-to-last stool, and the bartender—goateed and smiling—sauntered over and flipped a coaster onto the scarred oak.

"A Lone Star, please."

He had worn a dark suit to The General's funeral out of respect but had forgotten how cruel and unrelenting the Texas heat was in August. Worsted wool was consistently comfortable in Chicago, but not here. He had turned the A/C in his rental car to full blast during his way to the funeral in an attempt to dry out his shirt, but left the jacket hanging in the car. It was soaked with sweat and wouldn't be dry by the time he boarded his flight back to Chicago. Not in this godawful humidity.

First things first.

He took a sip of beer, then scanned the room in the backbar mirror. On his way over, he had passed by a blonde immersed in conversation with a man in a business suit, and full dilation now confirmed that she was an easy eight, or maybe even a nine, which eliminated her from consideration. Anything above a four or a five wouldn't grant enough leeway. Besides, the highball in her hand had a Shirley Temple tint, and she was dressed for the office, and even if that provocative face hadn't disqualified her, there was no way she would be around when he really needed her. She was probably on a lunch-hour tryst, seeking anonymity in a dive she normally wouldn't be caught dead in.

He passed on two or three more, then turned his attention to a redhead smoking a cigarette and sipping a gimlet in the booth along the wall behind

him. As a plain Jane, she qualified in appearance, but the size of the four empty glasses in front of her implied doubles, and she was undulating from the waist up like a snake charmer's cobra.

She'd be gone soon too, and not back to a job.

What he needed was a woman who would still be around in two or three hours when he really would need her. A woman with stamina.

He was on his second beer and considering recruiting the bikinied, lasso- twirling cowgirl on the Shiner Beer calendar taped to the cash register when she walked in. He watched in the mirror as she approached the bar in an unerring clip and took the third stool down on his left. She was a brunette, probably in her mid-thirties and with tired eyes, but there was still an aura of faded beauty.

The drink the bartender began mixing when he saw her walk in turned out to be a Gibson. She took a sip when it arrived, then pulled a pack of Marlboros out of her purse. The bartender held a flame to the tip of the cigarette she slipped between her lips, then turned toward the clatter of the stools being pulled out at the far end of the bar.

He watched in the mirror as she set her elbows on the dark wood and blew a thin stream of smoke toward the ceiling.

When her head came back down, her eyes settled into the netherworld of the mirror, and he knew she wouldn't be going anywhere anytime soon.

Well, hel-looo, Miss Drunk-ometer. When you hit a seven—aw, hell, make it an eight—it's time to give Virgin Mary a call.

#

He had always wondered how old The General was, and now he knew. The blown-up obituary mounted on the easel at the church presented his date of inception as July 6th, 1887, meaning The General would have been seventy-six in the summer of 1963. And now, after almost a hundred years on this earth, he was gone.

But not that summer. It was still in the air, radiating off the pavement just as it had when the parking lot that once fronted a scooter shop instead of this bar, as immutable as a recurring dream.

#

It was Pete who had called with the news of The General's passing. They didn't have much in common anymore—Pete had zeroed in on a law degree after they graduated high school—but had been close friends for too long for that to matter, staying in touch through occasional phone calls, randomly instigated and often alcohol-induced. Were it not for that, he would have missed the funeral. His parents had sold the house on James Place and moved to Florida right after his high school graduation, leaving Pete as his last remaining link to Fuller and the limestone hills south of the Nebraska River.

It had been seventeen years since he had dropped out of Texas College, married, fathered a son, and gone north for an airline job. His first stop was Chicago's O'Hare, where schlepping bags through a brutal winter inspired an escape to sales in Manhattan. Then, ten years later, a painful divorce and the move back to Chicago to his current office in the Loop.

After the service, he had told Pete there was something important he needed to tell him.

"Okay," Pete replied. "Let's meet up at Dad's old scooter shop."

That's what this seedy dive had been in '63, before the plate-glass windows were boarded over with plywood and the entrance partitioned to block out the light and the polished concrete floor was arrayed with Cushmans, Vespas, and Ducatis instead of cheap bar furniture coated with cigarette tar. Pete's father did well until cars started to shrink and scooter and motorbike sales to plummet, then held on as long as he could and finally shut the doors and went back to selling insurance. The building became a restaurant after that, then a florist shop, then a plumbing supply store, then God knows what.

He was in Chicago by then.

Before the divorce, in both Chicago and Manhattan, he had rented in neighborhoods that offered a short rail commute to his job in the city, and the corner bars, glass-fronted and inviting, were as essential as the churches and temples they often abutted, offering secular souls a spiritual refuge as well.

So different from Texas.

Rat traps, that's all these suburban bars amounted to, a species apart from the fancy downtown bistros packed with hobnobbing lawyers or the rowdy honky-tonks wailing along the country roads. Segregated by zoning from schools, churches, and anything else claiming innocence and purity, it was as if their sole purpose was to lure vermin off the roads and out of the public eye. They might occasionally change ownership or close to be brought up to code, but they would never lack for customers. Survival was assured.

He glanced at the Coors Beer clock above the mirror, then tilted his wristwatch into the light. The Coors clock was set to bar time, giving a fifteen-minute leeway to clear out the drunks before closing time kicked in.

Pete had said he had a court appearance that shouldn't take more than two or three hours, and he'd be over after that. No time at all, when juxtaposed against the twenty-three years that had passed since the Riverside Drive murders. What difference could a few more hours make?

He slid his eyes across the mirror to the brunette three stools down.

Good. Still a solid five, and still sipping those Gibsons away in a world of her own.

He brought his eyes back and let them sink into the mirror, like hers, in search of an escape from the meaningless laughter, the empty and wasted time, and soon the chaotic rhythms of a long past summer poured into the void.

It was as if the scooter shop had opened up behind him.

Late Spring 1963

CHAPTER 1

Through the splintered light of breaking sleep, the outline of the bomber was muddled, incoherent, even threatening to his slowly gathering consciousness. He pressed his fingertips to sleep-swollen eyes and massaged them to some degree of function, then returned his gaze to the ceiling.

Now the scene was familiar: the besieged B-17 banking into a shallow dive with a Messerschmitt on its tail and a Focke-Wulf attacking off the starboard side, unaware of the P-38 swooping in at two o'clock high.

He brought his head off the pillow and looked across the room. High in the opposite corner in dim shadow, the Lafayette Escadrille, led by Rickenbacker's Spad, was still battling for control of the skies over France, frozen in mortal combat with Baron Richthofen's triplane and the other German fighters that had been assembled and assigned to his squadron.

He kicked the sheet down to his ankles and lay motionless, savoring the subtle chill as the light sweat rose from his body, naked except for yesterday's Jockey shorts.

Location now established, he had yet to determine chronology, and for this, visual clues, if any, would be less obvious. He sat up in bed, folded his arms across his knees, and began to scan the dimly lit room for nothing in particular.

He didn't sense the pall of an impending school day, so Saturday morning was the first assumption, and then he shifted his focus to the walnut desktop under the battle-weary skies of France, seeking out the large stack of textbooks that always accompanied him home on weekends. His antidote for forgotten assignments was an overkill of reference; his locker at school was left virtually empty on Friday afternoons.

Nothing was silhouetted against the white plaster wall. The desktop was bare.

Now he remembered. The books had been turned in on Tuesday, the last day of school was Thursday, so this had to be Friday morning, meaning that Thomas Kessler was now a high school junior with the entire summer ahead of him.

Hot DAMN!

He slammed back down on the bed and drove his head into the pillow from the pure joy of it all, and was considering a return to sleep when he became aware of a dissonance reverberating through the window facing the street.

He looked over at his alarm clock. 7:43 AM, it read.

So THAT'S why I woke up so early.

Undisturbed, he was fully capable of sleeping away an entire day, or whatever portion of the morning his father's patience would allow.

He rolled to the edge of the bed, swung his feet to the floor, then stumbled over a boot on his way to the window. The room flooded with light when he raised the blinds, and when he knelt at the sill and pressed his nose to the screen, the heavy morning air was quick to divulge the nature of the commotion.

Across the cul-de-sac, from their chain-link pen in the backyard, Lowry's dogs were carrying on with more than their usual enthusiasm, given the time of day.

He retrieved the jeans draped over his desk chair, pulled socks and undershorts out of his dresser, a shirt from his closet, then stepped into the hall and entered the bathroom with his wardrobe clutched to his chest and the tops of his cowboy boots dangling from his teeth. After showering and dressing, he walked through the living room and into the kitchen, then pulled the back door open and stepped down into the garage.

It was The Colonel's garage, orderly and disciplined, and with the exception of a whitewashed plywood cabinet by the kitchen door, all rights of access were governed by strict rules of usage. His father had sorted and interred in a vast assortment of containers—coffee cans, cigar boxes, glass jars, tobacco tins—every bolt, scrap of wire, every washer, nut, and nail he had ever encountered, assuming some future use. Tools were likewise sorted and suspended on a sheet of plywood attached to the wall, and hisfa ther could detect a misplaced tool with an ability that Thomas found irritating, but inspiring.

Thomas leaned out of the open garage door and caught sight of his father, known to most as The Colonel, with pruning tool in hand, searching the spindly boughs of the live oak trees in the front yard for limbs lost to a rare hard freeze in March. His mother was nearby on her hands and knees, edging the stone walkway with a pair of grass shears.

He stood motionless until he was sure he hadn't been spotted, then eased back out of sight, glad that for now the garage was his. Malicious intent required secrecy, and he preferred the complete abandonment of a project to the creation of an impromptu fiction that would withstand his father's scrutiny.

He stood amid his available resources and pondered his objective. What would it take to disconcert an asshole dense enough to remain oblivious to a cacophony loud enough to wake up somebody halfway up the block?

It would probably take a bomb.

Or more precisely, a projectile. Like a grenade, maybe. Preferably loud, but not incendiary. Disruptive, but not destructive. And definitely of indeterminate origin.

A quick scan revealed some candidates for a casing. His mother's empty canning jars were on the shelf over the freezer, but were quickly ruled out. They might shatter when they hit the ground and would be too fragmentary anyway. His father's stock of empty coffee cans under the workbench was quickly discounted as well. The shards would bear the base commissary brand, and besides, the odds were good—no, excellent—that his father would notice the shortage. Then there was his own collection of spent cartridge cases in various calibers that would require little or no modification—simply pour in the powder, insert a fuse through the primer hole, and crimp the throat shut. The downside was that actual shell casings might raise the stakes. There was no point in bringing the Feds in on this.

The ululations down the street had settled into a chorus of low howls, and he felt his righteous rage ebbing. He needed to hurry.

His father's table saw was positioned toward the back of the garage in an area comparatively free of clutter, and beside it, a cardboard box full of wood scraps awaited their October transplant to the hearth as kindling.

Thomas pulled the carton along the floor to an open space in front of the workbench. His father had recently cut some two-by-fours to equal length for a masonry form for a limestone wall around his mother's rosebushes at the foot of the driveway, and he salvaged fifteen pieces before returning the box to its proper place beside the table saw.

He quickly hammered together two cubes, four nails to a side, with a sixth side left open to receive the explosive charge. For this, he relied on the generosity of an uncle in Minnesota who, five summers before, had bequeathed to him two hundred reloaded twelve-gauge skeet loads. They had already seen fifteen years of shelf life—his uncle had long abandoned the sport, and over half the rounds proved to be duds, but only the primers were bad.

Thomas swung the doors to his whitewashed cabinet open and groped along the top shelf until he connected with one of the worn cartons, then pried the lid open and drew out six shells. Five rounds yielded enough powder to fill the first wooden cube, and after drilling a small hole and inserting a Black Cat fuse, he nailed the last piece on.

Thomas wrapped the cube with duct tape pirated from his father's tool chest, then flipped it into the air to gauge the heft.

For the sake of experimentation, the second cube should be of a different design, Thomas felt, and he opted for a more potent version. Black powder had long been replaced by smokeless in ammunition, but it nonetheless possessed a volatility that would better abet mayhem. Little compression was needed to produce an explosion, and the billowing smoke that ensued always smelled like a fart.

He retrieved the can of black powder he used in his muzzle-loaders and old Colts and filled the chamber of the second cube, then installed the fuse and nailed on the sixth side. He still felt the need to add compression but had already depleted his father's duct tape to the acceptable limit. Then he saw something even better.

He walked to the back of the garage and removed two clothes hangers suspended over his mother's washer and dryer. He cut and straightened them, then bound the cubes tightly on all sides, twisting with a pair of needle-nosed pliers until the wire sank into the edges of the dry pine.

The arsenal was ready.

Thomas set his grenades out of sight under the workbench, then opened the door and stepped into the kitchen.

#

"Morning, honey."

Agnes Kessler had finished her yard work and was at the sink, rinsing pieces of chicken under the tap. She gave him a cheerful smile. "What's going on in the garage?"

"Hi, Mom. I just need a paper bag. I'm cleaning out my cabinet. You wouldn't believe the junk." He pulled up a chair and retrieved a grocery bag from the top of the refrigerator.

"Have you eaten anything this morning? How about some toast and eggs? We've got grapefruit."

"No thanks. I'll just grab something later. Thanks anyway, Mom." "Okay. Love you, honey."

"Love you too, Mom."

Thomas stepped back into the garage and bagged the grenades, then as he stepped out onto the driveway, he realized he had forgotten something and returned to the garage.

His father kept a large box of strike-anywhere matches on his workbench, and Thomas pulled five out and slipped them into his shirt pocket before returning to the driveway.

He had forgotten that the front yard was currently off-limits and froze in mid-stride as the sight of his father's tanned back came into view beneath a live oak as he was raking the trimmed branches into a pile.

Thomas darted back into the garage, then peeked around the door once again to make sure he hadn't been spotted. If The Colonel had seen the paper bag, his curiosity would have forced Thomas to expose the contents, and the mission would have had to be aborted. And even if he was able to explain why his wooden blocks were benign, he would probably have been drafted for yard work.

His father continued raking mechanically, and Thomas sought an alternate route. If the end of their cul-de-sac was twelve o'clock, then their house would be at ten-thirty. To the south of Thomas's street, one block to the east, was an identical cul-de-sac called Charles Place, and beyond that was Casey Lane. These three streets all fed into Ridgewest Drive, the major north-south artery of western Kensington Oaks. To the west of Thomas's block, also running north-south, was a long, gradually rising ridge overlaid with a jungle of thick juniper and cedar. Beyond this greenbelt, along the apex of the ridge, ran Crest Road, which rose out of Kensington Road from the south and ran the length of the ridge before falling back down at the northern end and sweeping to the east as Casey Lane.

Along the eastern base of the ridge, weaving in and out of the trees well away from the homes, a serpentine trail ran the length of the greenbelt. The origin of the trail was unknown, but toward the southern end, just beyond the neighboring cul-de-sac, a ramshackle shed housed the hulking, rusty pump that supplied well water to the thirty-odd houses along the ridge. Common wisdom deemed that the trail had been cut by the well-drilling crew, and it was consequently referred to as the "pump-path" in the neighborhood vernacular. Regardless of origin, it was an invaluable shortcut for students needing to reach the bus stop at the corner of Kensington and Crest Roads, where the southern end of the pump-path terminated. And for someone with a more hostile intent, the northern terminus of the pump-path spilled into the half-paved portion of Casey Lane, and Casey Lane was where Thomas determined he needed to be.

He stepped over the low limestone wall that girded the western edge of their property and mounted the pump-path where it passed along the base of the wooded ridge, some thirty feet beyond their property line. His departure would be undetected from the front yard, shielded by the trees and houses at the end of the block, and Thomas allowed the paper bag to swing easily from his left hand as he negotiated the overgrown trail, shoving the smaller branches aside with his free hand, ducking others too large to be handily bent. The buses wouldn't run again for months, at least not the school buses, and he wouldn't be sharing the trail with anyone but house pets and rabbit hunters, which were often one and the same. Sure enough, fifty yards down the pump-path Thomas encountered Hank Alder's beagle-terrier mix returning from a morning excursion, head lowered and tongue dangling as he trotted for home, not acknowledging Thomas's presence in any discernible way.

Thirty seconds and two hundred feet of tangled trail later, Thomas set the grocery bag at his feet, freeing his hands for a smoke as he stood at the edge of the unpaved half of Casey Lane.

#

The story came down to Thomas through a conversation between his father and the real estate agent who had sold them the house. Thomas was twelve when his family moved to "the hills," that so-called region south and west of the Nebraska River where the prehistoric fault that tore the ancient Texas seabed apart seventy million years before had vented the preponderance of its fury. Then, as now, he found most exchanges between adults to be boring and tedious, but this particular tale featured behavior bizarre enough to earn a place in his easily distracted memory banks.

Thomas, his father, and the agent were standing in the front yard amid the limestone rock and cedar brush that were soon to be raising calluses on the Colonel's hands. The talk was general and eventually touched on one of the peculiarities of the neighborhood . . .

#

. . . *"Mister Blaylock, you know that half-paved road a block over? I forget the street name offhand—might not have ever noticed it."*

"You don't need to remember it, Colonel. I know which one you mean. There's not but one half-done road around here. Lots of 'em underdone or just plain raw, but only one half-done." Mister Blaylock was a rotund and jovial man upon whom one could bestow every adjective bearing the curse of an indulgent middle age. Add a tacky checkered sports jacket and tobacco-stained teeth set in a broad and constant smile, and Thomas was attracted to him by nothing more than his total lack of conceit.

"Casey Lane's the name," Mister Blaylock continued, *"and the street lies almost wholly within the corporate limits of Kensington Oaks, all except for that little unpaved part you're referring to. That part's in the corporate limits of Granite Heights, and it just so happens*

the borderline of these two municipalities runs right smack down the middle of that little stretch of road, thanks to an oddball dogleg in the original plats." Blaylock paused and squinted into the summer sun, then pulled a soiled handkerchief from his hip pocket. He wiped his brow with a fresh fold before venting the contents of his sinuses. "Well, back when these hills started to show enough promise that paved roads seemed economically prudent, the developers stumbled onto this little bit of dual ownership in the survey plats, and Kensington Oaks asked Granite Heights to cough up for their share of blacktop. Remember now, we're talking about a strip of asphalt maybe ten feet wide and not even an eighth of a mile long."

"Well, Granite Heights didn't have any houses built along their little strip of Casey Lane—for that matter, they still don't—and the owner of that land is just sitting on it. It's not cut up into lots, and as far as I know, it won't be any time in the foreseeable future. So the boys over in Granite Heights said No to chipping in, and you really can't blame 'em. No point in laying good road down in front of raw cedar brake."

Thomas picked up a rock and side-armed it at a roadrunner that had darted into the yard with a lizard in its beak. The rock missed the bird, then ricocheted off a live oak stump and sailed over Blaylock's brown Studebaker, missing the roof by inches.

Thomas stiffened and waited for the conversation to tell him if his slip of judgment had been noticed.

"But if Granite Heights didn't want to pave their half, why would Kensington Oaks pave any of it?" the Colonel protested. "It seems to me that a half-paved road is no better than one not paved at all."

Thomas breathed out slowly and picked up another rock.

"Besides," the Colonel continued, "there's only that one house on the Kensington Oaks side. And so what if his driveway is on the paved side of Casey? What good is entering on pavement when you have to pull out onto rough caliche when you leave? Or white mud if it's raining? I'd like to know what the fellow who lives in that house has to say about it."

Blaylock produced the handkerchief again and widened his grin as he applied it to his constantly weeping brow. "Well, to understand that, I suppose it helps to know something of the feller who lives there. Man's name is Sherman, and he's one of the major builders in Kensington Oaks. Hell, half the houses on Ridgewest Drive were put up by him at a time when this area had its first real growth. He's done right well for himself."

Blaylock fumbled a pack of Lucky Strikes from his shirt pocket and shook out a cigarette, or rather two cigarettes: one fell beside his right boot while he placed the other between his lips. He glanced at the ground, pausing as if to estimate the degree of exertion for retrieval, then produced a book of matches announcing Sid's Olde Tailor Shoppe for Large Men from his coat pocket and lit up.

"Like a smoke, Colonel?"

"Thank you, no. I've my own when I'm so inclined."

Thomas's father smoked at least a pack a day, plus a cigar or two after dinner on most nights, but for some reason shunned tobacco when in the company of those not falling into the categories of family or friend, confirming what Thomas had already known: Mister Blaylock was not the type of person the Colonel would ever promote beyond a purely incidental relationship. He was too brash and undisciplined to be included in his father's roster of respectable and generally boring cohorts. But Mister Blaylock came highly recommended, and the Colonel never considered using anyone else while shopping for what he swore would be their final roost. Nobody, it was said, absolutely nobody, knew as much about the area and its real estate as Clayton Blaylock. But Mister Blaylock was, as his mother would say, a "hoot."

"You've been by that house, Colonel." Blaylock's smile didn't exactly leave, but it did fade noticeably. "Ever notice anything unusual about the decorum?"

Thomas caught himself in the instinctive act of raising his hand. He was sure he had the answer, but choked it back, acknowledging his father's priority in the exchange.

"Yes, I've had occasion to drive by that house. It's quite a home, probably three thousand square feet or more, and at least one Cadillac in the driveway. But beyond that, I don't recall anything out of the ordinary." "The bear?"

Thomas had shifted around to face the two men and was gazing timidly toward the ground. He knew the risks of entering into adult conversation uninvited and cloaked himself in the guise of unworthy innocence whenever he did so.

"Yep, that's it, all right, uh, uh—" Blaylock waggled a finger at Thomas, soliciting a clue.

"Thomas."

"Thomas! Right. Thanks, uh, Thomas. Ring a bell, Colonel?"

"Of course. The beast fills up an entire plate glass window. I've never been one to take note of hunting trophies—things like a waste of space to me—but you can hardly miss one that pretentious."

If Thomas didn't know what "pretentious" meant before, he thought he did now. Anyone driving by the Sherman house on the Casey Lane side was offered a full-length display of a Boone and Crockett polar bear mounted fully erect, with fangs bared and claws extended and reaching. The first time Thomas had found himself in its stare, he froze unblinking for whatever amount of time it took to realize that the bear was only some taxidermist's rendition of furious rage. He had passed the window hundreds of times since, but the bear never failed to command his attention.

"Well, that bear was bagged not too long after Sherman finished that house, and after it was installed, somebody, probably Sherman himself, tipped off the Fuller Dispatch about this record-breaking monster of a bear staring out of a plate glass window out in Kensington Oaks. And of course they sent out one of their greenest cub reporters to cover this little bit of local interest, somebody who wouldn't know any better than just to write down verbatim what he was told—didn't know to fish the waters a little bit deeper, so to speak.

"Anyway, the following Saturday the front page of the local lah-dee-dah section of the paper sports a big photo of Sherman and his bear, with Sherman holding a pistol across his chest and kneeling down beside an Eskimo guide, both of 'em smiling like Cheshire cats. The article is pretty short and dry, telling what part of Alaska the bear was taken in and the listing in the record books. Then the last couple of lines told that the bear was killed by two shots to the head with a twenty-two pistol. I seem to recall that the article mentioned that the bear was in the water at the time, but that was it.

"Well, hell, I thought, this scrawny little home builder was sure encumbered by a pair of muy grande huevos, if not a downright suicidal love of the hunt. That sort of thing always plays well in this part of Texas, what with so many deer hunters and all.

"So anyway, the whole town's properly impressed, me included, till about a year and a half ago. I'm down at James's Barber Shop on Arroyo Blanco Road getting a trim, and this feller in Charlie's chair spots the aforementioned newspaper article framed and hanging on the wall, grouped with several others featuring the shop's regulars that happened to get their picture in the paper. For meritorious reasons only, of course. There weren't any mugshots.

"Well, this feller, who was in town on business, just so happened to be on that same hunt with Sherman—hell, he recognized the bear in the picture first. Said it had distinctive markings around the muzzle. Anyway, this guy had never read the newspaper account, and he goes into talking about how this critter happened to back into the kind of bad luck only your mother-in- law should have."

Blaylock paused long enough to step over to the nearest live oak and crush his cigarette out on its trunk. Thomas sidled nonchalantly over to where Blaylock had been standing and sat down on a cedar stump, folding his arms across his knees.

The salesman set the live oak between his shoulder blades and continued: "Seems there were two hunting parties in whaling boats that day, the one Sherman's in and this fellow's. They had spent the day on an iceberg and were on their way back to the base camp when they come across this humongous bear out in the middle of nowhere—ten, twenty miles from the nearest chunk of ice big enough to hold him—and he's ninety-nine percent drowned by the time they see him. This feller says that was nothing unusual, that polar bears could swim like that for days, but not this one. Whether real sick or just real old, he wasn't long for this world.

"The rest ain't too hard to figure out. Sherman's boat was out front, and this bear starts paddling over to it with what little strength he's got left. And he wasn't a threat, this feller says. The gunwale was a good three feet above the water line, which was three feet higher than this bear was capable of climbing. The poor animal was just looking for something to hang onto, and he was more scared of drowning than he was of people.

"So Sherman's barking orders to the guides, and they're shaking out loops in their lassos, and this feller said he thought Sherman was doing what he would have done, that is, shore this pathetic creature up alongside and tow it to something solid to either die or resuscitate itself back into something worth shooting at.

"But as the bear gets close enough to get a couple of lassos on, Sherman leans over and POP! POP!—shoots that bear point blank in each eye with a twenty-two pistol.

"Okay, this feller says. The other option, the old coop-dee-grass—put him out of his misery, give him to the natives to feed and clothe their families, and earn their undying gratitude and a discount on the guide fee in return."

In spite of the obvious glee derived from his own oratory, Blaylock's inability to regulate his body temperature was forecasting a premature conclusion to his little suburban fable. With his jacket now soaked in sweat, Blaylock produced the handkerchief one last time, but with a more pronounced flourish.

"So Charlie finishes this guy's haircut and he unfolds himself out of the chair, says the last he saw of Sherman and his bear was back at camp as he was handing his duffel bags to the bush pilot taking him back to Fairbanks. Some of the Eskimos were trying to muscle the bear into an impressive pose while Sherman was setting up a tripod.

"And that's the end of it. The feller takes his brush-off, pays Charlie, and takes one last look at the picture on his way to the door. He just stares at it for a moment, real quiet-like, then shakes his head and walks out."

Blaylock inhaled deeply and wiped the sweat from around a victorious smile, by far his broadest yet, but this time he remained silent, his face frozen in rapture, and Thomas sensed his father's resentment of this obvious ploy to manipulate a response.

"That's all well and good, Mister Blaylock," the Colonel finally replied, "but what does all that have to do with the existence of that dad-blamed section of half-paved road?"

Blaylock's face wound down to a less playful demeanor, the hint of a smirk struggling to break the surface of his ruddy, wrinkled countenance. "Well, Colonel, my carrying-on was intended to help render a judgment as to what type of person would only half-pave a road to begin with."

Blaylock's face had just begun to draw up into its exaggerated grin, anticipating another pause, when Thomas's father shot back: "And just what type of person is that, Mister Blaylock?" Blaylock's half-smile stalled momentarily, then swelled into full bloom.

"A chickenshit, I'd say!"

#

Thomas pulled his pack of Kents out of the left front pocket of his jeans. Hiding his smoking from his parents required his tobacco products to conform to the contours of his angular physique, and this particular batch was on its third day of compaction. He pulled a wrinkled cigarette through the ragged foil and slipped it into his lips, then popped a match ablaze on his belt buckle and set the flame under the tip. When he drew in, the hot, dry smoke told him the paper tube had maintained its integrity.

Thomas rammed the cigarette pack back into his pocket, then looked east, up Casey Lane, a flattened hand to his brow to block the glare. It was clear all the way to the corner. He retrieved the grocery sack from his shoulder and started walking with the Kent dangling loosely from his lips, the hot smoke curling over his nose, bringing his eyes into a deep squint.

Goddamn Kents. Blaylock's Lucky was better than this.

Blaylock's Lucky. Thomas wondered if everybody remembered their first cigarette, if they remembered it the way everybody says you remember your first piece of ass. What a prize, laying there white and perfect and fresh between two chunks of limestone, beckoning to his latent manhood, a seductive, forbidden siren. Blaylock had turned to his car, the Colonel back toward the house, and Blaylock's Lucky was his. That evening, he had tried to smoke it while standing on the commode with his head next to an open window, but after two stomach-churning puffs, the cherished Lucky was flushed down the crapper.

Nothing worthwhile comes easy. The Colonel himself had said that.

Now Thomas's habit was limited only by availability and logistics, which allowed about ten cigarettes a day during the school week, twice that on weekends. He considered his limited tobacco sources, especially now that summer had arrived, and felt a subtle stirring in his gut at the thought of running out. *It's no big deal. It's not like I'm hooked or something.* Nonetheless, he promised himself to bolster his supply enough to get him through the summer, at least.

Thomas drew another dose of the acrid smoke into his lungs as he moved along the unpaved side of Casey Lane, the crushed limestone grinding under his boot heels. Still no traffic at the intersection of Casey and Ridgewest, where shared dominion ended and the caliche abruptly vanished under Kensington Oaks blacktop.

Thomas's strategy was hastily conceived and simple. First, navigate the cedar brake to a position within throwing range of the dog pen; second, launch the missiles in rapid succession (noting their effect for future applications); and lastly, although utmost in importance, abandon the vicinity in a fashion commensurate with the consequences.

When he reached the point in the road directly opposite the crescendo of yaps and howls on the far side of the thicket, he stepped onto the shoulder.

He had lucked out. An unusually arid spring had kept the undergrowth to a minimum and even offered several vague trails. The first one he followed led to a dead end, but the second brought him into a rough clearing that, while barely a yard in diameter, would enable an unobstructed launch in comfortable anonymity. It couldn't have been better if he had carved it out himself.

Through the thick screen of brush, Thomas could only confirm the rough outline of a tall chain-link enclosure set against the back of the red brick house, and there was no discernible movement or shape within the confined area that would translate into fur and bone. Just the yapping.

He knelt to one knee and removed the grenades from the grocery bag and set both on a limestone slab, fuses up, then pulled two matches from his shirt pocket and placed them between his teeth. He looked through the opening over his head, calculating arc and distance, and picked up the first, less potent grenade and began passing it from palm to palm, familiarizing himself with its heft, imagining the characteristics of its flight. His first impulse favored a blind launch into the open backyard, since he had no desire to hit the dog pen itself, but decided that would risk hitting a window or a sliding glass door—either directly or on the rebound from an unseen concrete patio—and increase his chances for a summer vacation in the Fuller juvenile facility.

Then he saw it—a large live oak at the northern edge of the property with branches that reached halfway across the backyard—an easy target that would receive his missile and pass it gently from limb to limb, as Thomas was now passing it from hand to hand, and deliver it onto green grass under soothing shade, to explode in whatever degree Thomas's design mandated. A fifty-foot lob angled slightly to the left of the benchmark ruckus of the dogs should do it.

Thomas garnered his resolve and rose to his feet. He plucked a match from his lips with his left hand and flipped the block around in his right, searching for the optimum grip. He swiped the match across his buckle with a shaking hand—it took three tries—and cradled the flame in the quivering cup of his fist until it stabilized. Then he took a deep breath, cocked his arm, and brought the match slowly over. His palms were dripping sweat.

The fuse erupted in sparks as soon as he slid it into the flame, and he arced the grenade out of the thicket.

Thomas dropped to his knees and watched the block tumble lazily out of the hole at the top of the thicket, a thin stream of smoke trailing in its wake, and as it fell from view, a wave of irreversible commitment, at once thrilling and terrifying, seized him. Seconds later, a dull *whump* could be more felt than heard through the tight thicket, and a churning cloud of gray smoke billowed quickly into view within the upper branches of the big live oak and swirled away. Thomas remained in his crouch until the frenzy of the dogs subsided, then picked up the second grenade, again setting his grip.

There was no sound of human activity on the other side of the thicket. He plucked the second match from his teeth and rose to his feet.

This time was different. Light-headed with adrenaline, he watched as if in a dream as a detached hand popped the match ablaze on the first pass across his brass buckle and held the frantic flame until it steadied. The dogs' howls were gone now, replaced by the machine gun-pounding of his heart against his eardrums, sealing out reality, consequences.

He lit the fuse and hurled the last grenade the way of the first. As the block left his hand and flew out of the thicket, events unfolded quickly.

The world returned with a distant yet recognizable clack and clatter—the unlatching and rolling back of a sliding glass door—in perfect concert with his final glimpse of the grenade as it plunged out of sight.

Thomas's senses came back with a jolt.

Next, a hollow *clunk,* as wood on concrete, told Thomas that he had missed the live oak.

Then, from the far side of the brake:

"Ho-LEEE SHIT!"

Thomas turned toward the half-paved road, moving methodically, precisely. Midway through his second stride, the impressive blast impacting the woods behind him was punctuated by the violent scrape and thud of the sliding glass door. A luxuriant cloud of white niter boiled into the air behind him, and bits of shattered pine fell over the thicket like a soft spring rain. As he stepped into the sun at the edge of Casey Lane, the dogs began again.

Thomas checked the urge to bolt as the adrenaline raced his pulse and threatened his control; again, the gritty clatter of the heavy glass across its track, barely audible through the insanity now radiating from the dog pen.

"I'M GONNA GET YOU, YOU LITTLE SUNUVABITCH! YOU HEAR ME? YOUR ASS IS MINE!"

Thomas's face flared to a broad grin at this affirmation of a successful campaign, and the insult was filed away for future retributions. He waited for a car stopped at the intersection of Casey and Ridgewest to move out of view, then crossed the half-paved road at a diagonal and began deliberate and instinctively timed travel up Grady Way, heading north, planting his boots one in front of the other in the perfectly formed concrete gutters of Kensington Oaks.

He was seventy-five feet up Grady Way when he thought he heard the muted slamming of Lowry's patrol car door, knew he had when the big Commando engine roared to life seconds later. He quickened his pace and watched it play out in his head: Lowry pulling the car onto the uneven asphalt of James Place; Lowry wheeling the big Plymouth through the broad circle of the cul-de-sac, then picking up speed for the short downhill dash to the stop sign at Ridgewest Drive. For the moment, the Plymouth's exhaust went silent.

He was two hundred feet up Grady Way and envisioning Lowry turning left onto Ridgewest when he lifted his hand in response to a salutation from an elderly woman he knew only as Miz Groves. She was on her knees in baggy denim overalls, planting bulbs in a newly turned bed along the edge of her front porch.

"Beautiful day, huh, Miz Groves?"

Miz Groves ceased undulating her fingers in greeting and wiped the gloved hand across her brow. "Yes, Thomas, but already warmer than I'd like. Well, enjoy your day."

"Yes, ma'am. You too."

As Thomas passed Miz Groves's yard, his mind beheld the Plymouth proceeding through the intersection and turning left onto the paved portion of Casey Lane. Then suddenly the bass rumble of the big V-8 was audible again, pure, unfettered by the thicket that had bought him thirty, maybe forty seconds of invincibility. When the pulse of the motor suddenly dropped to little more than an idle, Thomas knew Lowry was slowing for the turn onto Grady Way.

GODDAMMIT! Why couldn't the bastard go STRAIGHT?

Four houses down from Miz Groves's, Thomas mounted the gravel driveway of a split-level resting along the top of the ridge. The stones squeaked and ground under his boot heels as he bore down on his stride. He closed on the front door stoop in a suppressed panic, his finger pressing the doorbell well before his feet reached the straw welcome mat. Through the clustered, stunted live oaks in Miz Groves's front yard, he could see Lowry's blue Commando accelerate out of the corner and start rolling toward him, up Grady Way.

Again and again he pressed the doorbell, hearing nothing but dampened chimes through the thick wooden door.

And then, just as the nose of the Plymouth emerged from behind the sheltering oaks, just as Thomas began to feel as if his clothes were melting away from his bony, quivering body, the door swung open.

CHAPTER 2

"TOM!"

Thomas had thrust his left boot across the threshold of Bennett's front door as soon as there was an opening large enough to accept it, and the rest of him followed as quickly as the door's increasing angle would allow. Bennett stepped back with surprise and mild amusement playing on his tanned face until Thomas turned and shoved the door firmly back into its jamb with such rapidity that Bennett's right hand was left outstretched and cupped around a knob he no longer held. Then they faced each other, one flushed with indignation, the other with anxiety.

"Would you please come in, asshole? Why didn't you just knock the fuckin' door down?"

"Sorry, man. I . . ."

"BENNETT! Who in the HELL thinks a goddamn family of bellboys lives here?"

The menacing bluster booming through the open door along the second-floor landing belonged to Ernestine Caldwell, the irrepressible overseer of Bennett and his sister. Thomas began to weigh the possibility of better odds on the outside.

"Keep your goddamned shirt on, Momma. It's just Thomas."

"Well, tell the little shit to be more considerate of other people's privacy. Hello, Thomas." Thomas turned his gaze upward to the second-floor walkway that overlooked the living room, to the door always left ajar at the far end. Once, he and Bennett entered the living room from the deck along the back of the house after a round of shooting pellet guns into the woods, and he was afforded a glimpse inside Mrs. Caldwell's studio. The view was limited by the steep angle and the black spiral railing that always made Thomas think of licorice sticks, but he could make out a paint-smeared easel holding a heavy wooden frame which bore a canvas, the front of which could not be seen. Behind this, along the far wall of the room, high shelves were laden with cans and jars extending beyond his vision, suggesting a vast stock of whatever exotic potions were required to enable Mrs. Caldwell to do whatever it was that Mrs. Caldwell did. All Bennett ever said was that she painted some on her own, but most of what she did were restorations, leaving Thomas's imagination to paint his own portrait of Bennett's mother looming over some decrepit, ancient image and applying her restorative chemicals like a sorceress concocting a vile fate or flailing her own naked canvas with violent strokes of unfathomable hues.

Thankfully, Mrs. Caldwell had not been goaded into an appearance, and Thomas resumed breathing.

"Sorry, Mrs. Caldwell."

From the room at the end of the landing, silence.

Thomas's response had come in a wavering falsetto, and he glared at Bennett, whose enjoyment of his discomfort had erased any ill will brought on by the abrupt intrusion. Bennett was chuckling through a thin smile, eyes aglow. "It's okay, man. Momma likes you. Have a seat."

The boys stepped down into the sunken living room. Bennett spread out on the loveseat next to the free-standing fireplace with his neck and Achilles tendons cradled on the armrests, while Thomas took a more guarded seat on the sofa. In the brief, welcome silence, he consigned his eyes to a search for serenity amid the exotica of Ernestine Caldwell's living room.

For no obvious ancestral or cultural reasons, Bennett's mother was drawn to things Nipponese, and the motif in this, the largest room in the house, adhered obsessively to that theme: a rice paper dressing screen framed in gilded wood; Buddhas of marble, ebony, and ivory, some large, some minute, scattered artfully about the room; a huge one-dimensional painting of kimono-clad women with skin the color of cream strolling through a stark, metallic Japanese afternoon with their parasols open and shouldered, chatting mutely under tiered and shadeless cherry trees bearing vibrant blossoms that would never fade and wither. Through the plate glass doors leading to the stilted pine deck that overlooked the valley of cedar and juniper below, sparrows and wrens sparred for a perch at the seed troughs of a copperplate pagoda making languid rotations at the end of a braided chain. Ernestine Caldwell, with her straight black hair sheared at the shoulders and alabaster skin, blended with the motif as well; only during spirited American colloquy was the theme broken.

The serenity of the room was contagious, and Thomas swept away a bead of sweat rolling down his cheek with a hand that was beginning to steady.

"So how in the hell did you get out of doing yard work—throw a shit-fit or just murder The Colonel in his sleep?"

Thomas glared defiantly at Bennett, determined to retain his precarious hold on tranquility.

"Hey, if he doesn't snag me while I'm still in bed, I'll be damned if I'm gonna hang around so he can shove a rake in my hand."

"You snuck off from massa, didn't you?" Bennett countered. "You a ba- ha-ha-had liddle Tom, isn't you?"

Thomas chose to ignore this, turning his attention instead to tweezing the flattened pack of Kents from his left front jeans pocket with two nicotine- stained fingers. The pack broke loose with a sharp snap of cellophane, and Thomas pulled a rumpled cigarette from the folds, then held it to the light, looking for visible cracks or weevil holes.

"Hold it, Rastus. Here, try a white man's cigarette."

Bennett rolled onto his side and reached for the crush-proof box of Parliaments and a Zippo lighter resting on the end table. He shook out two cigarettes and placed one in his lips, then tossed the other across the alcove to Thomas. The Zippo clacked as Bennett flipped the lid open. He lit up, snapped the lid shut, then catapulted the lighter into Thomas's waiting palm in a lazy arc that took full advantage of the vaulted ceiling.

Thomas lit his Parliament, marveling at the soothing flavor of tobacco not yet caustic with age; at the fundamental dignity of being able to smoke without first barricading oneself in a bathroom with an open window. If Bennett's mother had ever forbidden his smoking, it was a battle she decisively lost. He stuffed the crooked Kent back into the crumpled pack, the pack back into his pocket under a rigid hand, then procured a brass ashtray from the coffee table and cradled it in his lap.

Bennett chose to change the subject, allowing Thomas his fragile tranquility: "I tried to call you about eight-thirty, man, but my goddamned sister's been talking on the phone all morning." Bennett set his cigarette in the corner of his mouth and reached down to the Princess phone on the floor by the loveseat. "Don't make any noise. Okay?" He slipped a thumb onto the receiver button, lifted the handset to his ear with his palm over the mouthpiece, then eased his thumb off the button.

"Did anyone just pick up a phone out there?"

Bennett's older sister, Angela, occupied one of the bedrooms along a sunken walkway that ran the length of the south wall, and it was Angela's voice coming to them now behind her latched door.

Bennett straightened on the loveseat, his eyes narrowed over an evil grimace.

"Did anyone just pick up the phone? Bennett? Mother?"

"Don't say *anything*," Bennett whispered. "She's talking to one of her queer boyfriends." The house sat silent for a moment, with only the faint chirping of the competing birds on the deck to stir the calm. Finally, a thumbs-up from Bennett indicated that

Angela had resumed her conversation, and Thomas was content to smoke his excellent cigarette and amuse himself by attempting to interpret Angela's dialogue by reading her brother's face.

By the time Thomas had crushed out his Parliament and returned the ashtray to its yellowed pedestal on the coffee table, Bennett's face had sunk into a pout and deep furrows creased his brow. He was gnawing the thumbnail of the hand cupping the mouthpiece.

"GA-hawed *DAMN!*" he finally announced, "These assholes have been on the phone over an hour now and half the time they're not even saying anything, just laughing at nothing or listening to each other breathe."

"So what? You don't need to use the phone right now anyway, do you?"

Suddenly Bennett shifted his vision off Thomas and his eyes widened, as if he had been seized by an undeniable force. "Yeah, I need to use it"—then, in a single movement, he arched his back, raised his buttocks, and brought the handset down and into the cleft of his pressed Levis—*"right NOW!"*

Thomas's tranquility vanished in a burst of delight as Bennett brought his brow and cheeks together in an exaggerated grimace and delivered a sustained flatulence of sufficient volume to produce an audible resonance in the sheet metal hearth suspended over the freestanding fireplace.

He then brought the phone quickly back to his ear and, speaking in a droll, polite tone, said:

"Excuse me. Is this a party line?"

Everything went still. Bennett snickered and returned the handset to the cradle, then looked over to gauge Thomas's response, which would have been one of raving critical praise if the sharp shriek of furniture being shoved aside hadn't penetrated the walls like a shot. Down the sunken hallway, a door slammed violently, followed by an uneven patter that Thomas took to be shattered plaster, and once again he contemplated flight.

"MMMMUUUUHHHH . . ." —the wail came at them like a locomotive in a tunnel, more substance than sound—". . . THUUUURRRR!" Angela, dressed only in her black bra and panties, burst into the room in wingless flight and alighted with a slap of her bare feet at the foot of the staircase, knuckles looking impossibly pale as she clenched the black railing. Her face was pink with rage and her body heaving as she drew in the deep breaths needed to fuel her rage. She seemed oblivious to the two boys, oblivious to everything but the enlistment of her formidable mother to her cause. Under other circumstances, the sight of any discernibly attractive female clad only in underwear would have launched Thomas into a state of feverish arousal, but given the situation, Angela might as well have been wearing a nun's habit.

"Muh-THERRRR! THIS GODDAMNED LITTLE BASTARD IS MAKING

MY LIFE A LIVING HELL!" Again Angela, but now with a sobbing plea in her voice: "Muh-huh-huh-ther. Puh-LEEZE make him STOP!"

As the doorway at the end of the landing began to darken in shadow, Bennett's defensive volley began. "THIS GODDAMNED

BITCH HAS BEEN ON THE PHONE ALL GODDAMNED MORNIN', MOMMA!"

Angela threw her snarling gaze onto Bennett, speaking in a febrile hiss.

"If Mother doesn't kill you, I'll do it myself, you goddamned little—"

Something, perhaps a sound, perhaps a presence, caused Angela to return her stare to the top of the staircase. Ernestine Caldwell was leaning against the iron railing, silent and omnipotent, glowering down at the combatants. She waited until she commanded the attention of first Angela, and then Bennett, who had instinctively followed his sister's eyes, then drew herself erect and started moving toward the staircase, her billowing black kimono barking a toothy whistle with each hurried stride of her short, muscular legs. Her coloring was Angela's—black hair and skin impossibly fair for Texas beyond April—but the remaining physical demeanor was hers alone, and it foretold her granite temperament. Short and heavily built but in no way appearing small or portly, she moved with the confident determination of an entity for whom the earth had yet to produce a natural enemy.

She paused at the top of the staircase, glancing only briefly at Angela before turning her cold, dark eyes onto her only son, who was failing to look defiant while cowering in the deepest recesses of the loveseat. It was evident that she didn't intend to spend time determining where to affix blame.

"God-DAMMIT, BENNETT! You little BASTARD! You just aren't happy unless you're picking away at the peace around here! Who

in the HELL do you have to call so badly that it just can't wait until your sister's off the phone?"

Bennett folded his hands in his lap to exude civility: "I needed to call Thomas, Momma. I wanted to ask—"

"Call THOMAS? Then just who in the hell is THIS . . ." —Mrs. Caldwell began descending the staircase, her splayed gold lame slippers beating a frantic tattoo on the tiled steps until she reached the floor, where the carpet turned the sharp slaps into ominous thuds, and Thomas's eyes crossed when a hand shot out of her baggy sleeve and a thickly enameled nail appeared within an inch of his nose—*". . . looking like he's about to SHIT all over himself?"*

Bennett jerked himself to his feet, snatching the box of Parliaments from the end table as he rose. *"Goddammit, Momma! You always side with Angela."* He had abandoned vacuous innocence for the indignity of the unjustly accused. "Come on, Thomas. We're not welcome around here."

Bennett stepped up to the front door and had his hand on the knob before Thomas was able to shake off his trauma and join him. Angela, apparently satisfied with her mother's handling of her grievance, turned and strode back to her room wearing a triumphant smirk.

Mrs. Caldwell was still standing in the center of the sunken living room, fists set on her ample hips and breasts heaving, looking very alone indeed. "Don't give me that false indignation crap, Bennett, and close that goddamned door! We're not finished yet!"

Bennett pushed the door back into the jamb, turned, and looked down at his mother with his arms folded across his chest:

"Listen, Momma. I really don't know what the big deal is, anyway. I mean, all I did was pick up the goddamned telephone to see if the line was clear." Before his mother could speak, Bennett threw his arms up.

"Hell, I don't have any idea what the shit-eating bitch is so upset about anyway. Do you?" Mrs. Caldwell looked uncharacteristically daunted. She looked down the sunken walkway to the door of Angela's room and seemed about to bellow out an oral summons when a muffled peal of laughter, gay and careless, reverberated through the plaster walls.

"Careful, Momma. You don't wanna interrupt Angela's precious phone call, do you? That's what you're supposed to be yelling at me for!"

Mrs. Caldwell stared at Bennett with a mixture of reproach and consideration. Finally, after a large portion of what Thomas would have deemed an eternity, she glanced one last time down the hall, to the door still being buffeted with giggles and trills, then walked over to the base of the staircase, shaking her head and mumbling expletives as she went. As she lifted her foot to the first step, she remarked back over her shoulder: "I'll have lunch ready about noon. If you're not going to make it, call if you can. Thomas, you're welcome if you'd like, with your parents' say-so."

"Thanks, ma'am."

With this, Mrs. Caldwell ascended the staircase in earnest, jaunting briskly up to the landing, her kimono emitting a shrill whistle with each uplifted knee. Her face still reflected will and resolve, but now the target of her intensity lay once again beyond the door of her studio. At the top of the staircase, she vanished behind a door crisply closed, but quietly, except for the snap of the bolt. Downstairs, in quiet harmony, the front door latch clacked home as well, and the faint squabbling of the birds on the deck and the gaiety radiating through Angela's walls did little to claim the sudden stillness in the house.

#

The morning sun had climbed above the houses and trees across Grady Way from Bennett's front yard, and Thomas felt the prickling sweat rise on the back of his neck as they moved toward the street. At the curb, Bennett stopped, threw his head back, and let out a shrill half-laugh, half-yell of triumph.

"Goddammit, Bennett, don't press your luck. What if your mother hears you?"

"Shit, Tom! What in the hell are you worried about? It's my ass, not yours. When The Colonel jumps your butt I just sit back and enjoy it, except when the old fart makes me leave. Boy, that pisses me off! Anyway, what's the worst she could do? Throw us out of the house?"

Thomas silently concurred with his friend's analysis. In the two years he had known him, he couldn't recall a single time when Bennett had actually been punished beyond the blaring and profane tongue-lashings, and he was starting to question his assumption that dire consequences were waiting just beyond those bellowed ultimatums. "Maybe you're right, but if my dad ever gets to yelling like that you can write me off! And my old man doesn't even cuss. If I talked back to him the way you do to your old lady, he'd kill me! Wouldn't say another word, just fuckin' kill me on the spot!"

Bennett hooked his thumbs into his pockets and continued: "Look, when you're home, you can't smoke, can't cuss, and don't dare stand up for yourself, and then you come over here, where you can do just about anything you damn well please, and let my old lady scare the shit out of you

. . ." He put a fatherly hand on Thomas's shoulder. "Shit, son, relax. Why do you take everything so fuckin' serious?"

Thomas ducked out from under Bennett's grip. "Okay, okay! So I'm a chickenshit. So your mother's just spouting bullshit. But if she ever does lower the boom on you, I just hope I'm around to see it." Thomas looked down Grady Way to the south, checking for Lowry's Plymouth, trying not to appear nervous. "Anyway, I'm tired of talking about it. Let's do something."

"So what do you want to do? Grab our bikes? If you didn't ride yours over, I'll pedal you over to your house to get it."

Your house. He might be lucky enough to avoid Lowry on the way over, but there was no way his father wouldn't draft him for yard work. He needed a distraction within walking distance, and nowhere near James Place.

"Naw, I got a flat on the front," he lied. "How about we go over to The Drop-off and see if we can hit the other side? Nobody's made it yet, but I came real close last weekend—came up about ten feet short."

"Okay."

The boys stepped off the curb and headed north, up Grady Way.

The morning became pleasantly balmy as the ascending sun brought southern breezes that would persist until noon, when the unrelenting heat would swell the earth and air to a leaden torpor. But for now the weather was bearable, even comfortable by Texas standards, and the mood lightened as they jaunted up the center of the narrow street. Occasionally they would have to time their steps so a passing vehicle would intercept them at an unoccupied portion of curb, between parked cars, but most of the time the street was theirs.

In the yards, women were tending their flower beds and window boxes. Had it been a weekend, men would have been outside as well, wielding mowers or hedge clippers, or in the driveway with their heads under an upraised hood, putting profane lyrics to a metallic melody. This year, a mild spring had heightened the enthusiasm for yard work, but it would be temporary, and by the time the first norther blew in, the trees and shrubs would be faded and dry and the grass scorched and coated in limestone dust. An occasional sprinkler, whirling impotently away, would be the only enduring industry.

A hundred yards up Grady Way, a small brown terrier with oversized ears and bared teeth charged to the edge of his master's yard and delivered a diatribe as the boys drew abreast. Once past the yard, and just as the dog was beginning to quiet, the boys spun and launched a counterattack, snarling and flailing in unison, sending the horror-struck terrier scurrying under the front porch.

Thomas and Bennett continued up the street, their laughter interspersed with the tenuous yapping of the humbled terrier cowering in the shadows behind the lattice, daring to expose no more than two inches of quivering snout.

"So when are you gonna get this car you've been talking about?" Bennett asked. He was sweeping his damp blonde bangs from his sweating forehead. "This traveling under my own power's getting old."

"Bennett, what in the hell do you have to bitch about?" Thomas carped, his cockiness restored. "You got your driver's license right after you moved out here, and there's two cars in your carport. I remember you told me that your mother bought the Volkswagen for both Angela and you. And since when does a girl's car have a red racing stripe?"

"And just how often do you see me behind the wheel of either one, asshole? Momma won't let me use her car during the day 'cause she says she might need it, and Angela gets first pick of the bug 'cause she's the oldest and sucks up to Momma the most, and even if she's not using it, Momma makes me beg anyway, just for the fun of it. And the only reason it's got a racing stripe is that's the way it came when Momma bought it used. Now quit changing the subject and answer my fuckin' question. Didn't you say you finally won the old man over?"

Thomas certainly hoped so. He had completed his school's driving course in his sophomore year and was fully licensed to drive before the term ended. The Colonel quashed all discussion of a second automobile while he was taking the course but indicated he might accede to his son's wishes "under certain conditional circumstances" with the coming of summer, assuming he had acquired his license by then. Of course, Thomas would agree to virtually anything for his own set of wheels, so he considered it a done deal, however nebulous the cost.

"Yeah. I think so. He told me to wait till school's out, so I kind of let it slide. I was sure surprised when he changed his mind—he was dead-set against a car till I was in college. He'll probably make me promise to make straight As next year if I want the damn thing and make me deliver if I want to keep it, or some such shit!"

Bennett was silent for a moment, then replied: "Well, at least we'll have wheels, maybe, at least till your first report card comes out."

Thomas agreed with a nod.

The boys reached the midpoint of their travel at the intersection of Grady Way and Ridgewest Drive, where the parallel streets merged with the north end of Grady Way hooking east into Ridgewest at a right angle. A hundred yards north of this intersection, Ridgewest began a gradual descent to the steep limestone palisade that steered the Nebraska River south—and then eastward as it flowed out of the hills. Thomas and Bennett swung single file into the right-hand gutter of the wider street, where half-acre lots predominated and the circular drives and two-car garages left the curbs free of parked cars. Thomas led the way, and their conversation was spirited and formless:

"... but if your mother calls you a bastard, that's bad-mouthing herself, isn't it? I mean, isn't she calling herself a slut?"

Bennett nodded thoughtfully. "Yeah, I guess that's why I don't take it personal when she calls me that, or son-of-a-bitch either."

Thomas glanced upward. He was hearing a subtle rumbling, like distant thunder, but the sky was clear and blue as far as he could see.

"So when she says to you, 'goddammit, Bennett! You son-of-a-bitch,' what she's really saying is, 'goddammit, Bennett! I'm a female dog!'"

This evoked a shared laugh. Vacant lots were replacing the houses now, and the sounds of nature were reclaiming the roadsides. But just under the chirping of the birds and clicks of the locusts and cicadas, still, that barely audible rumble, more felt than heard.

"But, hey! If she ever calls me a mother-fucker, I'm drawing the fuckin' line! Ya know?" Then, silence.

I guess he finally ran out of bullshit, Thomas thought, and sauntered on, assuming the break in Bennett's monologue would be brief. But the silence held, and after another fifty feet he halted and faced up the hill.

What he saw froze him in place.

A dozen yards up the road stood Bennett, also reversed and halted, his feet planted and fists clenched in defiance. The front bumper of Lowry's Plymouth was just inches off his right knee, the low rumble of the motor complimenting the visual drama.

Thomas walked reluctantly back up the hill to his friend's side. He avoided looking toward the car, choosing instead to study the rage in Bennett's eyes as they bored through the windshield.

Then Bennett spoke, and his voice came in a seething whisper:

"The goddamn son-of-a-bitch rolled up so close, my hand hit his goddamned fender on the back-swing."

Thomas sheepishly examined Lowry's brutish gray face through the glass. Beneath the brim of his hat, he was scrutinizing them with cold, prejudiced eyes. Finally, Lowry whipped a blunt finger across the dashboard, commanding the boys to step around to the driver's side window. Thomas stepped off obediently and was almost even with Lowry before he glanced back at Bennett.

Bennett hadn't moved; he was challenging Lowry's stare through the windshield. His eyes held steady as he plucked a cigarette from the box in his shirt pocket and placed it fastidiously between his teeth. He pulled the Zippo out of his jeans pocket, clacked it open, and ignited the wick with a flick of the wheel. When he lit up, he squinted against the smoke, but his eyes never blinked or left Lowry's, and when he finally started around the front of the car to join Thomas, his nonchalance seethed disrespect.

Lowry was sitting with his left elbow hanging over the edge of the door, as if to emphasize the Granite Heights Police patch on his shoulder, and he had cocked his large head at an ungainly angle so the brim of the sweat- stained Stetson would clear the open window. Thomas thought of a bulldog trying to force his way through a chain-locked door.

Lowry glared back at Bennett. A snake trying to mesmerize a sparrow. "Do your parents know you smoke, son?"

Bennett looked puzzled, then mildly amused. He took a slow, indulgent draw on his Parliament, closed his eyes and inhaled deeply, then exhaled the residue as a compressed stream in the direction of the rancid Stetson.

"I dunno," Bennett replied.

"What do you mean, you 'don't know'? What's your name, son?" "Caldwell."

"That's good for starters. Now, what's the rest of it?" "Bennett."

Lowry hesitated. "Caldwell Bennett?" "Nope."

Again a pause, and the sweat on Lowry's face began to run. Thomas didn't know how he could stand it, but Lowry always wore khaki trousers and a long-sleeved white shirt bound at the neck by a bolo tie. Sharp ridges running down his arms and chest indicated heavy starch, regardless of season. And the Plymouth wasn't air-conditioned.

Lowry's eyes were boring into Bennett's over the top of his aviator-style sunglasses. "Young man, I want your name, your full name, and all at once." The words came out so slow and low that they were more growled than spoken. Lowry was beginning to sound like a bulldog.

"Bennett Caldwell."

"Bennett Caldwell, *WHAT?*" Lowry's eyes were still sullen and predatory, but no longer cocksure. His sparrow was behaving more like a hawk.

Now it was Bennett who paused, producing a silence so dense that Thomas could hear his ears ring.

The tan line around Lowry's neck moved clear of the starched collar as he craned harder through the window, closing in. "It's not that difficult, son. Now, what were you taught to say when addressing one of your elders?"

Bennett diverted his gaze to his shoes in thoughtful deliberation.

Suddenly his face brightened and lifted. "Well," Lowry said.

Bennett cleared his throat, straightened his posture, and folded his hands behind him—

> *Bennett Caldwell went to town*
> *Riding on a po-nee,*
> *Needing someone else to mount*
> *Because he was so hor-nee!*

An enormous globule of sweat that had been accumulating on the tip of Lowry's nose finally broke loose, and Thomas and Bennett watched it descend to the hot pavement and land with an impotent splat at Bennett's feet.

It was soon clear that Lowry's composure had gone with it. A snap of the door latch brought their heads back up, and a quick step backward was required to avoid the arc of the blue sheet metal as the door flew open and rebounded off the stops. Lowry swung to his feet, almost losing his hat in the process, and gripped the top of the door frame, knuckles white and trembling. Lowry was big—over six feet tall—and his control seemed dangerously depleted. But so did his stamina; his gray countenance was tinged with red and his breathing had turned heavy.

"*GODDAMMIT, SON, this is no GAME!* Now, I asked you a simple question, and you're gonna answer it! *Do your parents know you smoke? YES OR NO?*"

"Which one?"

"What do you mean, 'which one'?" "Which parent?"

Lowry wavered once again, fearing the inevitable. Whatever he said would be wrong, he knew. He loosened his grip on the window frame and leaned back against the roof, crossing his arms over his chest in an effort to cloak his defeat at the hands of this impudent little punk. "Okay, wise-ass. Your father. And it won't do any good to lie to me, 'cause you can bet your bottom dollar I'll be speaking with him tonight."

"I got twenty-five dollars says you won't." Bennett's response was sullen, cocky.

"*What?*"

"I said: 'I got twenty-five dollars says you won't.' My father died when I was five years old" —Bennett gave Lowry a twisted, contemptuous scowl — "sir!"

Lowry moaned and folded into the seat as if he'd been hit in the stomach. As he lifted his hand to the steering column to twist the ignition key, Bennett stepped forward and pushed the door firmly shut. "And as for my mother, she oughta know I smoke, since she pays for 'em."

Lowry stared silently through the windshield, having no desire to continue a discourse that he wished to God he'd never begun.

He slammed the gear shift into drive, made a sharp U-turn, and jumped the opposite curb with the rear tires spinning. After he got the Plymouth back into the street, he braked the car to a stop, backed up to where the boys were standing, and angled his head back through the window to take up something he had overlooked—the reason he had approached the boys in the first place.

"By the way, young mister Kessler, would you mind accounting for your whereabouts this morning around eight forty-five?"

Thomas returned Lowry's stare like a deer in the headlights, his mind fumbling for an alibi. He was about to blurt out something, anything, when:

"Thomas was over at my house all morning, since before eight." Lowry kept his gaze riveted on Thomas.

"Not according to Miz Groves, he hadn't. According to Miz Groves, young mister Kessler here was walking past her house about that time, headed up Grady Way like he had a fire under his feet." Bolstered by his command of the facts, Lowry turned his shielded eyes confidently toward Bennett. "Now, Mister Bennett, or Mister Caldwell, or whatever your name is, you wouldn't be calling a sweet little old lady like Miz Groves a liar, would you?"

Bennett looked from side to side, then took the cigarette from his lips and leaned close to the open window and rested his hands on the roof over Lowry's head. When he spoke, it was with an intimacy that made Thomas feel like he was eavesdropping: "Oh, you can't much depend on anything poor old Miz Groves says anymore, since she lost her husband last year. Talk on our block says she plants more empty gin bottles in those flower beds than she does tulip bulbs."

Lowry's face slipped back into wearied resignation as he put his hand on the shift lever.

"I suppose there's somebody at your house who can verify your friend's whereabouts at that time."

"Only my mother. And my sister. Wanna ask 'em?"

Lowry ignored the suggestion, then looked past Bennett to address Thomas with his sinister growl. "I know you did it, you little shit, and if it's the last thing I do I'm gonna nail your ass." Lowry then backed into a driveway before Bennett could fire off a rebuttal, hit the throttle as he pulled back onto the road, and launched the Plymouth back up Ridgewest Drive with smoke boiling off the rear tires, the dual exhausts roaring harmoniously, and the boys watched as the car crested the hill and rumbled out of sight and sound.

"So THAT'S why you were in such a hurry to get through the door this morning! That's that asshole vigilante who lives across the street from you, isn't it?" Bennett was ecstatic. "What in the *FUCK* did you do?"

Thomas felt embarrassed without really knowing why. "Aw, his goddamn hunting dogs woke me up this morning, so I whipped up a couple of grenades and lobbed them into his backyard. It was no big deal. The first one barely went off."

"*The FIRST one?*" Bennett's face exploded with glee. "*No SHIT! Outta-fuckin'-SIGHT!* And then you just strolled right up the street, past Miz Groves's house to my house"—Bennett pantomimed the ringing of a doorbell, then looked timidly upward to an imaginary respondent—"Excuse me, folks, but I've just blasted a hole in my neighbor's yard, who happens to carry a shotgun in his car, and it being broad daylight and all, I was wondering if I might be able to come in for a moment before he blows me to hell or packs me off to jail?" Then he dropped the facade. "Hell's Bells, Tom! What made you think you could pull that off?"

"It wasn't like I didn't plan it out. And there wasn't anybody around to see me, unless you count Miz Groves, and she wouldn't have heard anything that far away, with the cedar brake blocking the noise and her being half deaf an' all. You weren't there anyway, so quit pretending you know so fuckin' much. Okay?"

Bennett smiled and shook his head, then turned and started back down the hill with Thomas obediently in tow. "Besides, I didn't expect the old bastard to come after me so quick. He opened the door before the second one even hit the ground."

Bennett wasn't moved. "And what if we hadn't been home to bail your ass out? What then?" Thomas hadn't even formulated a primary getaway plan, much less a contingency. He would plan five moves ahead in a chess game but managed his own affairs one discordant step at a time. His father was fond of pointing out this inconsistency, but Thomas stubbornly clung to his penchant for spontaneous and often ill-fated schemes, occasionally at a price. But not this time.

"I just knew you'd be home, that's all." Bennett let it rest. "Bennett?"

"Yeah, Tom."

"Is that true about Miz Groves?"

"Hell, no, but how's that asshole gonna find out otherwise—go up to her and ask if she's got a drinking problem? And I don't have twenty-five bucks and my old man lives in Louisiana, which Momma says is the same thing as being dead anyway, so maybe that one's half true."

CHAPTER 3

Thomas and Bennett continued their descent along the gracefully winding curb, passed the Fuller city limit sign at the northern terminus of Ridgewest, then turned east onto Riverside Drive, a well-maintained city road that fronted the high-end homes being constructed along the towering bluff that overlooked the western bank of the Nebraska River. Deep arroyos cut by the sparse but often torrential rains intersected Riverside Drive along its entire length, giving it the topography of a roller coaster rather than a staid residential artery.

The entrance to a trail opened at the top of the first and deepest of these troughs, and Bennett and Thomas were taking their breaths in heaves as they stepped over the rusted strands of barbed wire lying slack in the dust at their feet.

The bluffs bordering the Nebraska River were useless as grazing land— the sole source of water, the river, was inaccessible—and the only historical evidence of agricultural enterprise was a herd of feral Spanish goats several miles upriver that could yet be seen scattered along the ledges.

Anchored at the ends by iron rods driven deeply into bedrock and devoid of any conceivable purpose, this fifty-odd foot stretch of fence now lying twisted in the weeds and caliche was for Thomas a somehow personal enigma that he had no hope of solving.

Riverside Drive kept a consistent proximity to the bluff and the river, straying no more than a stone's throw away along its entire run, and the trail Thomas and Bennett now found themselves on—walking abreast in the parallel ruts, wordless with fatigue—was carved through a meandering path of minimal resistance, perhaps a hundred and fifty feet long. Thick junipers provided shade all the way to the river, and the boys stepped onto the twin-tiered stone balcony looming a hundred feet over the river somewhat revitalized.

Thomas walked to the edge and looked first to the west, to the gentle curve of the high wall as it steered the green water toward them from the bottom of the dam that held Lake Fuller, and then to the east, taking note of a solitary rowboat slowly making its way across the river from the northern shoreline a quarter-mile downstream. Finally, he looked across and beyond the thousand feet of sluggish water to the suburbs of West Fuller that spread out before him, to the steeples and incinerator stacks, the flagpoles and water towers, so familiar and logical in their locations above the surface of the interminable forest into which the town had been carved.

Such was the view from The Drop-off, the highest promontory along the Nebraska River palisade.

Bennett seated himself on the limestone shelf and lit a cigarette while Thomas crept back into the woods that fringed the lip of the cliff. A crumbling layer of rock emerged from beneath the compost of rotting needles and bark that held a stand of stunted junipers, and Thomas began breaking it up with the heel of his boot, looking for decent throwing stones.

When Thomas walked back to the ledge, he was wiping caliche dust from a smooth, dark rock with the tail of his shirt.

"I'm gonna give this one a try. It's the only one I've found that's worth a shit."

Bennett scooted over to clear the shelf, and Thomas retreated back up the path about twenty feet, then turned and ran back toward the edge. His body twisted and bent as he skidded to a stop along the top tier, and the rock sailed out over the river with a smartly snapped sidearm.

"All-*right*, Tom!"—Thomas was surprised. Praise of any kind from Bennett was rare—"That one might make it!"

It sure as hell better, thought Thomas, insofar as it was the only decent rock he was able to come up with while Bennett was sitting on his ass, savoring his Parliament. Rocks with good aerodynamics—usually stones worn smooth and flat by time and water—were rare this high up, and finding one was part of the challenge.

The throw had felt like a good one, and the stone rode level and true atop the dense air rising off the water. It maintained stability as it slowed and descended, hit the river with a slap a hundred yards from the opposite bank, then kicked into the air again, still flying flat and straight. It sailed another eighty feet or so, then rebounded repeatedly, halving the distance each time, until its momentum collapsed. When it finally sputtered to a stop and sank into the murky water, it was only three yards from the edge of the matted duckweed hugging the shoreline across the river.

"Not bad," Bennett said. "One more good bounce and it woulda made it."

Damn! Just one more skip and all the fame and glory would have been his. No one had yet reached the dense carpet of duckweed that flourished along the river's shallow northern shore, and though there were conflicting estimates as to how many stones had been hurled at this slimy, matted prize over the years, no one disputed the number that had failed to reach it. Being the first was fiercely contended by the mass of young men flailing through their pubescence in the hills south of the Nebraska River, but so far all claims had been dismissed for lack of a witness. And he even had that.

Moving to meet Thomas's attempt as if it were an unspoken challenge, Bennett let fly with the first thin sliver of limestone he encountered. It started off well enough, riding the hot currents like an airfoil, until the uneven air over the middle of the river flipped it onto its edge and it careened into the water with a barely audible pop seventy-five yards short of the duckweed border.

"Fuck! I'm getting bored with this shit anyway."

Bennett stepped down to the second shelf and reached for his hip pocket, then turned to look across the river. The teeth of a pocket comb played a descending scale on a welt as he slid it out of his jeans. He placed the comb deftly in the cleft of his long blonde hair, then brought his bangs over and secured the damp ends behind his left ear.

"Look, Tom. You can see our old house from here."

Thomas picked up a mediocre rock and let it fly with no enthusiasm, then stepped down to where Bennett was standing. The rock hit the water unnoticed less than a third of the way out.

The view downriver was vast but orderly. Only the largest and tallest of Fuller's structures broke the surface of the urban forest, and the Nebraska gently arced out of sight to the south about a mile downstream. The suburbs directly opposite The Drop-off revealed little other than the occasional steeple or water tower, and farther to the east the loftier structures of downtown Fuller could be seen through the haze of persistent heat. The small boat Thomas noticed earlier had traversed the river and was now moving slowly toward them along the riverbank below. Thomas could now make out the occupants—two men, one rowing gently while the other cast deftly into the boulders and dead trees that littered the shaded base of the bluff.

Bennett's eyes were focused on something above and beyond the river, something in the dense foliage west of the town.

"So, show me, Bennett! I don't know where to look. I've only been over there a couple of times."

Bennett moved closer to Thomas and leaned in with his right arm indicating a point somewhere along a ridge running parallel to the river about half a mile to the north. Thomas recognized the area, knowing it to be one of the older neighborhoods west of the town shimmering gently on the horizon a mile beyond the ridge.

Thomas canted his head, closed an eye, and followed Bennett's index finger.

At first, he could detect nothing of consequence. The hackberries, chinaberries, and other softwoods that once grew in the uneven land west of Fuller had been successfully eradicated, and the lush live oak forest offered only scattered glimpses of houses.

Thomas squinted harder into the trees along the ridge.

"See it? You see it, don't you? My goddamn arm's getting tired."

"Uh, yeah. I think so." Thomas didn't have an inkling. "So how can you be so sure that's your old house?"

"Because, dumb-ass, it's the tallest house on that whole hill, and that's the highest hill west of downtown, at least on that side of the river."

Unimpressed, Thomas was still sighting down Bennett's outstretched arm. He adjusted his aim higher up on the ridge. Now Bennett's finger appeared to be pointing in the approximate direction of a minute reflection, possibly part of a house.

"Hey, I think I see it, sticking out of those trees over there. It looks like a window or something."

"It *is* a window. It's under one of those little bitty roofs, like—it sits over a window that sits on top of the main roof."

"A gable?" Thomas interjected. "A *what*?"

"A gable. Like in that book, *The House of the Seven Gables*." The rendering of a Gothic house adorned the cover of the copy in the bookshelf at home, and The Colonel had to explain the title after he suggested Thomas read it for a book report. Thomas chose Dracula instead.

"*What house?*"

"Never mind," said Thomas. "Go on."

"Anyway, that's where we lived before we moved over here. That was Momma's room, the one with the window sticking through the trees. I didn't know you could see it from here, though." Bennett walked back from the edge and sat down on the top shelf with his knees drawn up under his chin. Thomas started to dig for his cigarette pack, but Bennett stopped him with a raised hand, then drew two Parliaments out of the box in his shirt pocket and tossed one over to Thomas. He was about to extend his right leg to access the Zippo when Thomas's cupped hands appeared a foot in front of his face. Bennett slipped the tip of his Parliament into the flame, then Thomas lit his own.

"That house has been in Momma's family for a long time. It was built by my mother's father's grandfather, or some such shit." Bennett took a drag off his cigarette, then sucked the smoke over his upper lip and into his nose. That was the way the French did it, he had once told Thomas. "Once, when I was a little kid, this guy from the city came by and said they wanted to put a plaque up in front of the house, but my grandmother told him the house was private property, that she didn't want people coming into the yard to read the plaque. Then she ran his ass off. Anyway, she got sick about five years ago and ever since all she talks about is how crappy she feels. I got sick of hearing her bitch, and she started accusing me of ignoring her. Anyway, Momma finally decided that living together in that house wasn't making anybody happy, so we moved out here and got my grandmother a live-in nurse. It's a neat house though, with lots of rooms and a big balcony over the front porch. Like those big Civil War houses."

"Are there any secret passages?" Thomas had heard somewhere that all old houses had secret passages.

"Naw, not that I know of, and I think if there was, I'd know it. But there's this one little room in the roof that my grandmother used to call her sewing room, and it had a staircase that was hidden behind a door, like a closet door, I guess, and if you didn't know where the stairs were, there was no way you'd ever find it."

"Cool."

Thomas looked back across the river at the ridge. Now he thought that he could detect the outline of a gable peering through the trees.

"What's that bunch of buildings just down from your grandmother's house, on the left?" Thomas was referring to a cluster of two-story limestone buildings grouped within several cleared acres along the southern-facing slope of the ridge.

Bennett paused, gazing over the river, remembering. "That's the Confederate Home, or at least it used to be. Anyway, that's what it still says over the entrance. It used to be for old rebel soldiers who were too sick or poor to live anywhere else, and later their wives, too. It's real old, I guess, and Momma said they should tear it down or use it for something else. She said once that there aren't any more soldiers left in there, maybe just a few wives of old men who were probably just bugle boys or something like that during the war. Anyway, I think they just keep it open for a few old women."

Bennett drew on his cigarette, then formed his lips into a circle and sent a procession of small vortexes rolling into the heavy air. Thomas counted seven before they broke up in the gentle breeze or simply slowed and fell apart.

"Hey, Tom. You know those long wooden buildings over there?" Bennett was pointing at a quarter-mile row of barracks lined up across the Nebraska from The Drop-off. "What are those used for?"

"Well, the school bus went by there every day when we were in junior high and the driver once said—"

Suddenly Bennett brought a hand up to silence him, but Thomas had heard it too—a distant clunking noise, hollow and deep, that seemed to fall out of the thick air and melt away. The boys exchanged puzzled glances, then Bennett got back on his feet and together they stepped down to the lower shelf.

Thomas spotted a man in a pickup truck unloading a Jon boat onto a sand bar downriver from the low-water bridge, but before he could comment, a hand closed firmly on his right forearm. Thomas turned and obediently followed Bennett's index finger once again—first, as it split the taut smile on his face, and then as it moved over the edge and pointed straight down at the water. The two fishermen plying the shoreline had worked their way upstream and were now almost directly under them. One was still seated, holding the boat steady with an oar driven into the sandy bottom, while the other stood and attempted to tie a cord to an overhanging branch. A second oar lay discarded in the bottom of the boat—without it, Thomas was sure, the skiff would have passed beneath them undetected.

The boys dropped to their knees and pancaked onto the shelf, then crept forward and peeked over the edge. Bennett was about to take another pull on his Parliament, and Thomas snatched it from his lips and crushed it out. "Goddammit, Bennett!" he said in a desperate whisper, "Don't do anything to screw this up! They might see the goddamned smoke. We don't get a shot like this every day."

Bennett ignored him. He was staring down at the river like a hungry cat, watching the standing man wrestle with the cord.

Suddenly the boys froze. The rear of the boat had drifted slightly around with the current, bringing the standing man's eyes in perfect alignment with their position on the stone mantel. If his focus drifted beyond his hands and the dead limb, he would be staring directly at them.

"*Oh, fuck,*" they whispered, in perfect unison.

The man fumbled for a moment longer at the tree branch, then finally gave the cord a jerk, sat down, and reached for his fishing rod.

"Man! For a second there I thought we were fucked," Bennett whispered. "Do you think they line up okay? Should we wait to see if they move to a better spot?"

"Naw, this is good. I think they line up purr-fect."

Thomas pushed himself back from the edge and jumped to his feet, giggling and clenching his fists. On two prior occasions, ducks had paddled into range under The Drop-off, and then there was that small gaggle of geese on one glorious spring day the year before. Also, later that same year, a big river turtle. All had strayed within range of the spot that repeated experimentation proved a large rock would land when manhandled to the edge and coaxed over. But he never expected good fortune to deliver human prey.

"Come on," Thomas commanded in a rasping whisper. "Let's find a good one quick."

They climbed back onto level ground and bounded down the path. "You look on the left,"

Thomas said as he stepped into the woods on his right. "The bigger and flatter, the better."

Thomas waded quickly into the brush, picking his boots up in long, high strides to avoid getting tangled in the green briars. He was thirty seconds into a fruitless search when Bennett called out from the path.

"I think I see a good one, Tom."

Thomas watched in amusement as Bennett tiptoed into the briars with his arms extended for balance. With his attention drawn to the floor of the thicket, juniper twigs were becoming entangled in his long blonde hair, then bending and snapping loose as he progressed.

Suddenly, twenty feet from the edge of the path, Bennett stopped and began flailing his arms about his head in wild, violent arcs:

"GODDAMNMOTHERFUCKINSUNUVABITCH!"

"Goddammit, Bennett, shut the fuck up! They might hear you! What's wrong, anyway?" Bennett was frantically running splayed fingers over his sweaty cheeks and hair, now matted with dust and juniper needles, then wiping his hands on his jeans. "Goddamn spider web right across my face! There's nothin' I hate worse than getting a goddamn spider web across my fuckin' face!"

"You city boys are pathetic, you know that? Look, when you first feel a cobweb on your face, just take a couple of steps back and go around it. It's not that big a deal."

Now Bennett was swatting at his jeans. "Oh, man! I've got beggar's lice all over my fuckin' pants, and . . . *holy SHIT!* Look at my goddamned socks! They're fuckin' *covered!*"

Thomas turned and started back toward the path. "Bennett, you've lived over here for what—about a year now—and you *still* don't have any boots. How many pairs of those shit-eatin' penny loafers do you own, anyway?"

"Okay, Davey-fuckin'-Crockett, I'll just let you wade in here and get the son-of-a-bitch if you want it. Come 'ere, wise-ass, and I'll point it out to you."

Thomas crossed the path and tromped indelicately toward Bennett, showcasing his footwear. Bennett moved over a step as Thomas came abreast, then extended an arm toward a spot deeper into the woods. "There it is. Just to the left of that cedar tree, behind that sticker patch." Thomas saw it instantly—a flat gray slab half-buried under rotted vegetation and topsoil, perhaps twenty feet deeper into the thicket.

"*Outta-SIGHT*, Bee-Cee! Wait here while I check it out."

Thomas started toward the rock with practiced finesse. "Thanks for clearing the cobwebs out, by the way."

"Yeah, well, I guess that means you owe me one, motherfucker." Bennett was slowly picking his way back to the path. "I'm gonna take a break. If you need any help, tough shit." Thomas made his way to the slab and cleared the vines and briars from around it with an arc of his leg. Amazingly, Bennett had done well. It was a good one—about the size of a trash can lid, and, assuming a reasonable degree of symmetry, at least a half-foot thick in the center. Thomas spread his feet wide and bent at the waist, then eased his fingertips under the far edge of the stone and rocked back on his heels, letting his weight do the lifting. The slab quickly broke loose from its dry bed, and he almost fell over backward before resetting himself.

With the slab held vertically, Thomas scanned the exposed bedding and saw nothing that could be put to use—just the expected ants and pill bugs, plus one fairly large centipede, about five or six inches long, that undulated into the brittle grass girding the shallow crater as soon as daylight swept over it. But nothing like a toad or a snake or a lizard that could be snatched up and flung back through the woods at Bennett.

He took a step back and brought the rock the rest of the way over, letting it pivot heavily to the ground. A scorpion scurried out of a cleft and quickly disappeared under a boot, and a final scan of the rock revealed no remaining life.

It was time.

Bennett had managed to pull most of the debris from his hair and was now sitting cross-legged on the top tier of The Drop-off, culling beggar's lice from his argyle socks. "Come 'ere," Thomas said. "If you still wanna go through with this, I'll need some help carrying this thing out of here."

Bennett rose to his feet and stepped back into the woods. Thomas managed to contain the sarcasm when Bennett finally arrived at his side, his blonde locks once again laced with cedar needles and a fresh crop of beggar's lice encircling his ankles.

"I can't believe my fuckin' socks, man."

"So throw 'em away. Come on, let's pick it up. Get on the other side."

Bennett looked down at the rock. "Are you sure it doesn't have any spiders on it?"

"No, Bennett, it doesn't have any spiders on it. Now, come on, we're wasting time. Get on the other side. Please."

Bennett positioned himself opposite Thomas, and together they lifted the rock clear from the brush and lurched toward the path like drunken pallbearers, fighting to maintain their footing. Twice they had to lower the rock to the ground to catch their breath and allow blood to flow back into their hands, and both were soaked with sweat as they staggered out of the woods and onto the path. Then finally, fifteen minutes after they had begun, the last lowering of the stone—at their feet on the second tier, within inches of the edge.

They dropped onto their stomachs and slithered to the rim. The boat was still there, one hundred unobstructed feet below, rocking softly with the casts of the fishermen. The appearance of both the craft and the fishermen was utilitarian. To Thomas, they looked like construction workers or plumbers or bricklayers—somebody who sweated for a living. Both men wore khaki trousers ("parochial school pants" was what their buddy Pete called them) and denim work shirts that looked like they'd been pulled from the bottom of a dirty clothes hamper, and leather boots. One man sported a tattoo on his left arm, and both looked as if they hadn't shaved in days. Their headgear alone gave them a clear identity—one wore a black baseball cap, the other an embattled fedora of nondescript color with a dark band of sweat abutting the brim. Thomas couldn't help but be impressed by how quiet the men were as they cast their lures, articulating each movement with surgical finesse.

"These guys take this fishing shit seriously," Thomas whispered.

As near as Thomas could tell, it was perfect. He had heaved enough objects over the center of the edge to know that the consistent point of impact was three feet out from the shore on longitude, and on latitude, exactly even with a decaying willow jutting from an accumulation of rock at the base of the bluff. The current was holding the stern of the tethered skiff about six feet from this spot—not too close for comfort, or at least Thomas's comfort, but close enough for the desired effect. The water was only about two feet deep at that distance from the bank, and Thomas had seen a rock weighing about twenty pounds—not a quarter of the size of the one on hand—generate a wave capable of lifting three large and instantly traumatized geese a yard above the river's surface.

The boys got to their feet, and Thomas stepped over and knelt beside the slab. The side that had been buried now faced up, and the damp coating of dirt had dried into a layer of dust.

"Look, we're here, and the boat's here"—Thomas cleared a path in the dust with a swipe of his hand and indicated the two points with a finger

—"and if we just push it over the edge"—the finger slid slowly toward the cleared path as he spoke, pushing dirt along with it—"then it'll tumble all the way down and who knows how it's gonna hit? It might land flat or it might just slice in. Or it might hit something on the way down. A tree limb or something. See?" Bennett nodded; he was staring intently at Thomas's finger. "But, if we pick it up and kind of hoist it over flat and level"—this time Thomas's finger doubled the distance with a shallow hop—"then it should stay flat and pancake in, and we don't have to worry about it hitting anything on the way down." Thomas stood up and wiped his hands on his jeans. "Okay?"

Bennett nodded. "Okay, Commander Kessler. Let's go."

The boys wrestled the stone aloft and inched closer to the edge. The blue morning sky had turned to a dazzling silver, and Bennett's soaked bangs were hanging limply over his eyes.

"Shit, Tom, my hands are dripping with sweat! I don't know how much longer I can hold on. Hurry up! Let's do this."

Thomas leaned forward and looked over the rim to the river below, and what he saw almost made him lose his balance. To his horror, the fisherman in the fedora was on his feet fumbling with the knot, and as Thomas watched in disbelief, the cord fell into a loose pile in the bottom of the boat. When the second fisherman picked up an oar and plunged it down into the riverbed, preparatory to shoving off, Thomas leaped from paralysis to panic.

"They're leaving, Bennett! COME ON ... on the count of three!"

Without waiting, he rocked his side of the slab back and then forward.

"ONE!"

Bennett, completely flustered and struggling to adjust to the accelerated pace, was a half swing behind by the time the rock lost its forward momentum, causing it to swivel drunkenly to the left as it swung out toward the river.

"TWO!"

Bennett had almost made up for his late start, and the two sets of hands that swung the massive stone toward the river the second time were more in sync, increasing the arc.

"THREE!"

The rock sailed out over the river, and the boys belly-flopped down and hooked their chins over the edge. For the second time that day, Thomas felt the adrenaline kick in.

From his place on the limestone shelf, Thomas's elevated senses perceived more than just a falling rock; it was as if he were watching a planet move lazily through a column of molasses-thick air and time.

The boat had been left to drift, and the slow current had brought it closer to the point of impact. *About five feet off dead center,* Thomas heard himself say in his dream state.

That evening as he lay in bed, Thomas would be astonished at the clarity of the memory of what he was now witnessing in a few electrifying seconds, at the details captured in the fleeting moment of impact: the round slab, his crude chart still visible in its dry coat of dust, shattering the stillness of the river with a slap like a gunshot; the grotesque mouth of naked riverbed bursting open under the stone in an exploding halo, sending cartwheeling strands of duckweed into the air; a pile of algae-coated stones

—relics of earlier campaigns—lying half-buried in the exposed mud; a small perch flapping madly in the air that had displaced the river, delivering a frantic series of tiny glints before disappearing into the receding froth; a decomposed beer can, torn and split by the trauma but still proudly displaying its brand—Lone Star—before the chaos reclaimed it.

The fishermen were struck twice—first when the initial wave heaved the meager craft over on its side and pitched Fedora Man and a nominal amount of unsecured fishing gear over the gunwale and into the churning water, then again, this time on the opposite side, when the water's inertia weakened and reversed as the round wall collapsed in on itself, leaving nothing but a dying brown eddy that quickly faded to green.

Thomas pushed himself back from the edge and stood, his heart pounding in his ears. He pulled his Kents out of his jeans with a trembling hand. "Come on, Bennett. Get back up. They'll see you." Thomas gently extracted a cigarette from his wadded pack and dug in his shirt pocket for a match. Last one, he noted, as he struck it on his buckle and raised it to the Kent. Bennett was still lying motionless on the shelf, and Thomas reached down and, with an ankle in each hand, dragged him back.

"Hey, man! Cut it out." Bennett rolled over and looked at his jeans. "Now I got white shit all over my Levis."

"Well, at least I got your mind off your goddamn socks. Why in the hell didn't you back off? Did you want those guys to see you?"

"So what's the big deal, anyway?" Bennett was on his feet now, beating caliche dust from his jeans. "They know we're up here—it's not like it could have been a humongous eagle turd or something."

"They know somebody's up here, but they don't know who! It's just plain stupid to let 'em see your face!" Thomas walked over to the second tier and took a seat. "And this town's not that big."

Bennett produced a Parliament from the box in his shirt pocket and coaxed the Zippo out of his pocket. The first spin of the wheel brought nothing more than a flat pop, and several more yielded only sparks. Bennett slid the lighter back into his jeans. "I'm out of fluid. You got a match?"

"Here." Thomas handed Bennett the Kent. "Use this. They didn't see you, did they?"

Bennett pressed the tip of Thomas's cigarette against his own and drew in, then held the Kent out at arm's length, twirling it analytically between his fingers. "Is this the best you can do? This thing's got more kinks in it than one of Aunt Jemima's cunt hairs." He gave the Kent back to Thomas. "Did you see that fuckin' fish fly? Man, that was outta sight!"

Thomas reached over and plucked the Kent from Bennett's fingers, considering his question answered. "Goddammit, Bennett, it was just dumb to let 'em see you when you didn't have to. What did they do after the rock hit, anyway?"

Bennett walked over and seated himself next to Thomas, then drew a foot up and started picking at his sock. "Well, if you weren't such a chickenshit, you'd have seen the guy still in the boat shoot us the finger, and I can't much blame him for that, considering what we did"—Bennett paused, ruminating—"but that other guy, the one in the funny hat, he just stood in the water and gave me a look that was equal to ten fingers!" Bennett cast a palm-full of beggar's lice into the breeze. "If looks could kill, I'd be one dead motherfucker."

Merciful winds were beginning to pick up from the southeast—gulf winds, they were called, even though the Gulf of Mexico was two hundred miles away. The strong currents were lifting the sweat from their knit shirts, tempering the oppressive heat. Thomas smoked his Kent in silence, alternately watching Bennett fuss with his socks—he had both feet on the shelf now, picking away with both hands, the Parliament dangling limply from his lips—and sweeping his eyes across the surface of the hardwood forest across the river. The sky was dazzling, limitless, with only a smattering of high, thin clouds—minor smears on an otherwise virginal palette—and when Thomas laid his back onto the stone balcony, he had to shield his eyes with a forearm. Soon a pair of turkey vultures floated from upriver and swooped casually in and out of his framed periphery, surveying the bluff in wide looping arcs, and Thomas unconsciously made a game of trying to anticipate the direction of the birds' next intrusion into his field of vision. Their flight patterns seemed to be centered on The Drop-off, and their gentle dives would bring them into a surprising intimacy before they would curl their wings and angle back out over the river, then circle back and sail back toward

Thomas along some untried route. The big birds were beautiful at a distance, at times allowing their glide paths to intersect only inches apart, but when they swooped in close, Thomas could see their bald, red heads, twitching nervously from side to side in search of putrefaction.

Thomas closed his eyes and brought his arm down from his forehead, sealing off the light and the buzzards, and thought of Mrs. Hatch, his algebra teacher from last semester. He would make a point of watching her walk in from the teachers' parking lot, those gorgeous hips twitching between that tiny waist and those long tanned legs, her teaching materials gathered up against her lavish breasts. But it was like with the buzzards— up close, in class, all you could see were her lazy left eye and the enormous black mole on her forehead.

Thomas smoked his Kent and lost himself in the buzzards' graceful passes through the hazy, flickering prisms that his damp lashes and squinted eyes had become. As they soared ever closer, he could begin to hear the whisper, the whoosh of their wings as they veered out over the river at the end of their glides with a single forceful flap.

Suddenly, a rock arced impotently into the path of one of the birds' tails as it swept by, clicking harmlessly on the rocks lower down on the bluff seconds later.

"You're not gonna be able to hit one of those things," Thomas droned, "and it wouldn't hurt 'em even if you did."

"I'm not trying to hurt 'em, just scare 'em away. They're getting too damn close."

Thomas's next drag tasted like filter—his indicator that a smoke was finished—and he crushed the fire out before flicking the butt over the edge. "You know, buzzards love beggar's lice. If you're not careful, they're liable to drag you over the edge by your socks."

Bennett ignored him.

Thomas brought his arm down from his brow and sat up. "How's about giving me one of your Parliaments, Bennett? My cigarettes are so dry they burn down before I can get much out of 'em."

Bennett snapped his still glowing butt over the edge, then reached for the box in his shirt pocket with the same hand. "Sure, but you'll have to light it yourself—my lighter's out of fluid."

"Bennett, you dumb shit! You just flicked our only fire over the edge, dumb-ass! I used up all my matches. Remember."

Bennett looked at the Parliament box in his hand, then up at Thomas, and a shared panic began building in their eyes. "*SHIT*, Tom! What'll we do? Rub two fuckin' sticks together?"

"Naw, let me try something first. Give me your lighter and a cigarette, just in case this works."

Thomas put the Parliament in his lips and began snapping the hand holding the Zippo as if he were resetting a thermometer. "I've seen my old man do this before. Centrifugal force or inertia or something pushes whatever fluid that's left into the wick. Keep your fingers crossed." The buzzards were still making their methodical and fluid passes, but now their efforts were taking them out over the river, about even with the edge of The Drop-off, as if their concentration had shifted to the riverbank.

"Looks like something has caught their eye," Thomas mused. "Probably a dead coon or something along the riverbank." He ceased the downward whipping of his right arm and thumbed the lighter open. "Well, here goes nothing."

Thomas arched his shoulders and turned his back to the wind, then cupped the lighter in both hands and brought it up to the Parliament. This was not the sort of suspense from which Bennett could derive any pleasure, and he distracted himself by stepping over to the edge and watching one of the birds as it sailed in from upriver. It passed about ten feet below the shelf, then soared back out over the green river.

Thomas thumbed the Zippo's wheel, and the wick caught the spark just long enough to produce a weak flame that sputtered out almost instantly, but not before he had managed to ignite a tiny portion of the Parliament's tip, and a series of sharp, desperate puffs brought on a glorious flame that consumed a half inch of cigarette before Thomas dared relent.

"*HOT* damn! Smokes all around," he proclaimed. "Here's your lighter back. From here on out, it's either chain-smokin' or no smokin'. That thing's dry as a bone now."

Thomas extended the lighter to Bennett's beckoning hand, then realized Bennett wasn't reaching for the lighter at all; he was rocking in and out over the edge, casting sporadic glances straight down, and his outstretched hand was bidding Thomas do the same. "Come here, Tom," he whispered. "You won't fucking believe this."

Thomas stepped over to the edge and looked down.

Fedora Man was no more than twenty feet below on the face of the precipice, clinging to the stunted vegetation struggling to survive in the barren strata of the wall, the blunt toes of his boots groping blindly for a footing in the crumbling limestone while he struggled for breath. His clothes were still soaked—sweat had probably replaced the river water— and the fedora still sat atop his head like a corrupted toadstool. The other man was far less adventurous, or vengeful. He remained seated along a generous ledge fifty feet below his cohort, a baseball cap pushed back on his head while he smoked a cigarette with little enthusiasm.

Thomas knew he should flee with his anonymity intact before the situation got out of hand, but something compelled him to remain with Bennett at the edge.

And then he heard Bennett's voice, soft yet rich in evil inflection, intone: "Well, well, it looks like Christmas came early this year."

As Fedora Man's head began to slowly, hesitantly, tilt back, the soaked hat dislodged from his matted hair and tumbled down the steep scarp. The creases in his face were filled with a compost of sweat and dirt, and there was nothing he could have said that wasn't already voiced by his expression: a terror of vulnerability and a self-loathing for having brought himself to such a tenuous, helpless position. And, of course, intense hatred. He was throwing it up at Bennett with every wordless heave of his exhausted breath.

"Come on, Bennett!"

Thomas had made the second shelf in two vaulting steps before he realized he was alone.

"Let's get outta here!" he called back. *"He's so fucking close you can count his nose hairs!"*

But there was no perceived movement from Bennett. He was standing at the edge, as if admiring the serene vista across the river, and the set of his elbows put his hands in front of him. Then his Levi's fell loose at the waist, and a thin yellow stream dropped between the toes of his penny loafers, then raced to the edge and arced into the air in front of him.

Thomas was trotting to the mouth of the path when the first shrieks of Fedora Man's rage and pain were torn from his throat by his inexorable and headlong return to the river's southern bank; he was ten feet into the sheltering cedar canopy of the trail by the time the weathered clapboard barracks across the water caught the first of his screams and threw it back to the limestone palisade; then more cries crossed and came back, multiplying and amplifying the agony until it was as if the damned citizenry of Sodom had chosen to cast the ancient burden of their sins upon the sluggish, lime- green waters of the good old Nebraska River.

CHAPTER 4

There was nothing—not even the knowledge of a void—when suddenly he was positive that he had been in the office at Mister Hansborough's Gulf Station, talking with his father and Mister Hansborough. But NO—a distracting sound, a bell ringing. When he looked up from his search for a source, he found himself standing outside Pete's family's big old farmhouse in South Fuller, south of the Nebraska dry grass pressing in along the soles of his bare feet, prickly.

It didn't matter; nothing really seemed to matter. He looked up at the porch, long with railings, dead white paint curling at the cracks, gray wood beneath Bennett and Pete in old rusted lawn chairs—once white too— sitting there on the porch, mumbling and giggling back and forth like silly girls. He raised his hand. HEY, he thought he said, his arm moving through the air slowly, TOO SLOW.

His friends rose, silent, dirge-like, to their feet, turned, and melted through the shadowed screen door, sand through a sieve. He started to follow, but as he brought his bare leg up to the first withered step, his name came to him: "Taahhhh-hahm," floating soft and musical on languid air. He stopped, arrested, curious—a sharp stir of hunger, but not hunger, not really. Maybe a sweet hypnosis. It owns me, the lullaby in the voice pulled him back from the porch, back from the dead screen and the hard boys like him, back into the yard. But not a yard now; a large field, the old two-story house looming over him, curving down at him like a kindly old man bent at the waist, offering candy.

The balcony along the second floor of the house seemed so high—higher than he thought it should be. Now it angled over him, allowing a view seductive and distant through the bedroom windows, over the peeling sills, past the faded cotton drapes moving soft and sleepy. Then, "Taahhhh-maas" and movement, this time with the calling voice swift, teasing in the shadows of the second window from the right.

He stepped forward a pace, but the house moved with him, shifting back, staying the same. "That's an old bedroom; nothing in there but old boxes," he said, maybe out loud. Allured, he started toward the porch, the house, the screen door, and the worn oak staircase within that would take him there. The warped boards of the porch steps creaked and bowed as he pressed his weight down, watching each placement of his bare feet along the splintering pine.

Then he looked up to the torn and rusted screen, reaching for the door pull, but he was at the rear of the house, centered on its girth—a gray and white expanse. He placed the fingertips of one hand on the weathered wall and brought them down cat-like, bringing tiny flakes of shattering paint popping, snapping like eggshells into his face, floating down to his feet still bare in the hot, gentle dust.

He turned his head and looked past his bare shoulders: one by one, yellow flat lawn rolled on forever. To his right, the old garage stood detached, an anguished parallelogram, once vertical slats angling like snake's teeth hovering jagged and rotten just off the yellow ground against a limitless empty sky. "Taahhhh-hahmmmmm."

"Tom, do you want me?" He stepped back at once, growing hard and desperate. The porch was gone; she must be here somewhere. He felt the stubble tingling of the lawn beneath his feet, the sun careening off the tin roof as the house arced over him again, showing him windows. He brought his hand to his brow, peering under it to the row of second-floor windows, drapes drawn and gathered. Then he saw Sharon Riley, looking as if she had been there forever, leaning out of the window, far left.

He moved over to be under her. Her arms straight, elbows locked, her breasts swelling toward him, held between her tanned arms. Her forearms angled out to tiny hands braced on the flaking sill, wearing the same red two-piece he had seen her in at the pool in Live Oak Park. Her wet hair, heavy and long, moved with the serpentine sway of her hips and breasts as she strode past—superior, untouchable. He was invisible.

"But she's different now," he thought. "Nice, come up, Thomas, come on up!" Though she seemed at the end of a long tunnel, he could see and hear her clearly, her voice high, sultry—a bell in the intoxicating light heat of a reality building after wandering lost and broken in a random void. He wasn't thinking, but a thought came to him as a question: *How do I get up there?*

He looked back to the window, vacant now, the frayed colorless drapes stroking the frame, the room beyond hollow. Then she was gone. "Yoo- hoooo, Tom! Over here!" He followed her voice again, now to the window at the opposite corner of the house. Moving across the yard, he set himself near the corner. He could see her now, dimly, as she held herself back from the light, flirting through the gloom. Her white smile was lucid, remote, reaching to him from the depths of the high, forward-leaning room.

She stood, hands held coyly on her hips, the severe red of her knit top sharp and bright against the shaded tan of her skin, almost black in the dimness. Vague, undeniable, he could see her rose-pink nipples and the dark joining of her thighs—forbidden, hidden. "Thomas, I've got to get up there!" He felt a thousand fingers of warm electricity squirming, trying to pull him apart, delicious torment.

Then Sharon stepped forward, flashing brilliantly in the glass, just a glance of breasts and pussy hair that vanished below the sill when she dropped to her knees. Her eyes—he hadn't seen her eyes, big and brown, holding his now. "Why don't you climb the tree?" Had she moved her lips? "What tree?" "Why don't you climb the tree?" she repeated.

He spun and retreated from the wall, from the house, then back to face the house again. It was there, to the right of the house, that he had known forever, and just off the corner, an enormous live oak that had never been there. But of course, it clearly was. He ran to its huge trunk, his strides carrying him in slow vaults across the yard. Then he was there, against the hard rough column with his bare skin.

He looked up; the branches spread out in all directions, and he could see a stout branch that swept upward to the second floor, to the window to Sharon. He looked back to the trunk—it was smaller, telephone pole-sized, perfect for shimmying, he thought. He mounted it feverishly, feeling it press against his nakedness, soft as he knew Sharon would be in the cool shade now, simultaneously hugging and crawling up the shaft and then onto the branch.

He was naked. "I'm naked," he thought, and it seemed somehow strange, but it wasn't really, and besides, it was irrelevant anyway. *Rap rap!* The branch knocked against the house, and he dragged himself up the branch now, toward the window. Through the mesh of branches and leaves, his body begged for release, bursting. He saw her, shamelessly pawing the air with an outstretched arm, begging for him, her entire upper body protruding from the ancient frame of warped slats.

Rap! Rap! "Rise and shine!" Frozen on the limb, electricity fading, he looked to Sharon. OH NO—she was still in the window. Did she say that? He heard her say it, but he knew she didn't, and she just looked bored, her arms and breasts down on the sill, elbows resting before her nipples, her cheeks cupped in her palms.

RAP! RAP!

"Daylight in the swamp!"

Only one person ever says that, he thought he said to no one.

It was a familiar, disturbing voice with no direction, and the exquisite surges were almost gone now, leaving his rigid body as the dream began to come apart. He looked below for an affirmation that it wasn't ending—for Pete or Bennett on the ground, perhaps. For anything. But he saw nothing; the yard was featureless, the scene blurred.

RAP! RAP! "Confound-it-all, Son! Wake up! We've got something to do."

Then it was over. Sharon and her white breasts and the leaves and branches and the faded cotton drapes collapsed into a swirling, featureless matte of dark orange light, and the sun-filled room poured into his opening eyes with cold efficiency. This new reality was not Sharon, but The Colonel; not an insanely sensuous tree limb but one of his pillows held fast in his thighs, the imprisoned and impersonal recipient of his aching erection. He had kicked his sheet into a twisted roll at the foot of his bed and exposed his legs, which were drawn halfway up and hobbled at the ankles by his Jockey shorts. At least The Colonel respected his privacy. He shuddered at the thought of the embarrassment an opened door would have brought.

"Okay, oh-*KAY*, Dad! I'm up!"

"Your mother wants to know if you want any breakfast." "Naw. Maybe just some juice."

"All right. Meet me in the garage after you're bathed and dressed." Then the sound of The Colonel's brisk tread down the carpeted hall.

Thomas rolled over onto his back, snatched the pillow from between his legs, and threw it hard against the wall. *"Gah-hod-DAMN! I don't fuckin' believe it."* The words came out in a low moan of defeat.

Just a few more minutes, and that stuck-up, cheer-leadin' bitch would've been mine.

Stripped of ardor, he lay spread-eagle on his bed. His eyes settling unconsciously on the B17, twitching against the cool flowing from the duct. What had it been? Three days? No. *Four days!* He had held himself back, had resisted choking the chicken for four teeth-grinding nights, through at least three showers, and God knows how many trips to the crapper, just so that he might once again experience the inimitable reality of a gen-u-ine, slam-bang, headboard-knocking, tooth-chipping nocturnal emission—the closest a virgin can come to the real thing—and The Colonel comes along and yanks him out of it.

Well, the next time Pete tells me I could fuck up a wet dream, at least now I can tell him who I got it from.

Thomas swung his feet to the carpet. He couldn't comprehend why his father would want him up so early. He'd been out of school for over a week and had slept late every day except the first one (he had Lowry's goddamn dogs to thank for that). Well, that day and last Tuesday as well, when his father had set the lawn mower outside his bedroom window going full blast at eight in the morning, then roped him into three hours of hauling rocks for one of his little stone walls when Thomas ran outside in his bathrobe to shut it down. He had to hand it to The Colonel on that one. But this time was nothing like that. His approach had been matter-of-fact and non-negotiable.

And where in the hell does he get that "daylight in the swamp" shit? We've never lived in a swamp.

Thomas retrieved a fresh pair of briefs from the top drawer of his dresser, then pushed his door open just enough to peek into his parents' bedroom. The whole house was quiet. He swung the door wide and stepped across the hall and through the master bedroom, animating the thin slivers of light seeping onto the floor through the blinds, then entered the bathroom and flicked the wall switch. The lights twinkled on, and he twisted the lock in the center of the doorknob. He showered quickly, dried with a few swipes of a clean towel, then slipped into his clean briefs, resisting temptation for the time being. If he could just hold off one more day, he theorized, surely Sharon or someone just as comely would enter his next deep sleep and deliver him from his monastic agony. He turned to the sink and twisted the cold water tap before applying the toothpaste to his brush, in defiance of his father's austere edicts concerning utilities, then defiantly applied too much toothpaste by squeezing the center of the tube rather than crimping the end. He brushed mechanically for less than twenty seconds, then rinsed with water sucked directly from the spigot. Thomas's haircut was supposed to be a flattop, but his hair was too fine to stand up without the aid of Butch Wax

—which he refused to use because he had never found a way to remove it from his hands after applying it to his hair—so his tonsorial regimen consisted of nothing more than several strokes of a hairbrush straight back across his damp scalp. Even this was wasted time, since his hair simply crept back into a featureless burr as it dried.

Lastly, he moved onto the carpet of the alcove that held his mother's vanity for what was as much a part of his daily routine as the shower and the brushing, a final morbid ritual that he forced on himself each morning like a passerby surrendering to the lure of morbidity in a wreck on the side of the road. He stepped over to the bank of light switches and flipped a second one up, and the fluorescent bulbs mounted high in the nook above the mirror crackled on with a splintered rhythm that bounced light about the room. When the shards settled into a unified glow, he set his feet into their usual spot in the alcove and looked up.

The image in the mirror reflected the description on the driver's license that Thomas had so proudly earned the previous February: fifteen years old (if you do the math); blue eyes and brown hair; five feet, two inches tall at eighty pounds. He had lied about the weight—he actually weighed only seventy-five pounds at the time—but probably no amount of lying would have made any difference, anyway. This rite of passage, this legitimacy that had initially made him feel older, didn't make him look any older, didn't prevent the occasional cop from pulling him over and waiting by the window with a cocksure smirk on his face while Thomas fumbled the license out of his wallet and handed it over. And it was always the same—the smirk would fade and the cop would hand the license back in a manner that was more astonishment than apology, and Thomas would tuck the license away in his wallet until the next time.

But he couldn't really blame the cops. It was a child who looked back at him from the mirror, a child who still got into the movies for the price of an eleven-year-old, who was not to be taken seriously by anyone, anytime, for a while yet to come.

Thomas had grown to detest the cruel caricature he saw in his mother's mirror each morning. To him, it was a subterfuge, an obscene misrepresentation of himself in a time long past, before cigarettes and driving and wet dreams about Sharon Riley. And though he tried to confront the image anew each day, bolstered with the objectivity born to each new morning, it was always Thomas-the-Child, frozen in time, looking forlornly back through the heartless glass, saying *this is not who you are, but this is who the world will see today.*

He studied the spare image in the mirror, highlighted by the soft glow radiating from the vulnerable, translucent skin that barely veiled the veins and arteries just under the surface, infusing his skeletal rib cage with the subtle undertones of white marble. His blanched skin differed from his bleached Jockey shorts in shade only—the intensity of the reflection back from the glass was the same—and the arms and neck and head, burned to umber by the Texas days, seemed detached, drawn into the gloom behind the light, leaving the stenciled body cleaved of upper extremities, suspended in a warm glimmer like an emaciated and headless mannequin in a department store window. His hip bones protruded like sharp knobs, setting off his indented waistline and enhancing the cadaverous appearance of his torso. And Thomas was thinking *I'd rather be dead than have that bitch Sharon Riley see me like this, and she was right, right to treat me like I didn't exist the other day at the pool in Live Oak Park, because I was there with all my clothes on and she was there without hardly any of hers, and she hated to show herself to me because I had nothing to show to her in return—*

—and he had used what he had taken from her and used it selfishly and without restraint that very morning and would again, and there was nothing she could do about it.

Ever.

Thomas scanned his small, gaunt face. He didn't bother to check for whiskers anymore. Like body hair, if it came, it came, but he was tired of leaning into the mirror and seeing only the veneer of pale down he had worn since infancy. He scraped the matte of fuzz from his face with his father's razor with just enough regularity to allow an affirmative response when asked by his peers if he shaved yet. Even The Colonel had expressed bewilderment at his lack of facial hair, and once offered a hypothesis involving his mother's lineage, which ran through the heart of the Carolinas—Cherokee country—and Thomas couldn't tell if he was joking or not.

But Cherokee blood or not, there was one thing for sure—there was no way Thomas was going to shower in gym class when school started again until he had some pubic hair. He'd put his old man on notice that he might have to give the coach a note, but that was *it*. Last semester he was the only guy in the class without hairs.

But he was growing, The Colonel insisted. The bathroom scale and his father's pencil marks on the door frame in the kitchen proved that he was, in the most literal sense of the phrase, "inching up." But he was still the slightest boy in his class by far (he probably didn't outweigh any of the girls, either), and he and his buddy Pete sort of went back and forth at being shortest, with Thomas being the tallest for the moment. Ever since he could remember, The Colonel had been preparing him for the inevitable difficulties of a sluggish maturation—telling him how he was short too at such-and-such an age—but his assurances were ringing hollow in the face of his mounting social awkwardness. He wanted it to be like in his dreams, where his body was just an obscure vessel, intangible and ghostly, and public nudity was less of a threat to his anesthetized esteem than an inadvertent fart.

Thomas bent toward the glass and forced a broad smile onto his narrow face to inspect the one area that was showing improvement. His upper incisors had finally begun to surrender to the weight of his lip, leaving him looking less like a rodent and narrowing the gap in the teeth that came in after he left his first set laying broken and bloody on an Alabama driveway eleven years before. Of course, he was losing a whistle, and a wonderfully accurate water pistol to boot, but he had outgrown the latter and hardly ever used the former. Besides, no price was too high to pay for an improvement in his appearance, however minor.

He drew himself erect and turned to open the door, leaving the impostor in the glass, then passed back through his parents' bedroom. Once in his room, he shut the door and scooped the Timex off his desktop.

Seven-thirty.

Shit, it's early! Anything before ten was early.

Thomas didn't know what The Colonel had planned, though he had a few ideas and deemed none acceptable. He pondered an escape as he wandered about the room assembling his wardrobe—first to his dresser for socks, then to his closet for a clean knit pullover, and finally over to the belted jeans draped over the back of his bent-wood rocker—all the while allowing his eyes to divine the room for something from which he could craft a diplomatic footbridge that would carry him beyond the garage and safely onto the brown powder of the pump path. Thomas dressed haltingly, his mind elsewhere. His scrutiny fell on his telephone. It was one of those old black ones that looked like a wedge of cheese or a piece of chocolate cake wearing a matador's cap.

I could call Bennett. We could make something up about my promising to help him do something this morning. Dad would never make me break a promise.

He walked over to his desk and lifted the handset to his ear. The dial whirred as he fed Bennett's number into it, and after a few clicks, it started ringing. It was picked up halfway through the third ring.

"Caldwell residence."

"Hi, Miz Caldwell. It's Thomas. Is Bennett there?" A moment of silence, then:

"Well, no, Thomas. He's not. I should think he would be at your house by now. He left about half an hour ago and said he was going over to your house."

Shit!

"Oh. Well, I guess he must have got held up. That's why I called. I'm expecting him. I'm sure he'll be here soon. Anyway, sorry to have bothered you, Miz Caldwell. Have a nice day."

"You too. And do me a favor, will you, Thomas? Have our boy call me when he gets to your place."

"Okay, ma'am. Bye."

Thomas walked over to the bed, picked up the knit shirt, and slipped it on.

I guess I'll try Pete. He's gotta be home, it being so early and all.

He slipped the shirt over his head backwards, pulled it off, turned it around, then pulled it back on again without being aware of any of it.

Naw, never work. He lives too far away. It would take him a half-hour or better to get over here.

Thomas stepped over to his walk-in closet and cast his imagination onto the workbench his father had built into it. Scattered debris from his various projects was spread across the scarred plywood, and the shelving over the work area was so crowded that the bottoms of cans and jars hung precariously over the edge.

He pulled the stool out from under the bench and sat down to pull on his boots.

I could say I promised Momma I'd clean up my workbench this morning. He'd respect that. He surveyed the hodgepodge of trash, treasure, and ongoing projects: accumulated bits of shrapnel dug out of the walls of the Alamo on trips down to San Antone; a nearly completed black powder cannon he was building around an old 45-70 casing; a half-finished painting of his favorite gunfighter, Bill Longley; a model P-51 ineligible to join the fray over his bed for a lack of wings; three fossils dug from the local limestone; a pair of rattlesnake rattles; a little wax Halloween pumpkin with a black cat inside that was really a candle, and Thomas could never bring himself to light it because Rosa, a colored maid his parents had employed when he was a toddler, had given it to him. He could no longer bring a picture of Rosa into his head; he only knew he still loved her. *What the hell am I thinking? I'd rather do yard work than tackle this! Besides, he knows she'd never ask me to do something like that anyway. She'd just do it herself.*

A deep shelf stacked with blankets and quilts was mounted over the clothes rod opposite his workbench, and he drew the stool over and mounted it, then thrust a hand into the soft folds of a Mackinaw at the bottom of the pile. After a moment of hidden manipulations, the hand withdrew clutching an unopened pack of Kents, and Thomas turned it over in the light of the caged bulb, inspecting the cellophane for weevil holes. The pack threw off dull cards of flat light as it pivoted, revealing no breaches in the clear film.

He crammed the Kents into his left-front jeans pocket and collapsed the corners with his thumbnails until it was a formless mound, then left the closet to retrieve his wallet from the desktop, but not before sweeping his loose change into the pocket not occupied by the Kents.

He was ready to go. But where?

He sat down on the bed, once more allowing his eyes to roam freely across his walls and furnishings, still confident, still knowing that the mechanism of escape was somewhere in the room, and that it would make itself known to him before his father's impatience brought the sound of his brogans back to the hallway. The Colonel was good at outmaneuvering him on those rare occasions when they played chess, but their daily jousts over control of Thomas's body weren't played on an open board under set rules.

Just twenty seconds later, the key to his deliverance appeared, as he knew it eventually would, in his walnut gun case, loosely swaddled in an oily cotton rag between the butts of two lever-action Winchesters. And it was sure-fire—a better ticket than he had any right to expect. He rose from the bed and stepped into the hall, snatching the hefty object from the gun case as he went. His lightening spirits brought a tune into his head as he jaunted down the hall, and he presented it to the world as a modulated hiss that bled out from between his front teeth like air out of a deflating tire.

#

"Mornin', Sugar."

Thomas's mother was seated at the kitchen table in a rare moment of inactivity, a cup of coffee in one reddened hand and a Camel in the other, both held aloft by a planted elbow. The smoke was curling past the gentle face and salt-and-pepper hair, then collecting in the lampshade hanging from the ceiling. They exchanged smiles, and his mother motioned toward the kitchen counter and a beaded glass of chilled orange juice. Thomas set his burden on the table, then walked over and picked it up.

"Pittletail finally came home this morning."

Thomas turned and saw the stub-tailed gray Manx asleep against the wall, its long hind legs spread out on an army blanket. He walked over to the cat and knelt down, running his free hand gently through the cat's fur, rolling its hide between his fingers.

"He was already at the garage door when your daddy went out this morning. He looks all right to me—I went over him before I put out his bowl. Of course, he's been gone for over a week, and if any of those bullets are fresh he might have already healed up."

Thomas was amused at his mother's terminology. They weren't really bullets, but an accumulation of lesser projectiles that the tomcat tended to collect on his forays. Before this latest disappearance, the inventory consisted of two shotgun pellets—probably number eights—embedded in the web of skin between his body and left hind leg; a single small ball— turkey shot or a BB—under the skin just behind the right front leg, and another in the scruff of his neck. He had also located several lumps of scar tissue that held no evidence and could have been due to other causes, but Thomas felt that they were all probably gunshot.

He gathered two legs in each hand and started to roll the cat over to check the other side, but Pittletail's head came sharply up behind the growled threat of a weary front-line soldier, and Thomas left the animal in peace.

His mother was shaking her head. "That poor cat sure has a cross to bear.

It's no wonder he doesn't like people, as much as he gets shot at."

"Yeah, but there's nothing we can do about it, Momma." Thomas took a sip of orange juice, then pulled a chair out and took a seat. "I've seen him in the woods around the house at night, and he really does look like a bobcat. If I didn't know better, I'd probably take a shot at him myself."

"What if he wore a collar with a little bell on it? Wouldn't people know not to shoot at him then?"

Thomas thought about this for a moment. "Naw, then he couldn't hunt, and he'd hate us so much for doing it, he'd probably never come home. Besides, it would make him look like a sissy."

"I suppose you're right. How's your juice? Can I fix you some breakfast? Your daddy said y'all would be leaving straight away, but I'm sure he won't mind waiting while you eat."

Leaving?

"Uh, no thanks, Momma. I'm not hungry." Thomas drained his juice glass, then got up and stepped over to the sink. As he was placing the empty glass under the water tap, he noticed some paper matches—it looked like a full book—lying between two potted cactus plants on the windowsill above the sink. He made sure his mother's back was still to him, then slid them into the pocket with the Kents.

"Dad didn't happen to mention where we were going this morning, did he, Momma?" He delivered his remark devoid of emotion—as inconsequential as the water gurgling over the rim of his glass.

"Well, I think your daddy would prefer that I didn't tell you, and I'm probably telling you too much with that. Anyway, it's best you ask your daddy."

SHIT!

He walked back to the table and picked up his parcel, then leaned over through the twisting column of smoke and delivered a kiss to his mother's cheek. "Well, I guess I'd better go see what he's got in mind."

"Okay, Honey. Whatcha got there? One of your guns?" "Naw, one of The General's."

"Oh. Love you, Sugar." "Love you, Momma."

Thomas started for the door leading to the garage.

"Oh! Tom! I almost forgot. Pete called about an hour ago and I got it on the first ring. Hope it didn't wake you—I told him you'd call back when you got up." *A lot of good that does me now.*

"Thanks, Mom. I'll give him a call when we get back."

He opened the door and stepped into the garage. The Colonel was at his workbench against the far wall, and Thomas sauntered around the front of their Impala to join him. Thomas would have been surprised to see his father in slacks and a short-sleeved shirt this early in the day had it not been for his mother's clue to his agenda. The Colonel was nearing sixty now and spent most of his mornings in khaki shorts and brogans, doing the yard work while the heat was still bearable. The unlatching of the kitchen door had signaled Thomas's arrival, and The Colonel watched him approach. Parts of his mother's vacuum cleaner were spread out on the workbench amid scattered tools and beads of solder. The Colonel was holding an electric motor in his hands.

"Good morning, Son. Glad to see you could join the living." It could have been humor, sarcasm, or both. Or neither. The Colonel was a master of shrouded innuendo.

"Morning, Dad. How's it going with Mom's vacuum? Figured out the problem yet?"

"I'll need to replace the brushes and bushings and buy a new belt, but other than that and a little solder, it's fine. We can pick up the parts while we're out."

The Colonel looked down at the shrouded hulk in his son's hand. "What have you got there, Tom?"

"It's The General's Dragoon. I need to get it back to him. We've had it over two weeks now."

Thomas's father lowered his chin and peered over the top of his glasses. The wisk wisk wisk of a lawn sprinkler at the edge of the yard ticked off the interminable seconds.

"Strange that you should decide you need to return it right now, when you were told before you were even out of bed that I wanted your time this morning. We finished that job over a week ago, and with school out you've had every day since to get it back to him."

"I *know*, Dad, but I told The General I'd have it back in less than ten days, and today makes eleven. It's just that I keep forgetting." Thomas countered his father's gaze with canted brows, oozing sincerity. "And you always told me a man's only as good as his word."

His father thought for a moment, then respectfully surrendered, defeated by one of his own homilies. "Well, I was never one to keep a General waiting if I could help it. Okay, but get back here as soon as you can. We've got somewhere to go."

"Where?"

"You'll find that out when you get back."

The Colonel pushed his glasses back over his eyes, then returned to placing his tools in their assigned positions on the plywood backboard, officially ending the conversation. Thomas said nothing and stepped out of the garage and onto the asphalt driveway.

There were precedents—other times when Thomas was denied details of his immediate fate—and as he left the garage his instincts were dictating flight. He walked across the driveway to the low rock wall bordering the property with forced restraint, then mounted the pump path with an accelerated gait, heading north.

He jogged lightly along, stirring the powdered dust at his feet, the wrapped pistol cradled between his chest and forearm like a cherished pet. Regardless of what The Colonel had planned, he was confident he could extend his parole beyond all reasonable bounds, given his distaste for the alternative.

Two hundred feet up the path, a peninsula of cedar and juniper encroached on the trail, and Thomas slowed and scissored down into a crouch, then entered a thinning in the thicket. Within seconds, there was no sight of him available from the path.

#

The ridge along which Crest Road had been laid was unusually symmetrical, running north to south as an elongated mound sitting atop the otherwise formless landscape like a freshly filled grave. It was the highest tract of habitable ground available for development along the eastern perimeter of Granite Heights, and the builders of many of the older homes on Crest Road chose the sites for the views they offered. The houses were generally large, of brick and stone, and constructed on lots of sufficient depth to provide isolation from the scant traffic along the spine of the ridge.

Crest Road, which began life as a dead-end street, was intersected by a county road that was eventually upgraded to serve the new development of Kensington Oaks and granted the title of Kensington Road. To appease the inhabitants of Crest Road who assailed the county commissioner's office with complaints of the increased traffic and demands for a northern access, a county bulldozer was sent in to extend Casey Lane westward, thus tying into the northern tip of Crest Road. But the county refused to pave it, and Granite Heights didn't feel compelled to improve a road that they had never mandated, so in time the winds and rains swept the caliche from the fissures in the shattered limestone and created a washboard that rendered Crest Road a "through" street only by the most liberal definition.

The water table had been tapped at the base of the ridge, and the pump-path had been cut to enable the laying of the pipeline that ran roughly parallel to Crest Road, threading in and out of the woods blanketing the eastern slope. The tract held within these two demarcations—Crest Road and the pump-path—was overlaid with an inordinately thick deposit of rich topsoil in an area otherwise barren, and the resultant greenbelt was impenetrable and towering, rendering the ridge virtually inaccessible along its eastern flank.

Two hundred feet from the northern edge of this prolific greenbelt, now defined by the primitive union of Crest Road and Casey Lane, was the oldest house on the promontory, sitting on the largest parcel of land along the ridge. Within this modest structure, assembled from materials quarried and cut from the chaotic hills that encircled it and nestled among flowering arbors of bent cedar, lived The General.

Thomas had heard talk of the kindly old army doctor and his wonderful repertoire of tales and props from the onset of his initiation into adolescent society shortly after his family's arrival, and the hearsay flowed unabated up until the day some six months later when a peer presented him to The General's court. From that day forward, it was Thomas whom The General found at his doorstep more than any other, grinning like it was Christmas morning and hoping the old man's quiet existence would tolerate one more unheralded call.

In purely linear terms, Thomas's house was no distance at all from The General's property—seventy-five yards north up the pump-path, then due west a hundred and fifty feet—but given the density of the greenbelt, the second distance was meaningless to anyone actually making the trip. There were two far more practical—albeit less direct—routes: he could bicycle to the mouth of his cul-de-sac, then turn left on Ridgewest, left again on Casey, and ascend the washboard hairpin at the end; or he could just stay on the pump-path all the way to Casey Lane and make the strenuous climb to Crest Road on foot. Either itinerary would deliver him onto Crest Road and the mouth of The General's gravel driveway, a hundred and fifty feet to the south.

For the first year of his acquaintanceship with The General, Thomas exercised these two options without much thought or complaint, given the subsequent rewards. But as the rapport between the boy and old man expanded and intensified, the irony—"You can't get there from here," his father would joke—and inconvenience began to grate. After he started shuttling the old man's rifles and heavy pistols back and forth, it became difficult, if not downright impossible, to navigate the rutted hill on his bike, and the long hike down the pump-path wasn't much better.

Then one crisp winter day, Thomas decided he had had enough.

He was in his room, resigning himself to another long slog up the ridge, when his festering resentment finally surfaced and exploded. He grabbed the bone-handled Bowie knife from his gun case and flew out the back door, past his startled father, then sailed over the stone wall at a full gallop and tore down the pump-path, launching himself into the impenetrable barrier of juniper, grapevine, and bramble with unbridled fury. When he emerged an hour later—scratched, exhausted, and victorious—the jagged, meandering tunnel in his wake had brought him to the edge of The General's backyard along the wooded hillside.

#

Thomas was only seventy-five feet into the thicket before the stagnant air and heat forced him to his knees. It had been two growing seasons since he had carved out the path, and reclamation by the trees and underbrush, in concert with his own growth, pushed him into a duck-walk that cramped his diaphragm and sapped his vitality. He dropped his chin to his chest and fought for breath with his heart pounding in his ears, sweat dripping from his nose. Breaching the greenbelt required at least one short respite, especially in the summer.

A tingling burn in his thighs soon drove him out of his crouch and onto his buttocks in the soft, rotting mulch carpeting the thicket. Thomas set his back against a mesquite trunk and straightened his legs, his boot heels gouging two black gashes in the deep compost that instantly came alive with crickets and cockroaches, scrambling for new cover. He pulled the Kents from his pocket, spun the sliver of gold cellophane, and tore open the foil, then brought the pack down sharply against the edge of his hand. The first cigarette tore when he tried to extract it, and he hurled the pieces bitterly into the brush. The next cigarette remained intact, and he lit it and filled his lungs with smoke, making it all worthwhile.

The dead air was heavy with dust and juniper pollen, hanging in the thick cover like a fog and muting the faint light further, giving the woods a sour pungency that made breathing distasteful and laborious. Thomas was disgusted with himself for not pruning the trail back earlier in the year when it was cooler; it was far too hot to attempt it now. But *I'll have a car soon enough* had been his rationalization. A car would negate the need for the passage altogether.

Thomas stuck the Kent between his teeth and unraveled the shroud from the old Dragoon. He pointed it into the gloom of the thicket and cocked the hammer, allowing the sights to settle on a phantom foe sketched by the shadows. Even with a two-handed grip, the heavy pistol was hard to hold steady, and he lowered the hammer down and wiped his sweat from the grip before shrouding the pistol once again.

It took less than five minutes for the oppression of the thicket to trump Thomas's lingering fatigue. He crushed out his cigarette and staggered abruptly to his feet, then lurched back onto the barely discernible trail like Quasimodo to his bell tower, his knees hammering his chest as the thicket forced his body onto his thighs. Branches and briars fought his free hand and pummeled his head and shoulders, and his eyes burned from the gritty sweat streaming down his forehead. Soon, an eruption of itching down his back and along the belt line of his jeans told him that the overhanging limbs were distributing twigs and cedar needles into the collar of his shirt, which drove him on even harder. Finally, dancing glimmers of sunshine began to enliven the drab colors of the stagnant woods at his feet, and Thomas slowed and lifted his head toward the top of the hill. The woods had opened, revealing The General's house in a swath of light breaking through the foliage along the crest of the ridge, and Thomas stepped onto the parched grass at the edge of the yard and straightened unsteadily, his chest heaving against the swaddled Dragoon. His shirt was hanging from his body like the placenta of a new foal, and he pulled the tail loose to dislodge the debris gathered at his waist. He watched a June bug fall free and bounce off the toe of his right boot, then stuffed the shirt back into his jeans and swept the cedar needles from his matted hair with a wet palm. Finally, bereft of further polish to apply to his presentation, he headed up the gentle slope.

Only the southern portion of the property had been cleared for The General's unassuming home and perimeter of rudimentary yard; the remainder of the elongated tract remained in its raw form. The house was constructed with white limestone blocks of various sizes, all precisely cut and assembled with a minimum of mortar. The roof was gentle in slope and covered with doughnut-colored pine shingles cracked and curled by interminable exposure, and wide eaves shaded casement windows framed in tarred pine with generous sills. There was no sliding glass door abutting a patio of smooth concrete, a feature ubiquitous to the backyards in the region; instead, an enclosed breezeway of wood and screen clung to the back of the house, footed by two limestone steps feeding into a procession of flagstones laid flush with the dormant lawn. There were no flower beds to weed, no hedges to trim, nor any evidence of ongoing maintenance anywhere in the yard; only a faded coil of hose encircling a spigot fifteen feet out from the back door, lying like a snake in a nest of tall weeds, suggested that once the grass might have been green.

While there were no embellishments to The General's picture, nor was there clutter about the grounds or encroachment by the surrounding brake tovdetract from the cohesion of the overall setting, the house and yard radiated an appeal and respectability wrapped in uncompromising simplicity. To the north, the dense woods that framed the yard to the south and east reclaimed the property, and a stand of oaks and elms that ran along the western edge segregated the tract from Crest Road, acting in concert with the western edge of the greenbelt to create a shaded walkway. But the view from Thomas's trail offered only the yard and the house, creating the illusion of a solitary dwelling nestled against a wooded hillside.

Thomas crossed the yard toward the screen door, and as he approached the first of the flagstones, he passed between the only visible concession to human indulgence—a pair of metal lawn chairs mounted on tubular steel rockers and finished in a thick coat of white paint, etched by time and the elements with a web of tiny, indiscriminate cracks so exquisite in their design that Thomas invariably slowed to admire them. Stretched across the armrests and backs of both chairs were the silken articulations of garden spiders, silent testimony to the territorial exclusivity of their weavers. Fifteen feet up the path from the chairs, he passed the only other manufactured structure in the yard: a broad Grecian birdbath mounted on a fluted pedestal, sitting slightly askew and encircled at the base by dead weeds. The exterior spoke of neglect, but the basin was scrubbed free of mold and algae, the water clear.

Thomas reached the limestone steps and vaulted both as one, planting his boots in the center of the abrasive rubber mat on the small stone landing, then rapped the frame of the screen door with the knuckles of his free hand. The pine was badly warped, and the door rebounded off the jamb in an uneven clatter, accompanied by the shimmering rattle of the slack screen. He could see that the door leading from the breezeway into the house was open and stood peering through the screen, patiently awaiting movement. Soon, a figure bled out of the obscured darkness.

"Well, hello there, young fellow."

The General stepped into the breezeway and moved slowly across the bare pine floor, then raised a hand and deftly flicked the hook out of its eyelet. "I've got to keep this screen latched or the crosswinds will blow it open and let the bugs in. Weak spring, I guess. Wipe your feet and come on in."

Thomas walked reverently through the door and waited while The General replaced the hook, then followed him back into the main house, hearing the creak of the hardwood floor under his boot with his first step up from the breezeway. Thomas loved that sound.

Besides the airy living area, there was little more to the modest residence other than a bathroom, a small kitchen, and dining nook, and what Thomas assumed were two small bedrooms—the doors were always closed—off the hall that led to the carport at the north end of the house. The building had been set atop the high ridge with the harsh climate in mind, and the east and west walls held large casement windows that would grant access to the cooling breezes flowing under the boughs of the large oaks spreading shade across the roof during the summer, or admit the warming sunlight after the same branches had shed their leaves for the winter. Over the years, these alternating forces had swept all strong color from the room, turning maroon to mauve, brown to tan, black to slate. The house, as humble and unobtrusive as the surrounding yard, was resplendent in the same weathered pastels.

"I bet I can guess what's in there." The General was pointing a feeble finger at the oil-stained bundle in the crook of Thomas's arm. "How did it turn out?"

"See for yourself, General." Thomas reached into the folds and took hold of the pistol's grip, then grabbed the edge of what was once one of his father's undershirts and spun the rag from around the pistol. The walnut and brass held tightly in Thomas's small hand appeared first, then the worn and pitted steel as the wrapping spiraled away. "It cleaned up pretty good, General, but we couldn't find a cylinder stop to replace the one that's missing, and Dad made me call every gunsmith in Fuller. Colt made three versions, and yours is the oldest—the cylinder stops are round instead of square." Thomas felt bad; he had told The General that he could return it to him in firing order. "That's what makes that part so hard to find. But you could probably have that part made if you ever want to shoot it."

"So why would I need a gun to shoot," he replied, smiling down softly at Thomas, "as long as it's got a story to tell?"

CHAPTER 5

This was where it had all begun, where the rusted steel of old guns and the blighted leather of gun belts stained with the sweat of men long dead had swept like the heavy air moving over the ridge and into Thomas's awareness like a lost dream restored. The reality of another time, another place, built by mere words from an old man, and together they would go back.

Thomas didn't know The General's full name, but a foot-long section of shellacked pine mounted atop the mailbox beside the entrance of the gravel driveway bore the name O'Grady. Thomas could only guess at his age, but The General had once told him that he and another underaged patriot had tried unsuccessfully to enlist for the Spanish-American War, so Thomas figured he had to be close to eighty. He had been raised in the hills— Thomas didn't know exactly where—and went through medical school somewhere back east, which accounted for the proper diction that quickly fell apart in the telling of his stories, which were rife with dropped consonants and colloquialisms, many unfamiliar to

Thomas. But his personal résumé prior to his military career was sketchy. The General didn't talk much about himself.

Thomas couldn't recall who was standing beside him on The General's stoop to moderate their introduction on his first visit; he only remembered how anxious he was, fearing a slight misstep might foster a rejection and deny his access to the fabled treasure trove within. Muffled gongs had brought a pair of bespectacled eyes to the diamond of glass set in the heavy oak door; then bushy white brows arced in a tacit smile and slid from view. Then the door creaked open, and The General, looking far more benevolent than Thomas could have ever imagined, invited them in.

He struck Thomas as a rather handsome man, with his sharply sculpted face and wispy white hair combed straight back over a taut scalp. His eyes, pale blue and lucid, danced energetically behind bifocals set in half-frames of fine gold wire, with thick lenses that made his gaze appear to float under his smooth white brow. His high cheekbones were tinged in red, and while he sported no whiskers or sideburns, an occasional shadow of white stubble would subdue the translucence of his cheeks. The top half-inch of his left ear was missing, sliced off so cleanly that it wasn't particularly noticeable, and his hands quivered slightly but constantly. While his gait was hobbled by a noticeable limp and his overall posture wilted, he nonetheless moved with a sense of quickness and vitality, as if the old body was being fueled by the energy of a younger man.

The General's attire was unvarying (as was The Colonel's—a proclivity of retired officers, Thomas assumed) and remained consistent from that first visit through all the others that followed: a faded poplin shirt left open at the neck, pressed but not starched, and tucked neatly into khaki shorts or pants (depending on the weather), a brown canvas belt, and tan suede shoes over white calf-length socks. During the colder months, he could be seen moving about his property or checking his mailbox wearing a faded field jacket that still bore his unit patch—a blue arrowhead—and OGRADY on the name tag over the right breast.

The General was not without his eccentricities. If he retained the names of his visitors, Thomas included, he never used them and addressed each one as "young man" or "young fellow" instead, as if it were a rank assigned to his entire cadre of inquisitive boys, a rank that they would hold until post-pubescence overrode their curiosity for the dying frontier and each vanished in turn, like the legions of fresh-faced soldiers who had rotated in and out of his acquaintance during his career. Thomas often wondered how many such as himself had fallen under The General's spell as the seasons washed over the hills and the years swelled into decades, wondered if the amiable smile of recognition The General bestowed upon him at every meeting was not for him alone, but for all of those who had left a part of their fleeting adolescence in his practiced care, disciples who would occasionally live again in anecdotes that invariably began with "I knew a young man once—" and progressed in a narrative devoid of historical moorings, leaving Thomas to speculate at the conclusion as to whether the incident related had occurred two weeks or twenty-five years before. Thomas hoped that he might even be enshrined himself someday as "a young man I once knew who liked to fix my guns," and would bask in the possibility of immortality as he worked on the old Colts and Winchesters at the workbench in his closet.

#

Thomas held the Dragoon out, and the old man took it in his smooth, shiny fingers, turning the heavy pistol over in his hands for a few moments before passing it back. "Hang onto this for a minute while I look for another one, assuming you'd like another to fix up."

"Sure," Thomas answered back, grinning.

The General smiled and began looking around the room, at the walls hung with the headdresses, blankets, and breastplates of Comanches and Apaches, and the lariats, bridles, and gun belts of the cowboys who would eventually displace them. Here the past was the present, not some scholastic echo from the somnolent depths of a text. And The General was the perfect curator, having shared those days of gunpowder and trail dust with his aggregation of relics, each consecrated anew as its story echoed through the room.

"I've got a piece somewhere that I think you'll find interesting. Now, if I can just remember where I put it." Among the relics, only the guns weren't given set locations and shifted about the cluttered shelves and doily-laden tabletops as their stories were spun out. A tall bookcase against the north wall seemed to provoke a recollection, and The General walked over and peered into the shelves. It was laden with antiquities—only one of the eight tiers was dedicated to the storage of books—and after a moment, he reached in and extracted a long-barreled six-shooter, then motioned for Thomas to join him. A Navajo rug silenced Thomas's steps as he crossed the room, granting his arrival a solemn formality. The General turned the pistol over in his hands for a moment to verify its identity, then lifted the Dragoon from Thomas's hands and set it where the other pistol had been.

"Old Sam. I'll never forget him," The General said as he held the pistol out at eye level with both hands, smiling. "Have a seat over there where the breeze comes in, young man, and I'll introduce you to Sam. And his brother too."

Thomas took a seat on the sofa along the west wall. A pair of blue jays were fighting over the birdbath in the backyard, screeching and slamming their breasts together, and he watched them until he heard the creak of the worn rocker next to the hearth.

"I know those damn birds are some of God's creatures, just like you and me"—The General was reaching for a smoking stand that held several pipes stacked like rifles—"but if I'd been Noah, I would have sailed without them." He had set the pistol on the coffee table while he prepared his smoke, and while Thomas had never seen it before, he was certain it was an 1860 Colt Army. The wooden grip was missing, but otherwise, it looked complete and functional. Thomas wanted to pick the gun up but knew better. He waited patiently while the old man packed his pipe.

After The General returned the leather pouch to the smoking stand, he began the slow, methodical process of compacting the tobacco to the correct density, and during that empty moment, Thomas's attention drifted to The General's left ear. He knew the story behind the disfigurement well, since it was The General's policy that his first story to every new arrival would demystify the injury, lest an undisciplined young mind be distracted from the recounting of more valuable parables.

It was a cold account of being blown out of a trench during World War One with a less fortunate soldier, told without passion or elaboration, and in the end, you knew it was flying shrapnel, hot and indiscriminate, that had excised the top of his right ear as cleanly as a surgeon's scalpel before boring into his right knee and producing the limp that few still living had ever seen him without. And then the tale would end with the lifting of his right hand to expose a dark lump under the skin of the palm, and the listener would be afforded an opportunity to caress the bone and gristle and seek out the hard fragment still swimming beneath the surface. *Can you feel it? Yes, that's it. Right there.*

The General drew the flame of a lighter he retrieved from his pants pocket into the meerschaum with practiced control, then retrieved the Colt, leaned back into the rocker, and turned the pistol over in his hands with eyes closed. It was a ritual Thomas had seen many times before. He knew, eventually, inevitably, his eyes would open, their gaze indeterminate and distant, and with his hands back atop the Holy Grail, the story would begin

#

"He was a good friend of mine, the fellow who owned this pistol. A Scotsman, tall and built like a whip, with hair the color of old copper. I first met him when Pershing was ordered into Mexico to go after Pancho Villa, not long before we went to war in Europe. He was a sergeant in the motor pool that supported our medical unit, and even though we didn't have much in common, we hit it off like total strangers sometimes do. After we went into Mexico, it was off to fight Kaiser Bill, and that mortar round landed in our trench about a month before the armistice. He was the last person to see this ear complete.

"His name was Seamus, which he hated, so he just called himself Sam. I was one of the few who knew his real name and always liked it, thought it had character. Anyway, Sam's people were from Tennessee, and his father had been an officer in General Forrest's cavalry during the war and had taken this pistol off a dead Union officer, then sneaked it past the Yankees after Appomattox by strapping it to his thigh and mustering out on crutches. Sam's father never did use it himself—Sam said his daddy carried a Dance and wouldn't trust a pistol made by Yankees anyway—but kept it just so he could say he didn't spend four years in hell for nothing.

"Sam's father married and started farming after the war, and it wasn't long before Sam's older brother came along. Sam wasn't born until about 1890—his folks used to tell him he barely made it through the gate, his mother being past forty when he was born—and after all those childless years since his older brother was born, Sam's parents probably hadn't figured on him coming along.

"Sam's brother—don't recall his name; probably never knew it—had got tired of plowing rows and lit a shuck for Texas like lots of Appalachians did in those days. His folks didn't want his brother to leave, but understood. He was around sixteen or seventeen, and back then that was as grown up as you were going to get, and they figured the wide open spaces of Texas would suit him better anyway, since he didn't care much for being around people and being alone suited him fine, as long as it wasn't behind a mule in a field. Anyway, given Texas's rough-and-tumble reputation, their father insisted he take this pistol with him, and it was strapped to his pommel when he rode off. Sam said his brother didn't really want it but just took it to shut their daddy up. Sam was about five years old when his brother took off for Texas, and after that his folks started treating him like he was cast in gold—even sold some livestock they could hardly spare just to buy him a pony." Thomas was enjoying this story more than the one that introduced the Dragoon. That pistol had been owned by someone to whom The General had not been even remotely connected: a soldier who had fought under Zachary Taylor in a conflict between Mexico and the United States that nobody in Texas much cared about, since Texas had already kicked the Mexicans' butts fourteen years prior.

A plume of smoke wafted to the ceiling as the old man relit his pipe, and his eyes fell once again beyond the room as he set his hands back on the pistol and continued:

"So once in Texas, this Sam's brother got wind that a big ranch out west in Pecos County needed a hand to ride fence. No breaking horses or driving herds to Kansas, no chasing mavericks, just making sure that the three hundred miles of barbed wire that circled the ranch stayed up and strung. It was a job no self-respecting cowboy would tolerate for more than a few weeks, so Sam's brother took the job and didn't do anything else for the rest of his life.

"Back in Tennessee, his folks would receive a letter about every three months, since that's how long it took Sam's brother to ride the whole fence line. He never had much to say since not a lot happened while he was on the job, but Sam said one letter told of a tornado he almost got caught up in, and another one he said he almost drowned trying in an arroyo after a gully washer. But mostly his letters just sent love and the overall feeling of a man at peace with himself and his God, out there under that endless sky.

"Then, about twenty years out, Sam's brother's letters stopped, and after a year or so of unanswered letters, his folks got one in the mail from the ranch owner. Sam said he was sure that writing that letter was probably the hardest thing the man had ever done. It rambled on for several pages about what a fine person Sam's brother was, about how he was dependable and sober and God-fearing and never exchanged a harsh word with anyone, at any time, and on and on, until finally there was nothing left to say except he was dead."

The General paused once more to relight his pipe, and Thomas shifted down on the sofa so that his knees would break over the edge. He hoped the toes of his boots would touch the floor. They didn't.

"The rancher said he would have written sooner, but it took a full year after Sam's brother rode off for the last time before they knew what had happened to him. When he didn't come back after three months, much less six months, everybody kind of figured he was probably dead but didn't know for certain. It seemed unlikely, but maybe he'd gone back to Tennessee or met up with another rancher who offered him better pay. Anyway, trying to find him was out of the question. It was hard enough to find a herd of cattle on a ranch that size, much less a lone rider.

"The hang-fire ended when his replacement found him. He was a young vaquero who drifted up from Mexico, and since he didn't habla inglés too well, he was more than happy to take a job where there wouldn't be anyone around giving him orders he couldn't understand. Two weeks out on his third circuit, he did the same thing Sam's brother had probably done— ridden his horse into a draw about a hundred yards from the fence line to water down in a branch that cut across the northern edge of the property. There, at the bottom of the draw, sticking out of the sand just above the high-water line, he found what was left of Sam's brother. A skull and one or two large bones—an ilium or a femur, I suppose, and this—"

The General's eyes fell back into the present, blinked once, then fell on the Colt under his quivering hands. He lifted it and leaned forward, the old rocker bending with him, and held the pistol out to Thomas grip-first. As the pistol moved from the half-light into the sunshine streaming through the window, the rusted steel turned from dull brown to bright nutmeg.

Thomas reverently accepted the pistol, and something else was revealed. The cylinder, barrel, and frame were pockmarked with dents. Only the brass grip and trigger guard were smooth and undamaged. When he ran his fingertips across the battered cylinder, it felt like a dry corn cob.

"Well, the Mexican knew his vanished predecessor had been well-liked by the patrón and didn't waste any time making a beeline back to the hacienda with the bad news. There was no way they could ever know what killed him. It could have been bandidos, but snakebite was probably more likely. ¿Quién sabe? When the rancher rode out to take a look for himself, nothing new was discovered, so they gave those bones a Christian burial beside the barbed wire fence that he had attended to for twenty years. They considered burying the pistol with him as well, but thought better of it since there wouldn't be anything to hand over to his family if they did. Besides, it was the pistol that had erased any doubt that it was Sam's brother the vaquero had found. There wasn't but one pistol that looked like it, and that's what the rancher used to nail a board crosswise on the fence post beside the grave to make a cross."

"All those little dents are perfectly logical, given the facts. Sure, Sam's family was Scottish, but Sam said that, in his brother's case, even religious proclivities played second fiddle to his frugality. Sam said that back in Tennessee his brother was front row, center pew every Sunday until the first time somebody thought he was old enough to put a little something in the plate and chose the more frugal option of reading the Good Book at home to commune with The Lord.

"Now, cowboys always hired on fully outfitted—it wasn't like the army, where you walk over to the supply clerk and draw whatever you need for your job—and for a fence rider, the unique duties of which consisted of little more than restringing loose barbed wire and staying alive, all the gear a man really needed besides a horse, saddle, and bedroll was a Winchester for shooting game.

"Well, the foreman waited until his new fence rider was just about to ride off on his maiden voyage before hoisting a fifty-pound box of staples up to him and mentioning the hammer requirement. No, he didn't have a hammer

—had never even thought about it. Well, that's okay, says the foreman, because the resident blacksmith's got a three-pounder he can spare for the highfalutin' price of one dollar. It's said Sam's brother got down off his horse, walked to the bunkhouse, and when he came back and mounted up, this pistol was stuck in his belt.

"So that old Army was his hammer. His Winchester disappeared along with his horse and the rest of his gear, taken by someone with enough sense to know a beat-up pistol would be nothing but dead weight."

"Sam's folks were too old to make the trip from Tennessee to settle their son's affairs, so Sam came down alone—and stayed, as it turned out. He wired home after he got to Texas, and the folks wired back saying they wanted to know how they could be sure it was Sam's brother that they buried, so Sam had to tell his father how his eldest son had abused his cherished old cavalry pistol. His father's answer—that his brother had put it to better use than the dead Yank he took it off—would be his last words, at least to Sam.

"Anyway, by the time Sam had settled the estate—about five thousand dollars, I recall, probably every red cent that cowboy ever made—Texas had gotten into his blood and he enlisted at Fort Sam Houston. Shortly after that, maybe a year at the most, we ended up in the same unit and were best friends till he died. After that same mortar round that took the top of my ear off killed him, his widow wrote me saying she'd sent me the old Colt because Sam always wanted me to have it if he went first. She mailed it to me after I got stateside, and I got it just like they found it out there in West Texas, with the wooden grips gone. Maybe they splintered and fell away from all those blows, or maybe they just rotted away. But there's one thing I can tell you for certain: that gun hasn't been fired since it was pulled off that dead Yank."

When Thomas picked the Colt up by its skeletal grip and brought the muzzle up, the hammer fell limply back to full cock. Thomas pushed it back into the receiver, then pulled it back down with his thumb in a slow, controlled pull. The cylinder rotated smoothly as the hammer went through its arc, then locked with a sharp clack at full cock. Thomas clutched it between the fingers of his left hand and twisted, trying to free it, but it held fast, locked firmly in place.

"You know, General, this gun's really in pretty good shape, considering what it's been through. The action's okay except for a broken mainspring, and I bet my dad could make up new grips for it."

The General smiled. "I knew a young man once who was as crazy about these old six-shooters as you are. He borrowed this one for a report he was giving in his Texas history class, and when he returned it the spring was broken. He felt just awful about it. Apparently, it got passed around in class and everybody just had to cock it—well, all the boys anyway. That's the last time I ever loaned any of these old guns out until you came along. With you, I know they'll come back looking and working better than they did when they went out." Thomas smiled, his face flushed with pride.

"Well, young man, don't feel obligated to hang around and keep an old man company. I know you've probably got a ball game to get back to, judging from the lather you were wearing when you knocked on the door."

"That was just from coming up the hill through those woods in this heat," Thomas said. "Anyway, I'll be getting my own car pretty soon. I'm a junior now."

The General's gaze shifted imperceptibly with this, moving over Thomas's left shoulder and through the window toward the road, looking thoughtful and a little sad, and Thomas wondered if his bravado had somehow been to blame. But before he could long ponder his culpability, the General turned in his chair, tapped the cold contents of his pipe into the glass disc of the smoking stand, and brought his smile back to Thomas with all its prior intimacy.

"Well now, I somehow didn't expect that particular rite of passage to occur so quickly in your case. How old are you now? Thirteen?"

"Fifteen."

"Fifteen! Well, I suppose there is more to your life now than playing ball, hunting rabbits, and fixing old guns. Do you have a girlfriend yet?"

This was a question that Thomas wouldn't have expected from the General in a million years. He slowly shook his head, without comment.

"Well, it won't be long till you do, if you're old enough to have your own car. Come with me, young man. There's something I want to show you."

The General grasped the armrests of the rocker firmly and, with a quaking, tight-lipped effort, pushed himself to his feet. When the trembling subsided, he stepped toward the back door, sprouting additional height as his spine and knees gained strength, and together they stepped down into the breezeway. There, the old man turned and said, in a light whisper: "I'll be right back."

Mrs. O'Grady—The General called her Lovey—must have been there when Thomas arrived, but he was not surprised that he hadn't noticed her. She was as nomadic as the General's guns, forever shifting within the quiet existence of their home, always dressed in the floral-print cotton dresses that it seemed every elderly Texas woman wore, the bright dyes of the bluebonnets and roses aged to the same hushed pastels as the cushions of the various chairs that shared her negligible form, each in its turn. Thomas had never really heard Mrs. O'Grady speak, not even that first day when the General had made a grand and sweeping gesture across the room toward the silent figure in the rocker adjacent to the cold hearth, introducing her as "my best girl." She had responded then as she always would, with a slight nod and a cryptic pursing of the lips that Thomas assumed to be a smile. She was a slight woman, with streaked gray hair pulled straight back into a tense bun that she would employ like a pillow against the high backs of the chairs. Her blue eyes, alert behind dainty gold spectacles, would infer little as they meandered about the room, falling most often on the walls displaying clusters of small black-and-white portraits, each held within an ornate frame that matched no other. Thomas had never been introduced to the people in these photographs—the General preferred artifacts to images

—but was nonetheless sure they were the couple's relatives. Thomas didn't know if they ever had children.

This morning she had settled in the south end of the breezeway, and the General walked over to her still rocker and bent slowly to her ear. Thomas could hear his lilting voice, muffled but discernible, softly asking her if she wouldn't be more comfortable inside—the sun was high now, the breezes turning warm. Her reply came as an indistinct, soft rebuttal that nonetheless conveyed iron resolve, and the General acquiesced to whatever was said with a respectful silence, then bowed and reverently placed the kiss on her forehead that he never failed to deliver whenever he left her.

Thomas stepped in behind the General as he tottered past. Once again the hook was flicked out of its eyelet, the screen door opened wide, and Thomas motioned through.

"There's something on the north end of my property that I think might interest you," he said, and Thomas followed him down the worn path that led to the storage shed that housed an arsenal that spanned two world wars: several generations of Mausers and Enfields, a 1903 Springfield, an M-1, and several machine guns. Thomas's favorite was a water-cooled Browning that he would have given anything to fire, but that was out of the question—the military required that the breeches of all fully automatic munitions kept as souvenirs be welded shut.

Beyond the carport, the footpath evolved into a shaded lane that split the length of the northern portion of the property, and they mounted the weed-choked trail in silence. Thomas reduced his usual scamper to a shuffle in deference to the General and let the old Colt swing to the meter of his step.

They had traversed this trail once before. It was shortly after they met, and the General had pointed out the strips of shellacked linen bearing the common names of the vines, bushes, and lesser species that flourished in the thicket so that his followers might better know the Buckeyes, Redbuds, and Cedar trees, and the Mustang Grape and Poison Ivy that draped them. Now the tiny swatches hung in the hot thicket like the remnants of an old land survey, their labels no longer legible.

At the end of the trail was an overlook fenced by ancient cedar from the gravel road that lay fifteen feet below, and beyond, the half-mile descent of the ridge to the Nebraska River palisade that overlooked the town. A cedar bench was set back from the edge, out of view of passing traffic, and Thomas sat down and laid the pistol in his lap.

The General rested his forearms on the top rail of the cedar fence and gazed out over the valley. Thomas stayed silent, leaving the General with his thoughts.

"It's been years since Lovey and I came down here, but this used to be our spot. The Overlook, we call it. All alone up here, at night—it was like we had the whole world to ourselves. There weren't any houses between us and the river back then"—the General swept a hand toward the line of homes set along another ridge that rose out of the valley to the east, the Caldwells among them—"and those didn't start going up until maybe ten years ago. And that big place up there on the hill to the left, maybe fifteen. No, back then you could come out here on a clear night, and it was just the moon and stars and the twinkling lights of a small town. Then in the fall, after the northers blew through and cleared the skies, we'd bundle up and come out here on those cold, crisp mornings with hot tea and a quilt and watch the cloud rise out over the river like a big white wall of cotton."

The General was framed against the infinite backdrop of silver sky and seemed to be scanning the horizon through the hot, humid air.

"No, it's not like it used to be, what with all this new construction on our side of the river. What used to be just a town is a city now, but I'll bet that cloud still rises out of the valley like it did when Lovey and I used to come down here on winter mornings. Anyway"—the General turned to speak directly to Thomas for the first time since they had left the house—"I just wanted to bring you over here and let you know that when you meet that special girl and need a place to be alone with her, you're welcome here. But please don't extend this invitation to anyone else."

Thomas wasn't sure how to respond, so he just rose from the bench and stepped over to the railing to take in the view. It was immense in its sweep, and he could see the rain-carved arroyos in which he so often hunted complete, knowing well each swell and fall of the cedar forest as it descended toward the Nebraska River valley.

Then he thought of The Drop-off and the trampled and ravaged stretch of ancient barbed wire fence that prefaced it.

"General, do you know much about what went on down there, on that land along the river? Was it ever used for cattle or horses, maybe?"

In spite of the heat, the General's lean countenance remained dry and statuesque except for a forelock of white hair adrift in the gentle breeze. He took a brief, inquisitive look at Thomas, then turned back toward the river and the town, saying nothing, and Thomas thought he doesn't have anything in his hands—maybe he can't tell a story unless he has something in his hands—maybe if I bring him a piece of the wire . . .

Thomas brought his focus back to the vista when the old man finally spoke.

"It was all river back then, and the only way across to this side was a ford just below where the dam is now. He was a strange bird, the fella who first—"

"HEL-loooooo, the house!"

A fist landed in Thomas's gut, and the nausea spread up his back and neck, tightening his scalp and bristling his hair. His first impulse was to vault over the cedar railing and slide down the crumbling limestone embankment to Casey Lane, then flee into the woods toward the river. But that would be unthinkable, to flee from the General like a whipped coward, dishonoring himself and the old cavalry pistol placed in his charge.

"I wonder who that is?" the General said.

"My dad," Thomas answered back with resignation.

The General placed a cupped hand against his cheek. "We're down here, Colonel, on the north end!"

Thomas turned to the south, toward the mouth of the path. "I've gotta go now, General"—his tone that of a condemned man receiving his last rites—"I should have this one back in a few weeks. But my dad's going to make the grips, and I don't know how long that's going to take."

As Thomas fell into the shadows of the brake, he could see the green felt hat his father had brought from Germany bouncing toward him through the vines that lined the path.

Then he turned and saw that the General was watching him leave, so he gave him a wave.

The General smiled and lifted a hand. "Say hello to your father for me, young man," he said, then looked back toward the river as Thomas continued up the path.

The Colonel had stopped midway up the trail and was now watching him approach. "I'm assuming the General thought his Dragoon looked up to par," he said, "and whatever that is tucked under your arm is our next project."

The Colonel's Impala was sitting in the gravel driveway, and Thomas opened the passenger door, slid in, and cradled the Colt in his lap.

"It was time we got going, and I thought I'd save you the walk home," the Colonel said. Then he swiveled in the seat, backed the car down the steep drive, and hooked the wheel sharply to the right as soon as he felt the rear wheels roll onto the pavement. Then the Colonel smiled as he dropped the shift lever into first and said, "And this way we won't have to worry about other distractions preempting our plans."

OUR plans? The sarcasm only fueled the pandemonium of scenarios already playing one after the other in Thomas's head, with each new version resulting in the same unutterable defeat.

#

As the Chevy dropped below the General's property and rolled onto the sharp dogleg that fed into Casey Lane, Thomas looked up the steep incline and saw the General framed by the empty sky, his hands trembling atop the cedar rail, and once again he lifted his hand in farewell through the open window.

But this time the old man didn't respond. He was looking toward the river, his eyes lost behind the thick lenses of the gold-rimmed glasses.

CHAPTER 6

Two bits an acre. A dry term and ludicrous if taken literally, inferring hyperbole and sarcasm whether uttered alone or suspended in rhetoric, and when it was said around Fuller, Texas, in the spring of 1924 and for some time beyond, it invariably brought a snicker at the expense of Otis Upshaw, a young ranch manager who plunged into land speculation by liquidating virtually everything his heretofore noble name could lay claim to for the appropriation and development of a crumbling and insidious wasteland. Too uneven and barren to farm, too destitute and perfidious to support livestock, and too lacking in natural amenities to be considered feasible for settlement by anyone refined beyond savagery, the area was known simply as the hills, to be uttered with the same tone of quiet contempt that might be used when referring to a confessed adulterer or a defrocked priest. No one knew for sure where the quarter-an-acre figure originated, or exactly how much Otis was actually paying for the land, since it had to be acquired in uneven blocks, from private owners in some cases and by proper claim, legal and binding, to the state land board in others. But the phrase became the official metaphor for one young man's folly, and it was uttered in the wake of Otis Upshaw's clicking boot heels for the better part of the decade.

But it was a gamble, in the purest sense. There was no guarantee that the dam of granite blocks being stacked across the Nebraska River would supply enough electricity for the robust expansion supporters promised; indeed, opponents of the project predicted only enough power to convert the streetcars to electricity, with the only benefit being far less horse crap on the prim boulevards of downtown Fuller. But Otis thought his hand was sound and answered all criticism with a smug smile. His development would be called Granite Heights—in honor of the new dam—and he lobbied for and won a contract for cheap Fuller electricity, cut meandering roads through the tangled jungle to access the low-water bridge being built over the ford just downriver from the growing wall of gray granite blocks, and joyfully handed out hundreds of business cards announcing:

Otis 'Two-Bit' Upshaw
SCENIC LOTS AND SOLITUDE
Dealing in Tomorrow

Otis's father, Elmer Upshaw, had been a judge, a tall Lincolnesque man who dressed like a circuit-riding preacher and often sounded like one too, spewing righteous condemnation down from his bench at the Barrett County courthouse just west of downtown Fuller at those whose acts, proven or supposed, would rouse his formidable demeanor. A widower with two young sons, he was active in most aspects of the community, serving on the school board, the city council, the PTA, even teaching history classes at Texas College when his schedule allowed and sometimes when it didn't. It was taken for granted that His Honor would eventually ascend to the mayoralty and beyond, possibly to governor or even U.S. senator, until one June afternoon in 1917, a Sunday, when his housekeeper found him lost in his own extensive library, an enormous blue welt on his forehead, muttering gibberish as he pulled the heavy words of the law from their shelves and onto his bare feet.

Whether the fall had caused the stroke or the stroke, the fall, could never be determined, and Judge Upshaw recovered well enough to once again cast his shadow down Fuller's more revered halls, it's true, but never again would it dance in fervent pantomime, animating the moral thunder that once rolled from his now twisted and half-fallen face. The town watched with solemnity as the passing weeks saw his resignations—some requested, others proffered—from every post he held, leaving him with little else to do but retire to his sprawling property along the riverbank west of Fuller and apply the lessons of fifty-five years of energetic life to the raising of his two sons, Otis and Gregory. Their mother, Mrs. Elmer Upshaw, as she had preferred to be addressed, was a slight, genteel woman, and as adoring and attentive a bride as any ambitious barrister could want before an inflamed appendix took her in 1908, a week before the sixth birthday of Gregory, their youngest. After her death, the infrequent parenting of their assiduous father and the relaxed supervision of the cadre of nannies and tutors engaged to chaperon the two boys failed to perpetuate Mrs. Upshaw's rigid discipline and cultural nourishment, and as the years passed they could be seen more and more in the fields, hunting rabbits and quail, or swimming in the river. But of course they were Skeltons, and grand expectations in sports and scholarship fell first upon Otis, who disappointed in the first arena by failing to realize anything near the physical proportions of his father at a like age, then in the second with a lackluster academic performance leading up to his graduation from Fuller High the month of his father's stroke, leaving doubts as to his intellectual capacities as well. Though quick-witted, fluidly conversant, and considered a pleasant companion by all, no one extended the conviction that other, more marketable gifts lay unseen behind the boy's convivial facade, and enough remained of his father's damaged perceptions to seize on his eldest son's deficits. The elevation of Otis would be his first crusade; Gregory had yet to enter high school—there was time before the need to rip him from the complacency of his childhood would be as urgent as in the case of his brother.

It was not long after the stroke had set Judge Upshaw adrift that Otis shuffled downstairs late on a squandered Sunday morning and found his father sitting alone in the kitchen, sipping a cup of hot tea from the good side, the right side, of his mouth while the other side sat drooling and indifferent. Otis, ever the respectful and compliant son, joined him at the table when bid to do so and sat in silence as the Judge explained to him what his life would become from that moment henceforth—a regimen of education and discipline along the same proven path that he himself had taken, to bring him to the moment and place of the father's fall, that the son might take up the lost torch of their common destiny.

It must be said that Otis tried. His abrupt accession onto the ladder to power and respectability was weighted with limited funds and a heavy course load that kept him at his books from each day's resumption of classes until his retirement at night, when sleep would overtake him before the warmth of the extinguished light would pass from the last inimical page. His weekends, once distinguishable from the remainder of the week only by the greater choice of companions with whom to join in revelry, were now dreary entombments in his father's library, where he would read the dour, somnolent tomes in a curriculum prescribed by the former judge himself, who was never farther away than his voice would carry, his ear would hear.

Otis carried his burden well and without complaint until the successful conclusion of his third collegiate year, when destiny once again accompanied him on a Sunday morning descent down his father's ornate staircase. The Judge allowed that Saturdays could be spent beyond the book-lined walls of the insufferable library, and Otis had spent the day before in the confines of his room, gazing out of the window at the swaying boughs of the live oaks that once delivered him safely to the ground for moonlit trysts with conspirators and sweethearts alike, searching in the infinite patterns of wind and leaf and wood for the whispered key to his salvation. Now Otis walked the length of the hall and entered the living room, where his father lounged in his favorite chair, reading. When the Judge sensed his presence and lowered his paper, Otis's discourse began.

Otis hoped that his father would cede gracefully, or that any parlance before the inevitable wresting of the reins would be charged with the same nobility and eloquence that he remembered from his early childhood, when his father, then a trial lawyer, would rehearse his courtroom arguments behind the reverberating doors of the library. Otis had steeled himself against a strong and judicious reaction by spending the previous night predicting his father's contentions and formulating a rebuttal for each, but as he stood articulating his abject loathing for his sequestered life and inability to elevate his regard for reading the law beyond the common drudgery it had become, the confidence that his father's silent audience was building in him collapsed into self-loathing with the first tear that crept from the old man's right eye and intensified with each one thereafter, until the insane paradox that the face became, flowing and ravaged by despair on the one side, dead and indifferent on the other, forced Otis's eyes to the floor at his feet, his fists quivering at his sides.

But Otis had spoken, and his father correctly sensed that he had indeed chosen, if not an alternate career, then at least an irreversible departure from the one he had obediently pursued the previous three years. For the next week or so, he was given to tacit brooding while Otis ran to no man's schedule, then turned his attentions to Gregory, who was showing no more intellectual prowess than his older brother had at the same age.

Otis was now free from the intangible shackles that had long restrained his abundant spirit, and his frequent absences and late hours in returning home and rising no longer brought rebuke. But his days were haunted by his failure, and he spent them searching aimlessly for some rewarding enterprise, some labor through which he could recapture the heart and eye of the Judge. And he walked their land.

The Upshaw homestead was a handsome property that befitted the cultured tastes and expectations of a gentleman of position, an impressive two-story antebellum situated atop eighty acres of rich farmland and pasture sloping gently to the south shore of the Nebraska River, three miles upstream from the heart of Fuller. The estate had always been a productive concern as well, employing hands and laborers whose skills coincided with the season, whether it be working the livestock, refreshing the land, or harvesting the fruit from the orchard. For Otis, life seemed measured in motion rather than time, with the years cadenced by the coming of the various crews of rough men who, for as long as he could remember, would hoist their calloused hands in greeting as they reined their mounts and teams through the whitewashed gate.

After the judge's stroke hastened Otis's conscription toward preserving the family's fortunes, even his frantic studies and cloistered weekends couldn't insulate him from the eroding level of activity about the pastures and corrals as well as within the very bosom of the house itself. Then, in 1919, his sophomore year, the gate passed April unlatched for no one, and the grounds were given over to unshod horses, scavenging chickens, and in a field upwind from the house, a cow rotting with her breached calf. The summer of the same year had passed through a rainless July before Otis realized that the Mexican pickers, their faces dark and careless under wide brims as they would rattle toward the river in their burro-drawn carts, had passed not down the narrow lane to the orchard for the harvest, but like the rest of his childhood, into memory.

That summer Otis began to force himself out of the house and onto their blighted acreage to take inventory of the damage his father's stroke had wrought beyond the confines of flesh and bone. He inspected the wasp-infested outbuildings, the stagnant troughs, and the skeletal, forgotten cattle languishing on barren range while high grasses bent to the breeze in adjacent fields. He mounted the orchard lane, straddling the tandem ruts cut by years of harvests but now hooded with nettle and milkweed, and strolled down to the pecan groves and beyond, to the river, to the willows that spread over the eddying shallows like towering plumes, dimpling the olive water with the frayed tips of the ropes that he had swung from as a boy. The tract of rich soil that had once been the orchard was now a harbor for all manner of air- and water-borne seeds and pods, creating a floral ghetto in which only the sunflowers burst triumphant above the fray, a hovering, shimmering blanket of gold above the mongrel thicket. The fruit trees, engulfed and withering, were now distinguishable only by the precision of their mutual placement and the remains of their forgotten progeny, dangling black and shriveled from each weakening, leafless umbilicus.

It was in early June, while returning from the river for the evening meal (prepared by the cook, still; she and a housekeeper were all that remained of staff), that Otis finally compelled himself to lift his eyes from the coarse trail to the top of the hill. Once the grand old house had shone like nacre in the western light as he returned from the river after swimming or fishing, and he selfishly shielded that childish memory by walking up the hill with his head down to facilitate denial. But look he finally did, and the final vestiges of his adolescence fell away as he beheld the once-imposing residence standing decayed and spent in the ebbing light.

As he climbed the steps to the porch, he noticed the railing was loose.

Later that same evening, after his father and brother had retired, Otis crept down the staircase and into the library. He crossed to his father's immense desk and lit the lamp, then turned to the massive shelves that could be seen behind the judge in his portrait hanging in the county courthouse. One by one, Otis pulled the heavy ledgers from their slumber, noting the chronology of each as he worked his way up and across. They had been kept in the old man's distinctive hand since his acquisition of the plantation at the turn of the century, and Otis's schooling had lent him a clerical literacy that guided him through the columns with an intimate comprehension. He swept through the volumes without sitting, noting many good years and some bad; he saw that the estate was a profitable entity for the most part, a worthwhile supplement to the already adequate earnings of an attorney and sitting judge. Only on the latest and final volume did he turn and take his place at the desk. He pondered the entries for over an hour, then quietly folded the log and returned it to its place in the dust along the highest shelf and left the room for the dark curve of the staircase. And so it was that Otis was irretrievably transformed, by the awakening virtues of blood and honor in the dark hours of the night, from a failed collegian to the apprentice manager of a sizable agricultural concern. His resolve allowed him little sleep that night, and he descended the staircase shortly after sunrise the next morning. He walked through the kitchen, past the startled cook, and onto the peeling, fretted porch facing the river. His inspection of the ledgers had borne testimony that his father's stroke had effaced more than his fire and eloquence—it had cost him the better part of his perspicacity as well—and the dwindling industry and employment on the Upshaw farm and the accumulation of Otis's college credits were not two disparate incidents. The judge had depleted his considerable savings and investments to replace the lost income from his various posts and legal ventures, then looked to the modest revenue generated by the plantation for the family's needs and Otis's education. This embezzlement of residual profits yielded a diminished operation with each passing year until it declined to the state in which Otis had found it in the final book, and he could feel the burden as he leaned low over the railing and watched the sunlight break over the roof of the house and paint a silhouette of their hilltop along the fractured limestone wall that faced them across the Nebraska, across a half-mile of ragged farmland. His father had apparently decided to seal the books on the malignant insolvency with the faltering entry of April 10th, 1919, the day the credits overtook the debits, handing Otis the somewhat heartening knowledge that the empty purse had been abandoned. There would be no battle to wrest it from the old man's hands.

Otis set to work after breakfast (with a new respect for the preparer of the meal; after questioning, she admitted she hadn't been paid for a month), spending the first day mending fence, clearing brush, and driving nails until the sweatband of the straw hat he lifted from a nail in the barn was stained with salt, and there was no letup as the week progressed. The stock were rotated to fresh pastures, the choked troughs cleaned, the orchard restored, and the fruit trees pruned or replaced. The chickens, long depleted by marauding snakes and foxes, were once again fed and secured, and they, along with the fish, rabbits, and squirrels dispatched by Gregory at the behest of his elder brother, provided cheap dinner entrées. In late August, Otis began the rehabilitation of the house and outbuildings as well, abandoning the fields for days at a time to wield hammer, saw, and brush until the western light failed.

As the weeks turned into months and Otis allowed the estate to absorb more and more of his time and energies, his motivation evolved. The redemption he had sought to mollify his shame had been lost in the wild fields that battled his mandate with a promiscuous fecundity; it was now proud defiance that drove him into the rebellious pastures with each new dawn, his fists flexing for the hafts of his tools even as he stole down the dark staircase. His original objectives—at best a salvaging of the family's reputation and the ransoming of their home from legal seizure by creditors—had been displaced by worries of early freezes and locating the most lucrative markets for fattened heifers and spirited colts. Otis no longer thought of his future as detached from the fate of the land; rather, his destiny was at his feet, from the time he stepped into the predawn darkness of the porch until dusk sketched the outline of their home onto the Nebraska River bluff before all sank into darkness.

Eventually, Otis negotiated a schedule of payments to keep their creditors at bay, and he began to consider other priorities, in particular, the restoration of his family's status in the only community that he and his brother had ever known. In truth, he cared little if the name Upshaw ever regained its stature in the town or the county or the borders beyond. If, in time, Gregory displayed an aptitude for attracting that intangible asset, then he would ensure that his younger brother be granted the same opportunities that would have been his had the Judge's coercion borne fruit. As for himself, Otis had no concerns beyond the barbed-wire perimeter of their eighty acres. Other things had changed as well. His father's attentions to Gregory left him with little time to dwell on the pain his eldest son had caused him, and he seemed not to notice Otis's activities, nor the fact that he now came in from the fields so late that he took dinner in the kitchen, after the supper table had been stripped and the library doors sealed to study. As for Otis, when he would straighten in the fields and allow his gaze to wander up the gradual flow of their land, the house seemed a vast sarcophagus, cold and abstracted.

October brought wind and rain to soothe the spent, turned fields, and Otis's efforts could now concentrate on their home and more domestic concerns. He worked through the winter, applying fresh paint, replacing broken pickets, and pruning the enormous trees, striving to get as much done as possible before spring pulled him back into the fields. And as he moved about the periphery of the old house, he would occasionally become aware of his father hovering behind a window, watching, his expression as vague as the smooth glass holding it in dream-like inference.

#

On an evening in early March 1922, Otis stood alone outside his bedroom on the upstairs veranda. By the light of a full moon, he poured himself a celebratory shot from a bottle of prized Kentucky bourbon that had been bequeathed to him by his father shortly before his stroke, as it had been to him by Otis's grandfather. It had fueled a pair of toasts to Otis's father in the course of a single year, thirty years past—the first, to his admittance to the bar, then the second, to his taking of a young bride.

Echoing through his bedroom from the vast foyer below, Otis could hear the front door lock engage with the turning of the cook's key, followed by the sound of her steps on the porch below, where she would sit and wait for her husband. He set the bottle on the railing and lifted the glass with a steady hand, holding it out to the night, to the silent fields and sleeping stock, then brought it down and sipped. Soon he heard the arrival of a team of horses, then the short bark and slap of leather, and he knew they were gone. His father and Gregory had left the library hours before for their beds. There was no doubt the house would be still.

Otis passed through his bedroom to the staircase, carrying the glass of amber liquid as if it were a sacrament. The window shades were drawn against the moonlight and the house dark, but no darker than when he began his workdays, and his step was confident. Once downstairs, he walked down the hall to the library, and the heavy door surrendered willingly to a gentle sweep of his arm, pivoting on massive hinges oiled beyond a whisper.

He crossed the room to the desk and set the brimming glass delicately on its broad surface, then switched on the lamp and walked over to the bookcase holding the ledgers. The one he wanted, the current one, was located on the uppermost shelf, and it required two outstretched arms and all of his height to retrieve it. Back at the desk, the generous cushion accepted his weight with a gracious, hushed breath, and he opened the ledger to the last entry and added another—the amount received earlier that day for a dozen calves. After calculating the new balance, Otis retrieved his glass and again raised it—this time not as a sacrament, but as a congratulatory toast to his own determination and effort, to this first time in three years that the Upshaw circumstances had escaped the cruel red lines of debt and registered a positive balance.

After five minutes of savoring the warm whiskey and the quiet winter night, Otis rose and returned the ledger to the shelf. When he left the library for the staircase, his step was bold, sounding heavily on the carpeted oak steps, and once upstairs, he pulled his bedroom door shut with the command of a captain at sea sealing the bridge. He had left the empty glass downstairs, upturned in the middle of his father's worn desk.

#

Otis was nine when his mother died, and during the graveside services, the pastor had spoken of Providence in justifying his mother's passing, making it seem as if it was a good thing, a right thing, to have happened. The inference in his words haunted Otis for weeks, and finally, he approached the Judge and asked about the pastor's intent. His father thought a moment, then replied without emotion that to a clergyman, Providence is Divine Destiny—the preacher was saying that Otis's mother had died because the Lord chose to take her—and it was up to Otis to decide whether to agree with the preacher or not. The answer has to come from within, he had said, and the answer takes time.

So in time, Otis had come to believe in Providence as an indiscriminate rogue, a faithless power that moves in its own way and time, whether disguised as a winning poker hand or a calamity. He had seen it strike his father down like a lightning bolt, with unrepentant cruelty, then step back, disinterested and uninvolved, as their world fell into ruin and decay. And so it was like the first stirring of Providence from a long slumber, like the quaking of a dying leaf against distant thunder, when on the first of November, after six months of stable enterprise, the following public notice appeared in the morning edition of the Fuller Dispatch:

#

To those citizens of the City of Fuller, Texas, and Barrett County, Texas, possessing title to properties abutting upon the shores of the Nebraska River as defined by the recorded flood levels; or those possessing title to land encroached upon by any of the creeks or lesser tributaries draining into the Nebraska River and thereby subject to the same aforementioned flood levels; or those possessing title to land that occupies an elevation within ten feet of the aforementioned flood levels with no natural or contrived barriers present to defend against rising flood levels in excess of the recorded levels; lastly, to all of those possessing title to properties of the above descriptions that are described by public survey to reside along the Nebraska River upstream from a point defined as one hundred yards upstream from a ford across the Nebraska River commonly and locally known as Fuller's Ford, which is situated approximately three miles upstream from the point whereby the Main Street Bridge accessing downtown Fuller, Texas, crosses the Nebraska River, who may, under reasonably conceived circumstances, deem their property vulnerable to flood levels in excess of fifty feet above the aforementioned recorded flood levels for the Nebraska River.

In conclusion, any and all citizens of Fuller, Texas, and Barrett County, Texas, claiming title to lands compliant with any or all of the above descriptions are hereby encouraged to attend a public hearing to be convened in the square before the Barrett County Courthouse on November 10, 1922, at 8:00 A.M. The subject will be the proposed dam across the Nebraska River and the benefits it will bring to all the citizens of Fuller, Texas, and Barrett County, Texas. Representatives of the Army Corps of Engineers will be present, along with elected city officials, to assist in satisfying all inquiries.

#

During the week that preceded the hearing, Otis stoically went about his duties, wrestling to keep his apprehensions at bay amid fears of lost land and bureaucratic apathy. The day of the hearing arrived under heavy rain, and he slipped under a poncho after a hurried breakfast and dashed across the soaked lawn to the shed housing his second-hand Ford truck. The engine started on the second crank, and after a few minutes to allow the engine to warm, he pulled onto the rutted drive that would take him to the winding farm-to-market road granting the properties along the river access to the town.

The route had been inundated by five days of rare, unrelenting rain, and the roar of the swollen Nebraska harmonized with the wind as Otis pushed the old truck over the concrete shelves spanning the flooded arroyos. After the first mile, the road angled away from the river and gained civility commensurate with the level of the land and usage by taxpaying voters. After three miles, packed gravel replaced caliche, and the random farmhouses girded by cleared fields gave way to urban dwellings of stone and brick on generous, groomed lots. Once inside the Fuller city limit, the homes and lots began to diminish, but what they lost in scope was made up for in sophistication, and the road earned the cosmopolitan title of Sixth Street after crossing Los Alamos Creek. By the time the uniform palpitation of cobblestones replaced the erratic thumps of the graded road, the homes had been reduced to prim cottages set on deep, narrow lots. Small but noble and unique, each bore some guileless, patent detail—arresting fretwork under the eaves; a front door inset with leaded glass; a roof adorned with lightning rods emerging from tripods of finely wrought ivy—that bestowed a unique identity.

The Barrett County courthouse was located on a hill to the west of downtown Fuller and, not coincidentally, just north of an enormous sinkhole, an immense depression of incalculable age that had been groomed as a natural amphitheater and mandated as a forum for official gatherings. A slow rain was still falling from the dark sky as Otis turned north from Sixth Street and climbed the last blocks to the courthouse, where the surrounding thoroughfares were already choked with the wagons, horses, and automobiles of his neighbors and fellow citizens who had concluded, rightly or wrongly, that they fell into the cryptic parameters of the public notice.

It took Otis a full twenty minutes to secure a parking spot within walking distance of the courthouse that would allow him to exit his vehicle without stepping into water higher than his boot tops, and upon his arrival at the square, it took almost as long to find a spot amid the throng that would place him within earshot of the dais. Then Slack Schulle, a neighbor whose property was a little farther downriver, noticed Otis weaving through the assemblage and hailed him to his side in the deep mud at the foot of the gazebo steps.

At eight o'clock sharp, the official contingent emerged from the courthouse in single file and crossed the street to the square. They were forced to step over and around members of their audience as they descended the flagstone steps to the gazebo in the sunken lawn and excused themselves repeatedly as they came.

When not engaged for official functions, the square served as a park, and his acquaintance with a good many of the gathered folk reached beyond memory. Otis had spent many a weekend afternoon and holiday there as a boy, lounging in the shade of the towering pecan and live oak trees while barbershop quartets and brass bands performed in the gazebo. Now, he saw few outright strangers in the crowd—mostly men older than he, pressed shoulder to shoulder in the interminable drizzle as the sagging brims of their hats channeled the rain around their heads and into the puddles at their feet. The scattered conversations were few, perfunctory, and strained, the talk of men too preoccupied with their own thoughts to hear those of others. Most of the men were familiar—ranchers and farmers whose properties abutted the Nebraska—but he also noticed the presence of men he knew to be cotton farmers from the rich flatlands that skirted the banks of the river north and east of Fuller. Otis reckoned they were there out of curiosity or, more likely, caution.

As they waited for the committee to complete their descent, the boughs of the trees began to reel and heave over their heads, tossed by a sudden cold gale—the first norther of the season had arrived to draw the morning even bleaker.

The last of the officials eventually filed past Otis and mounted the floor of the gazebo to take their prearranged seats in the semicircle of chairs arranged behind the podium. They consisted of the mayor, the county commissioner, two men Otis thought he recognized as state legislators, and four soldiers—two officers and two enlisted men—in dress greens with brass turrets affixed to their collars. Finally, a brace of Fuller policemen took their places at opposite sides of the top of the staircase and, at precisely 10:00 AM, the mayor approached the podium and brought the hearing to order with a whack of his gavel.

The mayor sensed the solicitous tone of the crowd and shunned the usual mollycoddling and politicking to proceed directly to the business at hand: an official verification of what had long been rumored, to wit, the intention of the City of Fuller to construct a dam across the Nebraska River for the purpose of providing a level of electrical power and flood control that would allow unprecedented growth and security from natural disaster.

But who would feel the immediate effects of the project? And what would these effects be? With the crowd thus primed, the mayor turned to the army contingent seated to his left rear and offered them the dais before taking his seat.

The four soldiers rose in unison and silently split into pairs. The two officers approached the speaker's lectern and stood at ease, while the enlisted men, both bearing corporal's stripes, strode to the rear of the gazebo and secured an easel and a large chart. A hum of recognition greeted the display when it was brought forward and assembled beside the podium—it was a surveyor's plat of the Nebraska River basin west of Fuller, Texas. Then the corporals stationed themselves on opposite sides of the easel to maintain the board against the gusting wind, and the ranking officer, a captain, plucked a baton from his waistband and snapped his arm sharply downward as he turned toward the easel. The baton tripled in length with a sharp metallic click. "Ladies—although I honestly don't see any of you out there—and gentlemen, concerned citizens of Fuller, allow me to introduce myself. My name is Edward Bouldin, and I am a captain in the Army Corps of Engineers, stationed at our headquarters in Washington, DC. I am here in response to a request for assistance by your local government here (he motions toward the seated politicians; they respond with a polite nod) and the governor of the fine state of Texas. I won't waste your valuable time nor submit you to this inclement weather any longer than necessary. My mission here is to outline the current plans for the development of your valley and answer any questions that you might have concerning your individual circumstances. Our, the army's, mission here is to provide technical support for the project only, so please hold any questions you may have concerning scheduling or finances for your elected officials. But first, a critique of the area as we now know it, followed by a rough analysis of the geographic transformations that will occur."

With this oral display of generic syntax and grammatical correctness so seldom heard in Fuller outside the confines of the college, Captain Bouldin cast his baton into the center of the Nebraska River above Fuller and sustained his proper monologue for the better part of an hour, only pausing for the contents of the easel to be renewed. Throughout, the audience stoically endured the chilly, ceaseless drizzle and gusting winds as the puddles at their feet deepened and the brims of their hats melted onto their shoulders.

The first chart that had been placed on the easel was illustrative of the current physical characteristics of the valley, quickly followed by a second that was a topographical repetition of the first, depicting the current recorded floodplain levels. The third included all of the river valley through Barrett County and was labeled with the dates, locations, and costs of prior destructive events, and a fourth outlined those areas currently most susceptible to future catastrophes. The narrative that accompanied these exhibits was little more than a rendering in statistical jargon of common knowledge and was taken with a condescending silence. The audience knew all too well the history of the Nebraska's threat—in some cases, the titles of ownership extended to Mexican land grants.

The fifth chart was noticeably larger than those that had preceded it—the aides had to struggle to secure it to the easel—and quickly brought voice and movement back to the crowd. They closed ranks even further, flowing down the embankment and pooling as tightly against the base of the structure as civility would allow.

The previous charts had shown the river as they all knew it, flowing normally within the limits of its natural constraints and defining the southern border of the town as it wound in a generally east-southeasterly direction toward the Gulf of Mexico. But in the last and largest chart, the historical floodplain along the river west and south of Fuller had been overdrawn with a crosshatched and convoluted blue stain, becoming linear only as it crossed the Nebraska just north of the low-water crossing known as Fuller's Ford.

The narrator stepped to the easel and raised his clear, cadenced voice above the blustering wind once again, and as the baton traced his discourse onto the wind-whipped plat, the audience leaned in, straining to assess their vulnerability in the ominous blue field.

Four hours would pass before the gavel fell again. The officer's presentation eclipsed another forty-five minutes, as he went on to explain the parameters of the completed dam and the projected loss of land. Many in the crowd remained tense and silent during this phase, simply waiting for the tap against the board that would verbally confirm what the graphics had already told them. Finally, the engineer turned to the crowd and consigned the baton and his hands to the small of his back, and the mayor rose and motioned the county commissioner to join him on the stage—the two state legislators had managed to slip away unnoticed—and they opened themselves to questions.

Initially, chaos won. Shouted demands for answers fused into an emotional roar that howled in from the drenched collage of felt, wool, and straw, and when a voice in the crowd was chosen, subsequent protests from the ignored prevented conversation. The mayor's frustration finally led him to scold the more zealous offenders, and the free and deliberate use of their given names resulted in a quieting of the remainder of the crowd, curious as to whom was being subjected to public censure. Eventually, an uneasy order prevailed and the exchanges resumed, droning in a staccato rhythm for the remainder of the gathering.

It took three more hours before all subsequent discussion was deemed ludicrous or repetitious, and shortly after noon, the gavel fell. The speakers and their entourage turned wearily toward the gazebo steps, and the ranchers and farmers slogged up the muddy banks of the reclaimed sinkhole and dispersed along the inundated streets with the silent carriage of shell-shocked troops. The final bomb fell almost as a postscript: construction on the new dam would begin the following spring, the formal announcement of which would appear in the public notices section of the Fuller Dispatch.

The rain had long overcome the gutters, but Otis had bigger things to worry about than the water seeping into his boot tops as he cranked the motor. He had long recognized the value of the graceful slope of his property, with its wide, gentle profile. The river was slow to climb the land during even the most ravaging floods, minimizing erosion and providing ample time for evacuation of stock and hardware, and recessions to normal levels were calm and gradual, allowing the deposition of good soil from upriver. Unlike some of his neighbors, whose steep properties had been eroded to bare limestone and grew nothing but juniper and cedar, Otis's land seemed capable of consuming as much moisture as the heavens and the river conspired to deliver and could feed more cattle and grow more crops than other properties four times as large. But what had been a supreme advantage could now well destroy him. In three years, Otis now knew, there would be a flood that would not recede, a flood that would bring the Nebraska a hundred feet above its current levels and leave him with twenty acres of dry land, give or take an acre, and a check for sixty acres of Lake Fuller mud at the county appraisal rate for farmland—an amount that might be enough to cover his property taxes for five years, given the higher rates for property designated as lakeside residential.

Otis steered the Ford out of the cold mist now moving over the square, where several small groups still huddled conspiratorially under the trees and the eaves of the gazebo, and pulled onto the nearest avenue that would take him back to Sixth Street, which in turn would deliver him beyond the rolling hills littered with the dwellings of those who had attached themselves to the town like a calf to a cow's udder. He now felt a deep exigency for the coarse road that would carry him beyond Fuller, a road he had traveled as a mute, awed boy seated between his blithe parents in their black surrey, the soft seat swaying drunkenly behind a brace of high- blooded mares; then later, as the older of two brothers with their widowed father atop the unyielding seat of a freight wagon, conscripted to humorless provisioning trips to town, eager only for the sight of Fuller between the bobbing tips of the mules' ears. Then the crude road seemed as constant and eternal as the Nebraska herself, knowing no master beyond the mood of the season dictating whether the whirling wheels threw ropes of mud or coated the trees in dust. It had taken him into Fuller by horseback for the entirety of his public schooling, and through his years of higher education as well, when he would rein his mare north at the edge of town and follow the Cooperton Road for the additional two miles to Texas College.

But the Cooperton Road was now called Mirabeau Road, and the edge of town had proven to be remarkably transient. Fuller was a mile closer to their home than it had been when Otis was a schoolboy, migrating westward at a rate of several hundred yards annually as an increasing percentage of the rural inhabitants were choosing to embrace the town as their caretaker. Otis motored along, and as the trailing edge of the oppressive gray sky overhead rolled away, the voices of his neighbors filled his head:

. . . what about the land we lose? According to the blue line there, my place will be losing pert near two dozen acres—hell, maybe more—and prime grazing land at that. Y'all gonna come up with a breed of cattle that will suck up catfish, or am I just shit outta luck? Mr. Schulle, rest assured that my office, indeed the entire

town council, has given untold hours in consideration of what consequence this wonderful asset to our county and community will have on those such as yourself, owners of land engaged in agrarian endeavors of our heritage, a heritage upon which the city of Fuller was established. Goddammit, cut the crap, your honor. Yeah, Eustas, this ain't even an election year. Yes, friends, careful consideration has been given to the potential loss of land and income, but my friends, please hear me out: after much discussion with the office of the county commissioner and the county tax assessor, it became apparent that the resultant increase in land values and the growth the new lake will bring to your area will more than offset your losses . . . and new enterprises involving swimming, fishing, and boating would now be available to owners of lakeside property, none of which Otis had the slightest interest in pursuing, any more than he wanted to sell off the remainder of his land as lake frontage or return to law school. He motored out of Fuller proper, desperately seeking a deliverance, a quid pro quo that would quell his latent hysteria. As he turned onto the last, the northbound leg of the journey home, he met the cold winds of the norther head-on, roaring and whistling all around him.

#

Otis steered through the gate and peeled his fingers from the wheel. His whole body ached with the cold. He crossed the lawn, climbed onto the porch, and read the thermometer mounted beside the door before stepping inside—it had plunged forty degrees below the reading he had taken upon leaving. But the sky was beginning to clear, and for the first time in days, he was able to gauge the time by the sunlight streaming onto the floor through the transom above the western entrance: four o'clock, he thought, given the angle of the light.

He walked by the closed library door and mounted the staircase. Five of the doors along the upper corridor were identical to those found throughout the house—tall, oaken, and ornate—but there was a smaller, sixth door built into the northwest corner. He twisted the porcelain knob, lowered his head, and stepped through.

In the center of the small room behind the door was a spiral staircase of steel and brass, and Otis swept cobwebs away as he climbed in the dim light. At the top, he threw the bolt on a hatch set into the ceiling and pushed upward until he felt the mass of lacquered oak fall onto two heavy brass stops that held it just beyond its point of balance. He climbed through the opening, closed the hatch, and rose into the howling wind.

Otis's father had purchased the property at an estate auction at a price that no one would have believed could win so considerable a piece of real estate. It had been established in the 1870s by a native of eastern Barrett County who, at the age of fourteen, had fled the poverty and work he shared with former slaves and followed the trail of cotton to the port of Galveston and a life at sea. Becoming enamored of whaling during his first New England port of call, he rose from cabin boy to captain over a long career, then retired and returned to Texas with his devoted wife some forty years after leaving it.

The home he built was of two stories, each with a wide, fretted porch that encircled the house. The roof was unremarkable as it rose from the eaves, set at a fairly aggressive angle and pierced by four chimneys and six gable dormers, two set to latitude and four to longitude. But whereas the expectation would be a continuance of the roof above these gables to a peak, instead a widow's walk of salvaged deck planking girdled by a low banister sat atop the house like a crown, built in deference to the woman who had spent countless hours awaiting the emergence of her husband's beacon on the horizon beyond Nantucket Harbor.

It held a history for Otis as well. Once, a lariat was anchored to each of the four corner posts of the railing, and every autumn, on a fair day, they would be uncoiled to encircle the chests of the Judge's two spry sons as they stepped onto the roof to clear the gutters of leaves and the eaves of wasp nests. Otis never felt threatened by the chore—the shingles were of cedar, and the gnarled grain of the wood had been so extracted by the elements that his footing was always sure—but the ropes had been installed to appease the concerns of their mother, who further insisted her husband position himself on the ground with the understanding that he would somehow catch them were the ropes to fail. The Judge concurred, even after her passing. In his youth, Otis could count the structures visible from the widow's walk on the fingers of one hand. Within Fuller proper, only the municipal water tower could be seen, hovering over the center of town on a knoll just to the east of Main Street, and on windier days, when gusts would open fractured windows in the dense treeline along the ridge, the defeated standard atop the flagpole at the Confederate Home flew in unanswered defiance for those valorous souls no longer capable of venturing beyond its shadow. The only other structure of sufficient height to breach the dense forest as it stretched north and east to the horizon was the residence of Douglas Enfield, a decorated Civil War veteran and founder of Enfield Cartage. Before the railroads drove him into an early retirement, he had amassed a fortune supplying Barrett County with manufactured goods brought up from the Galveston docks by freight wagon. In honor of his Scottish roots, he had built a castle atop a tall bluff skirting the western edge of Los Alamos Creek, and its twin turrets of red brick could be seen not only from the widow's walk but from any point west of Fuller. Finally, where the Nebraska River converged with the base of the limestone wall that steered her to a more easterly course, a lively white froth marked the wide shallows created by the placement of hundreds of flagstones, some still showing the gouges of the plows that had unearthed them. This was Fuller's Ford, visible from the southwest corner of the widow's walk.

By their third annual pilgrimage up the twisting staircase and onto the eaves, the boys had made a competition of locating new structures. It was Otis who first spotted the gradual blooming of the belfry on the new courthouse, protruding from the edge of the shadowed depression that held the courthouse square; Gregory claimed the tiny stalks a mile north of downtown that proved to be the construction cranes erecting the Texas College administration tower that would grace the horizon the following year. Otis had finished high school the same spring his father contracted gutter maintenance to the crew that came annually to prune the large trees surrounding the house, but by that time, the boys had long abandoned their rivalry—there was simply too much of Fuller to inventory.

Otis walked over to the eastern edge of the widow's walk, and suddenly the wind lifted his hat twenty feet into the air. Otis watched it cartwheel out of sight behind the trees, sailing toward the Fuller road.

The roof was one of the few remaining fronts of Otis's crusade. The gutters were filled with mulch, and dozens of abandoned wasp nests quivered against the wind under the eaves. The surrounding trees needed paring—he could hear the branches rapping the sides of the house—and while the once expansive view was now obstructed, the whipping branches still revealed in glimpses that the town had become a city. Downtown Fuller now stretched unbroken from the river to the college campus two miles to the north, and hundreds of chimneys and clapboard gables violated the forest that once surrounded the town in a virginal sweep. Los Alamos Creek was insinuated by the sudden dominance of trees over the land west of her rambling cleft, but Otis knew this to be a fleeting vision. Soon, bulldozers and survey crews would be carving out the roads that would eventually bring the houses of those who would bear the children who would attend the new schools marked by rising incinerator stacks of red brick.

He knew they were coming. It was only a matter of time.

Otis smiled when he spotted a former neighbor's windmill, due east and a thousand yards away, still spinning madly in the wind, trying to outrun time. He had laughed when old Matthews struck his deal two years earlier, when the county wanted an easement across his property to link the farm- to-market road along the river to another county road being brought in a half-mile to the north. Matthews asked only for cattle guards at points of entry and that the artery bear his name, to which the county agreed. When Otis first learned of it, he saw the naming of the street as a childish act of ego, but now he understood. Randolph Matthews sold out a year later at a price rumored to be obscenely high and retired to the small east Texas town that reared him, and if his only legacy of a lifetime spent along the Nebraska River was a few stenciled street signs among the hundreds of homes that would eventually obliterate what had been some of the best range in Barrett County, then so be it. Let the town move across his property like locusts in a wheat field, eating everything in sight. At least his name would survive.

Otis walked over to the west railing and in his imagination filled the valley with water. His land—or what would be left of it—would be desirable; there was no doubt. Few of the tracts fronting the lake would be closer to town, and none would possess his gentle shoreline. As far as Fuller was concerned, growth was uninhibited to the north and east, where the land flattened into cleared farmland. But Fuller people weren't flatlanders— if they were, they would have built their town on the blackland prairie twenty miles downriver, and Fuller would be just another gin town, another hole in the cotton belt.

Otis looked across the Nebraska to the shattered limestone rising out of the dead fault line, a hydrophobic range of impotent soil and worthless, stunted timber. The land beyond the melodic purl of Fuller's Ford was as it had always been—barren, exiled, forgotten.

But none of that really mattered. Eventually, they would have to cross the river.

He turned and opened the trap as the shadow of the house faded away.

#

The following week, Otis returned to the campus of Texas College, auditing classes on geology, engineering, and architecture. On weekends, his roan mare could be seen crossing Fuller's Ford in the morning and not returning before last light. Hunting trips, his neighbors assumed.

The heavy rains continued into the winter, and Otis sold his mature herd at market in December, then replaced them with a hundred head of weaned calves in February. By March, every structure on the Upshaw property that could separate a steer or heifer from available graze was removed—not even the picket fence that surrounded the house was spared—and in May, he acquired several tons of baled alfalfa from the buyer of the Matthews land by simply volunteering to haul it away, then purchased another fifty head of calves to help dispose of it. Gregory became available to husband the herd with the end of the spring term—their father's condition had gradually deteriorated to a vacillating state of dementia, and home studies had all but terminated—and was surprisingly eager to trade academics for spreading hay and monitoring the cattle for blowflies, freeing Otis to acquaint himself with the hills across the river as they appeared within the frayed binders of the Barrett County deed records.

In late July, Otis made his first purchase of land south of the Nebraska River—over fifty acres for less than the cost of a single yearling calf. The tract had belonged to a recently deceased Negro porter and resident of Griffintown, a small enclave of freed slaves and their descendants located just north of Sixth Street and less than a mile from the Barrett County courthouse. The late man's heirs had no use for the land—no family member still living had ever laid eyes on it, Otis was told—and quickly accepted the first offer from the pleasant white man swatting moths under their porch light.

By August, Otis was in an industrious rhythm. Tuesday through Friday mornings were spent at the courthouse researching deeds, followed by afternoons and, if necessary, evenings locating title holders and tendering offers. Weekends were reserved for agrarian pursuits, with Mondays spent selling the cattle needed to fund ongoing appropriations. There seemed to be no common denominator among those he sought out, nor was their station in the community any indicator as to the size or desirability of their acreage. The owners were rich and poor, city- and country-dwelling; white, brown, black, and—in the case of a tract owned by a Comanche whose grandfather had convinced the county that his descendants were Mexican— red. The only thing they seemed to have in common was an eagerness to sell.

Otis ran out of cattle the second week of January 1924, after amassing over two thousand acres of tumultuous and cedar-choked limestone, including all of the southern shoreline of the Nebraska River for a mile upstream from Fuller's Ford. And another big hurdle was cleared that month: the county completed a two-lane bridge across Fuller's Ford (Otis had been forced to finance half of it) that would grant Otis's contractors and customers more direct access than the circuitous route through Live Oak Park. There were still acquisitions to be made—the plat of western Barrett County that he had tacked to his bedroom wall still revealed scattered acreage within his targeted empire that he had yet to consecrate with flat swipes of charcoal—but they were untitled and uncontested. They would bear him no cost, barring whatever legal fees would be accrued by the act of staking legal claim, and fell to a low priority. It was land no one else wanted, and there were dozens of houses to be built.

In the latter part of the same month, The Judge suffered another stroke that left him comatose, and before he slipped away in early March, Otis was well into liquidation of their homestead. The land that would survive the construction of the dam was sold to the highest bidder, while the house itself was purchased by a wealthy local investor, torn from its bedding, then sliced up and carted into Fuller to be reassembled to a higher grandeur atop a knoll overlooking Los Alamos Creek, northwest of town. Written into both contracts was a provision granting Otis a gratuitous lease of six months, time enough for the construction of a new residence atop a high, level mesa in the new development of Granite Heights. Initially, Otis had envisioned a simple house of native stone—he and Gregory would be the only inhabitants—but in the third month of construction, the increased appraisals on land near the planned lake precipitated a tax increase so devastating that many of Otis's old neighbors sold out and opted to follow him into the hills, producing a sustained surge in business that compelled the addition of a den and second hearth to the existing floor plan, as well as two bedrooms and a bath overhead.

#

Otis's enterprise went well for several years, fueled in large part by the flow of Fuller expatriates. Many were enraged by the burgeoning taxes; others simply wanted to maintain the rural way of life the new dam had taken from them. Eccentrics and isolationists were also seduced by the dense lots and secluded dwellings Otis scattered along his caliche roads, and while competitors accused Granite Heights of courting artists, bootleggers, and anarchists, a large majority of buyers were simply responding to prices that halved the cost of a comparable home north of the river. That the roads were subject to flooding, the electricity prone to failure, and fire and police services ostensible at best mattered little to Otis's clientele, to whom he was acutely attuned. By the summer of 1925, he had changed the motto on his business cards from "Scenic Lots and Solitude" to "Solitude and Serenity."

The last of the granite blocks quarried seventy miles to the north and brought down the river by barge was laid in May of 1926, completing a final tier that brought the dam to an even one hundred feet above the Nebraska River bottom, and by October of the same year, the floodgates were opened for the first time when the reservoir threatened to eclipse her basin. During this same period, Otis's customer base (oddballs and skinflints, in his own terms) seemed to disperse, and Granite Heights saw sales fall by twenty percent month-over-month. Conversely, the fulfillment of promises that encountered unanimous cynicism under foul November skies almost four years before had propagated the first real boom in Fuller's history. Cheap, reliable power was bringing commerce and jobs to the sweep of rolling land between Fuller and the new lake. New construction included homes, schools, churches, and the city's first exclusive country club, featuring tennis courts and a nine-hole golf course, three holes of which would be played on onetime Upshaw farmland. Existing salaries and wages rose, alleviating the burden of high mortgage rates and taxes, and the dusty roads and gnarled juniper-strewn hills west of Lake Fuller were once again relegated to wasteland in the public consciousness. By the new year, only rarely would a hesitant prospect drop by the Granite Heights sales office and sign his name to a contract that Otis would type up on the spot.

Granite Heights continued to flag as Fuller boomed. Soon, the stagnant market, combined with higher wages and increases in the cost of materials, eroded the tax base until routine maintenance on the cruder roads, which were prone to erosion due to the arroyos, fell to the bottom of the county's priorities. Three weeks of unusually violent thunderstorms in the fall of 1928 gutted every low-water crossing in the hills, and lawsuits filed on behalf of his marooned constituents constrained Otis to hire, at his own expense, tutors to circumnavigate the distended arroyos on foot or horseback and conduct in-home study sessions for the stranded children. Only after Otis agreed to have provender and dry goods brought in by mules was all litigation halted. By the fall of 1929, Otis was disconsolate and embittered. Not yet thirty years old and looking into an abyss for the second time in a single decade, he was spending more time assuaging creditors than drawing up real estate contracts. Appropriately, he was sitting in the law library at Texas College going over the state bankruptcy statutes when the news of the stock market crash came.

Initially, Otis knew not where this latest act of Providence would lead, only that it had plunged a multitude of those who had been flourishing, some at his expense, into the same churning waters that he had been treading for some time. The few suppliers and construction companies he owed that were still extant were no longer hounding him for money he didn't have. Contrarily, the independent and cynical nature of those settling in the hills had spared them from the financial ruin ubiquitous along the opposite shore, and with few exceptions, mortgage payments continued to arrive on time at Texas Farmers Bank and Trust, the only lending institution in Fuller willing to involve themselves in what other banks had considered a folly. To an institution that had spent the last forty years bankrolling cattle and cotton in a drought-prone county, Otis's scheme to develop the hills hadn't seemed particularly risky at all. But there were still no new sales, and in spite of his enviable solvency, Otis feared that it would be a matter of months—perhaps a year at the most—before his cash flow would stop and his ledgers slip into the red.

CHAPTER 7

Lewis had managed to mold the rebellious little clot into an adherent mass by rolling it between the sweaty tips of his thumb and forefinger, and now held it furtively in the pinched space between the right leg and the passenger door. A covert glance revealed it to be gray and surprisingly large in the dull light, a single nose hair spun into its surface.

"There goes that shit-headed colonel and his pin-headed little shit-of-a- son."

Lewis brought his eyes back up and through the windshield, his curiosity piqued by the sudden hostility in Lowry's oral meanderings. The Plymouth was still halted on the unpaved portion of Casey Lane at the four-way stop, and his gaze leveled just in time to see the roof of the Kessler's Impala drop out of sight where the road descended into a deep arroyo.

The two uniformed men had just completed a loop—north on Ridgewest, then back to the intersection via Grady Way and Casey Lane—that had been appended to their usual itinerary at the beginning of the summer, apparently due to some incident that Lowry related only in incoherent profanities along the Grady Way leg of the circuit. Lewis mentioned on their maiden pass that it was out of their jurisdiction, that the blacktopped half of Casey Lane and everything north and east of it was in Kensington Oaks, and since they were members of the Granite Heights Police Department, they really didn't have any authority there. Lowry had just looked across the seat at him, his thin lips held with the disdain of an indentured babysitter discovering that his four-year-old charge had messed his pants. "Let's just let me worry about that, Lewis," Lowry had said.

"Since when did you become such an authority on the gawd-damned law?"

Just then, the Impala reentered their vision, undulating in the heat rising off the hood of the Plymouth as it nosed onto the shallow slope to the crest of the opposing ridge. The two men sat at the stop sign, watching The Colonel complete the climb out of the arroyo. As the Chevy leveled, they could see the abbreviated silhouettes of the occupants through the rear window: the hatted and stiffly erect head of The Colonel, his hands appearing as symmetrical lumps as they gripped the steering wheel—the epitome of control—and beside him, the barely visible nub representing his son.

"Ever wonder where your tax money goes, Lewis?" Lowry's forearms were resting atop the rim of the steering wheel. They still hadn't pulled into the intersection. "Well, there goes a goodly part of it right there. That cocky bastard probably isn't much past fifty, and he collects a full colonel's pay for puttering around in his yard, building his little walls and stepping in dog shit, when he's not chauffeuring that scrawny little juvenile delinquent around."

Lewis allowed his attention to shift back to the hand lurking between his leg and the door when the tone of Lowry's discourse became apparent, since his own lack of actual employment or, for that matter, his need of it, disqualified him from voicing a like resentment. He could only keep quiet, lessening the chances that Lowry would recall his enviable circumstances and turn on him like a coiled rattler.

Lewis cocked his index finger under the tip of his thumb and snapped it hard once, then two more times in quick succession, hoping to jettison the small lump onto the floorboard. Still, the small gray ball remained, taunting him from atop the well-chewed nail of his index finger as if held there by a magnet. Lewis fought the compulsion to transfer it to the seat or the door panel. Lowry would find it, he was sure.

"I know it's a fuckin' Saturday, but shit, every day's a fuckin' Saturday for that goddamn asshole."

The Plymouth finally lurched into the intersection. Lowry cut the wheel hard right onto Ridgewest, mumbling quietly to himself as they headed south, enabling Lewis to devote his full attention to the parasitic lump. The simple possession of a handkerchief or a sheet of tissue, and his predicament would never have evolved; for that matter, he could have just left it as it was—an unobtrusive blockage in his left nostril that could have been tolerated for another hour or so, eventually to be blown into a few stiff sheets of commercial toilet paper procurable in the restroom of whatever coffee shop or gas station their bladders would eventually drive them. But hindsight was pointless; what mattered now was avoiding Lowry's phenomenal powers of observation. It was as if his dark, probing eyes encircled his entire head.

#

Lewis Upshaw had never squandered much of his considerable idle time reflecting on these disagreeable interludes in his life. Lowry's abuses were, for the most part, circumspect and private, and mutated into intimate conspiracy during those rewarding intervals when they would become a team—Officers Lowry and Upshaw—jointly exercising their lust for the authority they so cherished. But if a time ever came to place blame, the case could be made that it should settle on the stooped shoulders of Amos Marshall and that time five years before when he burst into a Granite Heights city council meeting with hellfire in his eyes and firewater in his belly to face down the mayor, who was also the only person in attendance who had any idea who he was. Amos Jackson Marshall was one of the oldest citizens of Granite Heights, both in age and term of residency. A former economics professor at the State College in Fuller, Marshall had been a virtual hermit since the Wall Street debacle of 1929 plunged the greater part of his considerable inheritance into a fiscal abyss, and he fled south, across the river, and away from the college and the banks and the brokerage houses to four hundred cedar-choked acres along the southwestern border of Granite Heights.

He took up exile in an abandoned, ramshackle farmhouse set beneath the trees along the highest ridge on the property, well back from the road, and considered himself insulated from any remaining perils. The possibility that a greed just as potent and pure was waiting for him in the purple hills west of the Nebraska River never occurred to him.

Otis first encountered Amos Marshall during his college years, when Amos was a graduate student in economics and instructed freshmen and lagging sophomores out of no higher motivation than ego. He was from the older, "near-west" Fuller, the son of a stolid banker who had wed the most eligible heiress in town and amassed one of the largest fortunes in Barrett County before both were washed from their Packard in a flash flood shortly before the American entry into the Great War. With the discovery of his parents' bodies two counties downriver three weeks later, Amos became, at age twenty-three, the sole scion of his family's assets, if not yet a practicing millionaire. According to his father's will, the inheritance would remain in trust until Amos earned his doctorate and attained the age of thirty. In the interim, he was expected to survive on an allowance of three figures monthly.

Virtually all of Amos Marshall's students, Otis included, despised him for his superior demeanor and flippant responses to all questions, no matter how legitimate or well parsed. Perfect work and attendance were required to avoid an F, while the grade of B went only to those students corrupt enough to grovel for them, and an A required a bloodline leading to the upper echelons of Fuller society, although occasionally an attractive coquette would qualify as well. When he abandoned teaching upon earning his doctorate, not a student or staff member missed him, and he was rarely seen after cloistering himself inside the family mansion to await the coming of midnight on March 20, 1924.

Amos had observed the machinations of Wall Street with his academically honed eye long enough to be convinced of his clairvoyance and began moving his inheritance into the market as soon as it passed into his hands. Real estate, bonds, precious metals, even his mother's jewelry were liquidated and poured into stocks. In two years, he doubled his inheritance, and by the summer of 1928, it had doubled twice more. The week before it was all swept away, the value of Amos's portfolio was approaching ten million dollars.

Certainly, it was a time of calamity for all involved in business and investment, but no one in Fuller would have disagreed that Amos Marshall had the hardest fall with the least moral cushion. What torments he endured between that October and the following February, when he walked into Otis's real estate office at the intersection of Granite Heights Drive and Red Bud Lane, were his to know, but the physical transformation was so dramatic that Otis failed to recognize the man he glimpsed less than a year before at the county courthouse. The stresses of financial collapse had shriveled the features of the portly graduate student like sunlight on raw beef. His clothes now hung on his frame like a flag in still air. The arrogant, shining face with the high forehead that once so faithfully reflected the overhead classroom lights was lined and wan, and when he spoke, it was with a high, thin voice hinting at hysteria, alternating between condescension and despair.

Amos Marshall laid out what Otis decided could only be a plan of escape or exile—an act of salvation it certainly wasn't. With what he had been able to salvage from the forced liquidation of his assets, he wished to purchase a tract of land large enough to insulate him from the Society of Man, preferably with a dwelling thereon, existing to whatever degree of humility his limited resources decreed.

Otis leaned back in his chair when Amos quieted. He set his boot heels on the edge of the scarred desk and gazed at the ceiling with his hands entwined atop his belly, waiting for his salesman's clock to tell him when it was time. After a minute, Amos's lips started to quiver, and Otis swung his feet back to the floor, slapped the desk with his palms, and, smiling broadly, assured Amos Marshall that he had just the property for him.

#

That night, Otis, Gregory, and a Barrett County deputy climbed into Otis's truck and plunged into the maze of bulldozed roads. After an hour of constant jarring amid curses from the deputy, Otis pulled onto a pale caliche trail blocked by a crude gate. The men unloaded in the moonless gloom; a single kerosene lamp was lit, and the wick spun down until there was only a ghostly pantomime of two men loading shotguns against the uneven cedar walls. They stepped through the slackened gate and mounted the trail, Otis and the deputy abreast in the twin ruts, and Gregory with the faint lamp, twenty feet behind.

The path was level for a hundred yards, then banked sharply to the left and met head-on the base of the ridge that by day defined the southern horizon of Granite Heights. The men ascended the hill in the lambent glow, the limestone luminescent and muted, through a series of treacherous switchbacks that brought sweat to their foreheads in the cool winter night. On the steeper grades, the exposed limestone strata offered false steps that would collapse beneath their boots, and twice the deputy was brought sliding down to his hands and knees before he followed Otis's lead and left the path at these junctures for the thin margin of low brush that bordered the shoulders of the trail. It was twenty minutes before the ground leveled out onto the edge of a clearing at the top of the rise.

At the treeline, forms suggesting leaning and broken outbuildings moved in and out of the lamplight, and a clapboard farmhouse appeared in the center of a clearing, still but for soft flames dancing on shaded windows and gray smoke curling from a leaning chimney. Otis and the deputy crossed the clearing, stepped onto the porch, and up to the screen door, hearing voices on the other side. Otis rapped twice, then both men stepped back to allow for the arc. Inside, the voices stopped. Several minutes passed with no sound from the house except for the small bumps and creaks of deliberate movement, then the paneled door swung in and two men and a woman assembled behind the screen. Discussion followed, and Gregory's description would provide frightening theater later: how the conversation ensued quietly at first, then flared into anger within the house, bringing the barrel of the deputy's shotgun to bear, then more civil discussion. Finally, after more than twenty minutes of negotiation, Otis and the deputy stepped down from the porch and returned to the warm glimmer at the mouth of the trail. The doorway had never been breached; no shaking of hands had occurred.

Three withered, elderly people stood in the doorway and watched the glow of the lamp fade from the ridge. Then they turned and began moving through the house, giving orders and gathering up belongings. When Otis drove Amos Marshall up the jolting trail to the house the next morning, the only trace left of the Pratts, all sixteen of them, was the warm ashes in the wood stove.

#

Otis had made this same pilgrimage five years before, unarmed and naive in the radiant light of a spring afternoon. It was to be his first encounter with one of the clans that had first begun to cross the river from the hills when his father was still a young man, cracking their twenty-foot whips above the ears of gaunt and mismatched mules as they forded the Nebraska River with loads of cedar posts, exploiting a market that was created when the flatter land north of the river had been settled and cleared for cattle and crops. They were a welcome change from the Comanche war parties that began conducting sporadic raids on the town upon its forming in the days when Texas was a Republic, killing and scalping men and snatching women and children back across the flagstone ford, their cries echoing and dying in the hard arroyos that left no trail to follow. By the 1840s, persistent petitioning of President Houston to deal with the problem led to the encampment of a company of Texas Rangers in a grove of willows and cottonwoods a hundred yards downriver from Fuller's Ford, along the north shore of the Nebraska. Barracks were constructed the following year after it became apparent that success would only come after a long campaign of harsh retribution, and it was not until 1877 that the hills were considered safe and the unit reassigned.

The purging of the Comanches should have diminished the apocalyptic cast of the hills, but their threat lingered in myth, and the hills remained vilified and avoided, offering nothing beyond memorable sunsets and fodder for tall tales. Then, in the fall of 1890, the first wagons loaded with cedar posts rolled onto the north shore at Fuller's Ford, signaling the arrival of several clans who would become known as "cedar choppers," as if the term had been lying dormant in the bowels of the provincial vernacular, only awaiting the appearance of those souls from the primal swamp of dead civilizations to whom it would apply. They would pull onto the rutted farm road and rattle and bounce all the way to town, the patriarch slouched forward in the sprung seat, his wife seated wordlessly at his side with no fewer than one babe at her breast, the older children perched atop the stacked posts like basking lizards. They seemed somehow more alien than the Comanches, whose brutality held no mystery, and they crossed Los Alamos

Creek and entered west Fuller in solemn exile, oblivious to the dogs snapping at the heels of the mules and the jeering throngs of children assailing their flanks. Two blocks from Main Street, the procession would turn south to the farmers' mercantile that spread out over four acres just north of the riverfront, where the cedar posts would be bartered for dry goods and supplies.

The cedar choppers treated the general populace with catatonic indifference and kept strictly to business with the merchants, who said they spoke like mountain people and were probably from the Ozarks, hissing and spitting consonants sewn together with vowels pulled from their sinuses. They carried neither Bible nor pistol—although the stock of a shotgun or rifle often protruded close to the driver—and when not staring at the road ahead, they were returning every gaze as if it were an insult.

The cedar choppers had no interest in cash, swapping their cords of gnarled, stout cedar for common staples in tenacious bargaining sessions that left the establishment feeling defeated, which in most cases it was. Transactions were ratified either verbally or with a slow, reticent nod, and a hand was never extended. Finally, muttered orders were given to the waiting clan to facilitate an aggressive unloading and reloading of the wagon, then the town's youth would gather again with the first lash of the reins and the circus would begin anew, ending only when the final wagon would roll from the water on the opposite bank at Fuller's Ford.

The 1920 census recorded no less than four distinct clans of cedar choppers, and only the merchants with whom they dealt could differentiate one from the others—to the general citizenry, they were indistinguishable subspecies of the same animal. The Yarboroughs had appeared first, then the Snavelys, the Pratts, and lastly, the Sweets. The Dickensian names seemed to support an Appalachian background, but there was no correspondence to verify the identity or literacy of their bearers, and pronunciation by phonetics eliminated alternative spellings and hence, origins. When Otis committed his material fate to the domestication of the hills, he anticipated encounters with these families, but as it turned out, all had settled beyond Otis's targeted properties with the exception of the Pratts, who had squatted on a tract of land adjacent to eight hundred acres Otis had purchased from descendants of Griffintown freedmen. The Pratts had been living an anonymous existence atop a ridge that prefaced the steep plunge into the narrow valley of the Arroyo Blanco, and Otis's first visit to the weathered pine house was to tender an offer to the inhabitants, whom he assumed to be holders of title. Posing as a lost hunter, he established their probable status through small talk, then bid them a good day and retreated to the Barrett County courthouse to determine the owner of record, who turned out to be another resident of Griffintown. After an effortless acquisition, Otis revisited the clapboard house. When the door opened, he held up his pristine deed for theatrical effect and declared his ownership of their house and property, and then, in the same breath, stated that they would be allowed to stay on, rent-free, under the condition that they would harvest their cedar only from areas designated by him and would do so without question.

The offer was met with a long silence that Otis took as a tacit agreement, and when he held out his hand, Jeremiah Pratt just nodded once and closed the door.

#

Over the years, the Pratts had cleared many a lot and roadbed in fulfilling the terms of their unwritten lease, and their eviction from a home that had spawned untold generations wasn't without remorse. But Otis had always shot straight with them in the past, and his assurance that the utmost would be done to accommodate a satisfactory resettlement led to their peaceful retreat down the long escarpment to the banks of the Arroyo Blanco, not knowing that their fate hung on Otis's assessment of Amos Marshall's competency, or lack thereof.

The following day proved Otis to be right on every count—right about Amos Marshall's acceptance of the old house without further exploration of the three hundred acres that surrounded it, which would have revealed the deep, flood-prone bed of the Arroyo Blanco gouging the length of the tract and the displaced family of cedar choppers camped out on the broad, flat stones that curbed her north shore; right about his acceptance of a contract that Otis had drawn up before morning's light, a contract unremarkable except for the carefully buried waiver of timber rights; and right in his belief that his survey crew could excise a dozen acres from the southwest corner of the tract and have it recorded at the Barrett County courthouse by noon, deeded to one Jeremiah Pratt.

Amos had seen the property for the first time that morning, even as Otis's surveyor was cutting out the Pratts' acreage half a mile further down the ridge, and the transactions were completed and notarized in time for Otis to race down to the creek bed in the red dusk of that same day and hand Jeremiah Pratt his deed. This time there was only the nod of his head—there wouldn't be a door to close until the arrival of cooler fall weather.

Otis knew that he hadn't seen the last of Amos Marshall—the amount he received for the flawed tract was at least three times as much as the land was worth—but that didn't sully his drive into Fuller the next day to deposit his funds and pay off every debt he had. When he returned to his home atop the limestone mesa that evening, he drove a brand new Buick.

The fleecing of Amos Marshall would herald more than the immediate benefits of corporate and personal solvency, for while the shifting economic polarities of the opposing shores of the Nebraska would continue their inherent see-saw flux, never again would the viability of Granite Heights and the fortunes of its founder fall into serious jeopardy. True, sales languished through the remainder of the decade, then stagnated even further after Pearl Harbor and remained depressed through the war, but a random generational rhythm had allowed the Upshaw men to leapfrog every armed conflict since the War of 1812, and Otis and Gregory remained in the hills and nurtured their tax base, waiting for the resultant post-war boom that would keep three generations of Pratts busy clearing lots of mesquite and cedar.

#

Kensington Oaks was established in 1946 by Stanley Hartsfield, a former Army Air Corps liaison officer and Fuller developer who saw potential in the flatter, more complacent land just west of Live Oak Park, across the Nebraska from Fuller. Despite initial concerns, Kensington Oaks never seriously threatened Otis's market; Hartsfield's development targeted a more exclusive clientele with high-quality homes featuring amenities not available in Granite Heights at the time. To the contrary, Otis came to realize that the corporate limits of the two communities blended so seamlessly that he could poach some of his neighbor's prospects by offering upgraded homes of brick and stone along their mile of shared border.

In June of 1948, a reporter walked into Otis's real estate office seeking information for an article, and a week later a two-page story on Granite Heights appeared in the Sunday edition of the Fuller Dispatch. The article detailed the area's colorful history and dramatic terrain and contained quotes from several residents, including one from a retired army medical officer named O'Grady, who said he preferred the two college professors, three lawyers, and fellow physician he had for neighbors to his previous isolation. And throughout the article, the stigmatized, denigrated wilderness into which Otis Upshaw had sunk his birthright and soul was awarded proper noun status, and the barren purgatory known as the hills became, in the twinkling of a typesetter's hand, The Hills.

The day after the article ran, Otis ordered new business cards reading:

Otis Upshaw
THE HILLS OF GRANITE HEIGHTS
Land of Untold Promise and Fulfilled Dreams

#

Then came a new decade and an influx of young married couples that forced Granite Heights to create a school district in anticipation of population projections for children of elementary school age, an increase that would surely obviate the terms of Otis's long-standing contract with the Fuller Independent School District. The projections for junior and senior high school students wouldn't put an excessive burden on the Fuller system for some years to come, it was determined, but the first six grades would be dropped from all future agreements with no offer of mediation. To complicate matters further, the school board elections that followed (in which, to no one's surprise, Otis was elected President without serious opposition) had the adverse effect of illuminating the political vacuum under which Otis's dictatorship had flourished, however benignly, for over twenty-five years, and he was compelled to renounce his feudal tenure and actively campaign for powers once held outright. Vexed but hardly defeated by these niggling technicalities, Otis went on to retake the mayoralty and bring a sympathetic council with him, forming a coalition he would maintain through two more races over the next twelve years.

Perhaps the distant thud of hand-whetted steel against green cedar when the weather permitted—and most days it did—was accepted by Amos as necessary to sustain the smoldering rage that was all he had left to give his life purpose. Or perhaps the Pratts' consideration for his life of solitude, an existence different from their own only in its singularity, kept their work along the perimeters and outward-facing hillsides of the tract, well away from their old home.

Regardless, Otis would be midway through his third term before he would encounter Amos Marshall again, and it didn't have anything to do with cedar choppers or timber rights.

Otis had seen Amos Marshall occasionally since their transaction, but only in the literal sense. The first time was in 1939, when they passed while Otis was returning home from Fuller on the ranch-to-market road. Amos was driving his dilapidated Model A truck, and his eyes and hands were locked in their purpose as if by unadulterated will alone would the old Ford be prevented from spinning in the road and scurrying back to the destitute certainty of the cedar-choked ridge. Then several more times after the start of the war, with Amos driving to or returning from town, always along the same route, always the hands of the driver gripping the wheel as if in a rage.

And once, in the late afternoon of an April day in 1946, Otis was sure he saw a woman seated alongside Amos as the truck sputtered toward the sunset. Only the back of her head was visible through the rear glass, but the dying sun brought out a deep iron rust in her hair that was common to every Pratt that Otis had ever met.

#

But every other time Otis had seen Amos Marshall, he had been alone, as he was on a hot summer night in 1958, when he burst into the Granite Heights City Hall during a scheduled weekly council meeting and the two men faced each other again for the first time since Amos signed away the dregs of his inheritance. Ironically, time and the agenda were the only variables: the structure that served as city hall had begun life as Otis's first real estate office before being drafted for municipal duty, and the last shared words of the two men had passed over the very same desk, through the very same corridor of air.

It had been the usual boring meeting prior to Amos's entrance, with the usual contingent complaining about bad roads and low water pressure. As Otis and two underlings sat feigning commiseration, Amos bolted into the room looking exactly as he did on his drives into town, only now his fists held no wheel and his lips were moving:

"GODDAMMIT, SKELTON! All these years I've never asked a thing from you or any other soul on this God-awful earth, but I've got people *FORNICATING* on my land, and I won't stand for it! *DO YOU UNDERSTAND ME?* I won't! And by God, you're going to have to do something about it! *That's the LAW!*"

Otis sat frozen at his worn desk as the only two women present gasped and rose to leave. He was only vaguely aware that Amos was talking; the spectacle of what the man had become held him in cataleptic wonder. Amos Marshall was no more than a bearded, hatted skeleton draped in drawn flesh, his cold, tiny eyes blazing out of the darkness of their sunken hollows, and all Otis could think was *he's gone feral. I knew he was crazy, but I'll be damned if he hasn't gone feral, too, just like a goddamned hog. I would've never believed it could happen, not in a million years, that this filthy primate is the splay-footed pansy who used to erase his blackboard with his pinkie finger stuck out like my mother used to do when she sipped tea . . .*

Otis didn't stay quiet for long. He wasn't used to being dictated to at city council meetings or anywhere else, and was quick to stand and fire a retort:

"Don't go telling me about the law, Mister Marshall"—Otis's voice was low in volume but laced with resolve—"You're making some pretty high and mighty demands for a man who hadn't paid his taxes since Harry was a haberdasher. By law, you don't have any more right to be on that land than—well, than those so-called fornicators you're crying about."

Amos Marshall was struck dumb. He stood stock-still beneath the ceiling fan, and as the odor of his sweat- and whiskey-steeped flesh spread through the room, Otis watched the hate in the man's eyes turn inward, on himself— for wasting his inheritance; for letting Otis clean him out and deed away his privacy; for forging a perennial misery that he would never escape. And he barged into this meeting, only to fail again. He no longer had the resolve even for flight, and as he began to quiver and his eyes welled up, it was enough to move Otis Upshaw to charity for the first time in his life. He motioned the rest of the room toward the door with a sweep of an arm, then sat down and clasped his hand atop the desk.

"Okay, Mister Marshall, tell me again what your problem is, and go slow. I'll see if I can do something about it."

Amos Marshall waited for the room to empty, then reeled out his grievance in a confused ramble. It seemed that the trails that crisscrossed Amos's acreage—footprints of the Pratts' cedar harvests—had been discovered and put to a new use by those for whom Otis had once been required to build an elementary school. The intervening years had blessed these same children with drivers' licenses and pubescent urges, and every Friday and Saturday night their headlights would veer off the ranch-to-market road and flicker through Amos Marshall's cedars. Then the headlights would halt and die, and unrestrained laughter and the devil's music would pierce the shroud of dark forest and luminous stone, annihilating the quiet of Amos's tomb on the ridge. When asked for a justification for the charge of fornication, Amos only said that he had found "obscene leavings" as evidence, and Otis chose not to pursue it further.

It was close to ten o'clock before Amos Marshall finally turned and slunk out to his old Ford. Otis rocked his chair back against the wall and watched through the open door window as Amos bent to the crank. The engine answered several labored attempts with a weak huff before finally coughing to life, and as Amos chugged back into his world of infinite gloom, Otis remained behind his desk, his chair against the wall, pondering. He could care less whether Amos paid his taxes or not, but his complaint amplified a problem that Otis knew he would eventually have to address—his community's lack of law enforcement.

Officially, it was the county sheriff's job to police Granite Heights, but that entity was staffed to handle a large rural jurisdiction; the unofficial attitude was that if Granite Heights wanted to suckle Fuller for utilities and residents, well, then Fuller could do their policing too. But in order for that to happen, Granite Heights would have to be incorporated into the city itself, which would result in higher taxes and the sacrifice of autonomy that no one in Granite Heights, least of all Otis, wanted to relinquish. Amos Marshall had a legitimate right to complain of trespass, and assuming he even had a telephone with which to call in a complaint, which Otis was sure he didn't, it would be hours before the county would respond, if at all. And posted warnings were useless; teenagers were akin to armadillos when it came to honoring property rights. For now, it was just Amos complaining, but he wasn't the only owner of a large amount of acreage in Granite Heights who valued his privacy. The situation wasn't going to get any better.

#

The following morning, a notice appeared on the community bulletin board along Granite Heights Drive in front of the city hall:

WANTED!

Volunteers for the Establishment of a Granite Heights Police Force Applicants must be qualified and in possession of all required equipment A desire for selfless community service a must

Interviews will be given at the Granite Heights City Hall on Thursday, June 26, 1958,

following the conclusion of the regularly scheduled council business.

Signed: Otis Upshaw, Mayor

Otis never actually believed in the possibility of an unpaid, self- supporting police force—he had already worked out the budget considerations and projected costs of a professional organization—so the appearance of two applicants at his desk on the afternoon of that same day left him in stunned silence.

The younger and shorter of the pair certainly needed no introduction. He was Otis's nephew, Gregory's only child, and Otis shook the soft, extended hand wordlessly as Lewis stuttered out his rehearsed speech. Unlike Otis, whose romantic encounters never extended beyond rumored affairs with ladies inhabiting the lower tiers of Fuller society, Gregory had taken a wife in 1933—a pretty, compliant girl whom Gregory had known since high school—and as a wedding gift, Otis awarded the couple a large red brick home on a lot positioned lower on their hill and adjacent to the existing drive. Over the years, Gregory's lack of initiative had been offset by his loyalty, and while he never pursued any endeavor of his own, his willingness to subscribe to his older brother's agenda had proven him to be invaluable as an indentured aide, available at all times of the day or night to perform the more menial machinations that were nonetheless essential to the Upshaw enterprise. Their only child was Lewis, born one year to the day after his parents' union, and he proved to be predictably modest in his ambitions. In the six years since his graduation from Fuller High, he managed only to acquire a real estate license—which he never found occasion to use—and to populate his parents' backyard with a teeming warren of rabbits that was kept from overflowing only by the judicious bleeding of excess stock into the surrounding cedar thicket, where it would quickly perish by predator and perpetuate an endless plague of swirling buzzards that gave their hillside retreat a Gothic aura.

But Otis himself had displayed deficiencies of ambition when held to his father's high standard, and like his father, he saw no call to allow his disappointments to override family bonds. Besides, he was just glad to see Lewis actually applying for a job, paid or not.

Otis had never met the other candidate, a resident who had recently bought into the part of Granite Heights that melded so seamlessly with Kensington Oaks. His name was Mike Lowry, a war veteran and part-time postal worker, and Lewis's senior by fifteen years or more. In answer to a request for his qualifications, he proclaimed himself a survivor of many a deadly encounter with the nation's enemies, and Otis—sensing a looming medley of vainglorious war stories—pointed out the lateness of the hour and requested a moment for thoughtful deliberation.

Lowry was an unpleasant man with a crude, swaggering manner and would have been dismissed out of hand had he been applying for a share of the public coffers. But with so little, if anything, at stake, he was accepted along with Lewis, primarily because Otis assumed that it would take at least two men to constitute a police force. And they had met Otis's minimal requirements—that is, both were sane, sober, and displayed a willingness to outfit themselves at their own expense—and had schedules that would allow a high degree of flexibility. Otis had no doubt as to Lewis's availability, and Lowry assured Otis that the part-time postal work with which he supplemented his disability income left him with plenty of time to contribute to the community's welfare.

Otis swore both into service using a Gideon Bible and an oath pulled from the pages of a Zane Grey novel, then ushered them out the door.

#

As soon as they were equipped and without explanation, Otis ordered the Granite Heights Police Department to target trespassers on Amos Marshall's land, and they proved up to the task at hand. That first weekend, the two men—Lowry in his army khakis, a .357 Magnum on his hip; Lewis in an army surplus outfit of a similar cut, carrying a .38—confronted eight carloads of potential fornicators on Amos Marshall's land and returned them to their parents with the advisement that second offenders would be turned over to the Barrett County juvenile authorities.

As the summer progressed, the pair became so ubiquitous that by the start of the school year, a Granite Heights teenager was more likely to be found at home darning socks on a Saturday night than shedding his innocence along Amos Marshall's moonlit ridge.

As time passed and Granite Heights prospered, Lewis Upshaw and Mike Lowry worked hard and long to combat their replacement by salaried mercenaries, and when Otis Upshaw served out his final term as mayor and handed the management of the business over to Gregory in 1962, had anyone asked him to itemize his greatest accomplishments, the establishment of a pro bono police force would have been near the top of the list.

#

"So, is that Sam Browne new, Lewis? I don't remember that flowery design before."

Lewis glanced self-consciously down toward the gun belt buried under his belly roll.

"Yeah, it's new. My other one was still good, the one with the weave pattern punched in the leather, but this one's got a lot more features. It's got a little holster for my cuffs, plus a loop to hold a flashlight. Or a billy club, maybe. Anyway, the flashlight I got now just falls through, so I'll probably get a bigger one next time I'm downtown."

"Well, that's real interesting, Lewis, but I think I'll stick with what I got. All the patrolling we do is by vehicle, and it's just not that much trouble to reach over and pull the light out of the glove box." Lowry eased the Plymouth up to the stop sign at the intersection, then cut the wheel a sharp right on Kensington Road. A bus had just passed by and filled the car with fumes of burnt diesel, and Lowry accelerated through the acrid smoke, savoring Lewis's silence. "And don't tell me your pockets are so full of your granddaddy's money that you don't have room for handcuffs anymore."

They never patrolled in Lewis's highway fully equipped 1961 Plymouth anymore, unless Lowry's car was in the shop. Lewis's Uncle Otis had bought it at a state auction on behalf of the City of Granite Heights—it had logged only 22,000 miles before the model was phased out and replaced with new Fords—and Lewis eventually refused to use it for team duty due to Lowry's unending cracks about nepotism. Of course, the exclusive use of Lowry's vehicle was fine, providing that Lewis keep his gas tank full and pay for tune-ups and tires, to which Lewis readily agreed. But things were better now than they were two years ago, before Lewis's uncle had agreed to fund matching uniforms.

As they approached the intersection of Kensington and Crest Roads, Lowry slowed for a half dozen or more women climbing off the halted bus. They were of varying degrees of darkness and dressed in starched uniforms of white or pastel, and two of the women paused their Spanish chatter and nodded curtly to Lowry as they passed in front of the Plymouth on their way across the road.

"I'll be damned," Lewis exclaimed. "I didn't know Fuller ran a bus route out this far. We must be a mile and a half from the city limits."

Lowry smiled and waved to the younger of the two women as they stepped onto the lawn along the opposite side of the street. She returned his smile coquettishly.

"Well, this is as far out as they go," Lowry said. "From here, the bus goes on down to the ranch-to-market road, then straight back into town, nonstop. There are only two buses scheduled on this route—this one in the morning, then another at about five or six in the afternoon. A lot of nigger and Mexican domestics work out here who can't afford to own a car and also keep their husbands bailed out of jail, so the city throws its money out the window by running half-empty buses back and forth twice a day. It's just amazing what a little well-placed campaign cash can do, but what the hell."

Lowry started to pull around the bus, his eyes still fixed on the twitching pink hips of the younger chica. She had separated from the other woman and was skirting the edges of the lawns as she walked east on Kensington. He was debating which to toss out, a friendly buenos días or a coy hasta la vista, when he heard Lewis intone:

"What about her? You're not gonna try and tell me she's a domestic."

Lowry looked back to the north side of the street. A young black girl was coming toward them from across the wide lawn that fronted the sprawling ranch-style brick home sitting at the base of the ridge on its southeast corner. She was neatly dressed in the style of a schoolgirl on vacation, in a simple summer dress adorned with golden flowers, but she moved with a voluptuousness and feminine purpose that held their gaze until she disappeared behind the waiting bus.

"She must have used that path that runs along the base of the ridge," Lowry said. "It comes out right beside that house, along the edge of the backyard. This here's the school bus stop too, and the kids all up and down Ridgewest and Casey use that trail for a shortcut during the school year. By God, that's the first time I've ever seen 'em pick somebody up on the morning run, though."

Lowry watched Lewis remove his hat and strain for a view through the high windows of the bus as the Plymouth passed at a fast idle. "You know, they say a roll in the hay with a nigger gal will change your luck for the better, Lewis."

Lewis hadn't heard a word Lowry said. As they cleared the front of the bus and Lowry pulled back over into the right-hand lane, Lewis placed his hat back on his head and was about to turn in the seat for a final look when he spotted the outside mirror positioned on the front of his door, just inches from his right hand. He reached out and manipulated the chrome rim of the glass with subtle nudges of his index finger until the receding image was the shimmering brown and gold of the girl still on the ground in the cool shadow of the bus, pulling change from a small shoulder bag.

Lewis was watching the hem of her skirt climb the dark calf that had lifted her small foot onto the first high step, when:

"*GODDAMMIT, LEWIS!* If you're looking to change your luck, you can start by putting that mirror back where it belongs. And that piece of snot back on the end of your finger too, goddammit, or that nigger gal won't be the only one around here needing a ride home."

CHAPTER 8

The Colonel had been able to elicit little conversation from his sullen son beyond a discussion of repairs needed on The General's latest pistol, so he wore the subject for all it was worth as they motored along Kensington Road, headed toward town. The talk (or, more properly, The Colonel's monologue) had progressed to the type of wood on hand that would be suitable for the pistol stocks, and Thomas was wishing to God his father would shut up as they passed the stone wall bearing the wrought-iron signature of Kensington Oaks. A hundred yards down the road, at the edge of the Fuller city limit, sat the police pistol range, built in the early thirties to quell a nervous citizenry after two of Fuller's finest emptied their pistols at a trio of bank robbers without so much as chipping the paint on the stolen Packard in which they were fleeing. The range itself was a masterwork of simplicity—two massive parallel walls of native rock and mortar fifty yards long, ten feet high, and over a foot thick, set a hundred and fifty feet apart and bordered on the north by a hillside pulverized to white powder along its base by three decades of gunfire. Opposite this makeshift backstop and tying the southern ends of the limestone ramparts together was a narrow, wood-shingled canopy sheltering a row of shooting stands. Downrange, two rows of metal racks were set atop berms to hold the targets.

Thomas took comfort in the familiar sight of the old black Oldsmobile sedan parked under the live oak canopy in the cliché parking lot. It was owned by the range master, an obese, unsmiling police sergeant who had managed to distill his uniform down to an issue shirt, a baseball cap, and a badge. His presence meant that the range was open, and while regulations limited the use of the facility to law enforcement personnel only, this rule, like the dress code, was ostensible. When not in official use, polite civilians and respectful juveniles were allowed through the hallowed gate of the chain-link fence that separated the parking area from the firing line, and Thomas could not have been more respectful of the range master if he had been President of the United States.

The Chevy dropped into the low-water crossing just past the range and climbed out onto the flatter land that signaled the end of the hills. Thomas's father halted obediently at the stop sign where Kensington Road terminated, then took a wide looping left onto the eastbound lane of Arroyo Blanco Road and Live Oak Park opened up around them. He had depleted his monologue, and considering the receptiveness of his audience, saw no reason to pursue another. As for Thomas, he never considered asking about the purpose of their trip, since even something as innocuous as an outing to buy school clothes would be cloaked in vague and mysterious generalities ("Well, let's just say it's something we've been neglecting to do.") or simply evaded ("Not to change the subject, but did you clean out your closet like your mother asked?") and leave him more frustrated and no less enlightened.

There was nothing to do but use the silence. Besides, Thomas was pretty sure he had pegged his fate. He squinted into the glare of the high sun on the windshield as the brick homes and pruned oaks flickered by.

The summer of 1951 was one of heat and pliant voices murmuring innocuous conspiracies behind flower-covered walls; of reclining before a massive wooden cabinet and watching a tiny glass window that held a puppet with a huge, deeply-bowed mouth and cowboy clothes but no hat or gun; of racing dutifully to the corner gas station to buy Uncle Ray's Raleighs from a vending machine that took the quarter entrusted to him with a simple act of gravity, then resisted all manipulation of its gleaming chrome knob as if he were a thief; of sitting on the porch of the house on Trade Street and mindlessly watching the cars motor past while Uncle Ray cut the Raleighs in half to slow up his smoking, which even Thomas, at age five, knew was pointless, since Uncle Ray chain-smoked the little ones too.

His father, then a major, had taken an assignment in Germany at the beginning of the summer, and Thomas and his mother went by train to Charlotte, where they would stay with one of her sisters and her husband until quarters had been arranged overseas. Of eight children—four boys and a like number of girls—born to Thomas's maternal grandparents, only two had allowed life's circumstances to carry them beyond the borders of the Carolinas: the youngest son, who had followed his wartime Marine enlistment with a civil service career, and Thomas's mother, who had forfeited her heart to a journeyman pilot forced by The Great Depression to pursue his vocation on the opposite side of the world from Mecklenburg County. They were married in Manila in 1937. His mother's people were many and well-rooted in the red Carolina clay, and Thomas's inability to sort out the droves of cousins, in-laws, uncles, and aunts left him flustered and timorous whenever company came calling, but he was not expected to sustain conversation and the attention paid him was generally brief, leaving him to lounge undisturbed as the grown-ups chatted while their rockers massaged creaks from the pine floor of the old clapboard house. Evenings he liked best, when after supper his mother, aunt, and uncle (whose two children were grown and gone—a daughter to marriage, a son to the navy) would assemble in the backyard under the mimosas, willows, and sycamores with their lawn chairs arranged to best capture the prevailing breeze. Then they would wait with tinkling glasses of iced tea and talk in the southern manner of rounding the hard edges from their words until, as the light and heat would wane, members of the extended family would assemble at random and unannounced, settling along the back porch steps or onto chairs brought down from the house as needed, and on some nights particularly cool and bright, onto blankets spread over thick grass still warm from the day's heat. And all the while, the women would flit purposely about in long dresses of floral cotton, moving from house to yard with pitchers of fresh iced tea until, finally, they too would sink into chairs or onto the lawn.

The men were all handsome, Thomas thought, in starched long-sleeved shirts with cuffs folded back to their elbows, vests unbuttoned, and ties pulled loose with a uniformity that suggested a common ancestry dictated dress in the same way that it receded hairlines. These nights moved like undisturbed smoke, not ending so much as diffusing, and then he would be carried off to bed, where he would *pray the Lord my soul to keep*. And the last thing he would have heard if he did, indeed, *die before I wake* would have been his mother's soft voice making lullabies of *Good Night, Irene* and *Go Tell Aunt Rhody*.

They had been in Charlotte for a little over a month when a telegram arrived detailing their itinerary, Prior to shipping out, his father had settled all affairs and orchestrated the shipping of their material goods, including the cherished 1949 Lincoln, leaving Thomas's mother with the singular responsibility of obtaining the required inoculations. That evening, Agnes Kessler steeled herself for the candor she and her husband agreed upon in the rearing of their child, and the following morning announced over breakfast that the day would be spent driving over to Fort Bragg to receive the required immunizations for overseas travel.

"What's 'munizations?" Thomas had asked. "It's another word for shots, honey."

"How many?"

"I'm not sure. No more than five, I would think. Maybe six."

Nothing seemed amiss as the household piled into Uncle Ray's old Pontiac with faded paint (Uncle Ray's projects had long monopolized the garage) and headed east, drifting on the tranquil sea of southern life and failing to recognize Thomas's lethargic silence for the catatonic state of terror that it truly was. By the time the front tires of the Pontiac settled against the border of staked railroad ties skirting the dispensary parking lot, Thomas had emerged from his state of shock and crawled onto the deck behind the back seat, wedging himself firmly against the rear glass by thrusting upward on all fours, a maneuver borrowed from the lizards he ran to ground among the rocks back in Texas. When it became evident that no degree of reason would penetrate the boy's blind terror, Uncle Ray reached in, gently seized Thomas's left ankle, and leaned back. Four minutes of steady pressure later, an explosive extrication easily broke Uncle Ray's waning grip, and before anyone could make a move to stop him, Thomas had shot out of the car and fled across a broad parade ground. As they were getting into the Pontiac, Aunt Annie said she thought she saw his feet disappear under an elevated building about a quarter-mile away.

It took about fifteen minutes of careful peering into the shadows to find him and would have taken much longer had not several of the servicemen quartered in the barracks been curious as to why a group of civilians would be snooping around under their building. It was a young towheaded private, eyes still heavy with sleep, who finally spotted Thomas, or rather his eyes, shining out of the beam of the flashlight the soldier had carried on guard duty well into the morning hours. The building was set against a shallow hill, and Thomas had dug in where the crawlspace had narrowed to under two feet, awaiting the next campaign.

Uncle Ray's physical limitations—and tacit phobia for bites or stings— eventually forced a crisp dollar bill from his wallet as bounty to anyone willing to brave the diminishing corridor hung with spider webs and wasp nests and retrieve his nephew. It took five minutes and the doubling of the reward, but finally a Georgia farm boy—thin as a whip and sufficiently homesick to be seeking ways to earn bus fare—stepped forward and pocketed the money before disappearing under the barracks. He returned in remarkably short order dragging a limp Thomas, who was resisting only passively, through dead weight, as if barbarous insurgency against a stranger was forbidden by some unwritten code of misconduct. As soon as he was seized upon by the hands of his family, however, passionate resistance resumed, and he was wrestled back into the Pontiac.

Back at the dispensary, he splayed his limbs across the frame of the entry door like a cat being pushed into a bucket of ice water, and once inside, it took no less than an additional four pairs of hands to hold him onto the gurney until leather straps were secured to replace them. Then the sharp, alternating stings in his shoulders, and it was over; the bindings fell away and a silent nimbus of hostile eyes was glaring down at him.

"Castrating a bull would've been easier," his uncle had said, without humor.

#

The Colonel didn't learn about Thomas's scandalous behavior at Fort Bragg until the family was reunited in Germany several weeks later, when the matter had grown cold, and since Thomas's mother left the business of discipline to her husband, punishment was limited to a stern lecture that Thomas took as an implicit pardon. Only in the ensuing years, when the Colonel would occasionally shanghai him for mysterious outings, would he learn his true punishment—that with every trip rode the possibility of boosters for tetanus, typhoid, and plague, held in anonymity by the Colonel's glib small talk until the final hard turn into the dispensary parking lot. And the fact that it rarely ended like that provided little comfort.

As they were driving through the park, a pair of girls wearing two-piece swimsuits dashed across the road a hundred feet in front of the Chevy. Each had a damp towel draped over a tanned shoulder, and they were apparently heading home from Arroyo Blanco Springs. Thomas followed them furtively until they slipped out of his peripheral, but it was more of an instinctive reflex than an act of conscious lust. His friend Pete liked to say that it's hard to enjoy a fall out of a tree since you don't have much to look forward to, and all Thomas could think about was hitting the ground. They left the park with the crossing of the short bridge spanning the Arroyo Blanco a quarter mile upstream from its juncture with the Nebraska and entered South Fuller. Here, as along the northern shore, the river had dictated the growth of the town. The older structures, primarily small residences dating from the same period of expansion that had populated both sides of Sixth Street as far out as Los Alamos Creek, lay atop and beyond a ridge along the base of which Arroyo Blanco Road had been laid. It was no coincidence that the course of this sudden elevation followed the gently flowing river to the north—before the construction of the dam and the stabilization of the Nebraska's flood levels, the ridge fixed the southern boundary of the uninhabitable floodplain.

Few of the establishments and businesses that had sprung up on the swath of reclaimed land between the ridge and the south shore had been there for more than twenty years, and none could claim a seniority that fell within five years of the Nebraska's taming, due primarily to the river's lingering menace and legal entanglements concerning ownership. But by the end of the Second World War, all restraints had vanished, and the area, now lush with the pecan, oak, and willow trees that thrived in the rich loam of the old floodplain, was annexed and zoned for commercial use by the city. Along the half mile of Arroyo Blanco Road between Live Oak Park and Mirabeau Road were two barbecue restaurants, a garage, a sprawling community of travel trailers, an amusement park offering the unsophisticated thrills of small collapsible roller coasters and Ferris wheels of the type usually seen in migratory carnivals, two filling stations, and James's Barber Shop, where every male of the species residing in the hills had his hair cut with the exception of Thomas's father, who got his trimmed at the base.

The Colonel slowed the Chevy as they approached the green light at the intersection of Arroyo Blanco and Mirabeau. "I'm going to pull into Frank's here for a moment, son. It won't take too long. Then we can be on our way."

Thomas remained in his dumb isolation as the Chevy coasted through the intersection, and the Colonel wheeled a sharp right onto the stained concrete apron of Frank Hansborough's Gulf station, then feathered the clutch until the left rear fender came even with the regular gas pump.

"I'm going to step out and say hello to Frank, Tom. You can wait or come along—it's up to you."

Thomas nodded once, and his father opened the door and stepped out. There were no other customers at the pumps, and Thomas was wondering if the station had been left unattended until he followed a muffled expletive to the row of disabled cars parked adjacent to the restrooms behind the office. There, at the front of a hulking Buick sedan, a profane, grease-smeared Jonah was struggling in the maw of a whale. Thomas knew by the absence of buttocks that it was Mister Hansborough.

"There he is. I'll be back in a few minutes, son."

Thomas turned in his seat and watched as the Colonel left the shade of the pumps and stepped across the sunlit concrete. He took a position at the fender opposite Mister Hansborough and ducked his head to clear the gray fedora as he leaned under the hood.

Shit! Can't we get this over with, old man?

Thomas lasted three minutes. When the clock in the dashboard read eleven sharp, he laid the General's pistol in the seat as if some sacrosanct deadline had elapsed, then jerked the door handle sharply up, slipped out, and walked over to the Buick.

Half a dozen soft drink cases were stacked unevenly against the shallow curb girding the back of the property, and Thomas pulled one off the top of the pile and joined the men at the front of the Buick. He placed the case upside down beside his father's feet and stepped up, then stuck his head under the gaping hood.

"I thought you were going to stay in the car?" "I never said that," said Thomas.

#

It took a few years for Thomas to figure out why his father would tolerate, much less consciously pursue, the company of Frank Hansborough. The two men appeared to have even less in common than did the Colonel and Clayton Blaylock, a man for whom the Colonel had manifest disdain. They had met in the mid-fifties, when Thomas's newly retired father had dabbled unsuccessfully in real estate and Ruby Hansborough, Frank's wife, had been an associate in the firm acting as brokerage for the Colonel's business. Physically and materially, the Hansboroughs were completely polarized. Ruby was large and rotund, given to elaborate suits in garish colors accented with lavish cosmetics and costume jewelry, and coiffed to an additional three inches over the two she already held over her husband. She was at all times imperturbable, commanding, and mannered. Frank, on the other hand, was a blade-nosed scarecrow of a man who seemed perpetually in the initial stages of a nervous breakdown. He sustained motion—even when seated, his feet would twitch, his fingers drum—without regard to motive or necessity, and would degrade any discourse to its vilest four-letter interpretation. On those rare social occasions when he would be required to dispense with obscenities, he would speak low and haltingly, like an immigrant struggling with a new language. His receding, thin hair was the color of broom sage, heavily pomaded and swept straight back across his sunburned scalp, and a defeated waddle hung between his chin and prominent Adam's apple. His face was gaunt and creased by a constant clenching of the jaws, which projected either a grin or a grimace (which was open to interpretation) under mercurial blue eyes behind sweat-streaked lenses. Chain-smoking Pall Malls had highlighted the tiny fissures etched into the surface of his chipped teeth, complementing the spider veins that veiled his face and the arteries running like cords along his bony arms. Thomas loved to say Mister Hansborough's name softly to himself, to feel it roll over his tongue and caress his lips like the moist smoke of a good cigarette. *HAHNNNS-burr- ohhhhh.*

Mister Hansborough didn't look or act like someone with a name like Hansborough. It seemed to Thomas that a name like Pratt would have been far more appropriate. Or better yet, Snavely.

When together, the Hansboroughs neutralized one another. She would relax and allow a bit of crassness and ribaldry into her conversation, while he would defer to his wife until those times when his input was imminent, then present it with attempted modulation and restraint, as he did in the company of Thomas's parents when an informal game of bridge brought the two couples together for one or two evenings a month.

But the Colonel had folded his hand in real estate over five years ago, and the bridge games died without the workaday infusion of shared interest that the Colonel and Ruby Hansborough brought with them to the card table, eliminating the only logical denominator that would bring the two men together. Yet for anyone driving by Frank Hansborough's Gulf station on the southeast corner of Arroyo Blanco and Mirabeau, it was not uncommon to see the Kesslers' maroon Impala parked among the dead pickups and junked sedans that dwindled down to bare frames over the months and years as their parts were picked away.

#

Mister Hansborough was draped over the fender of the Buick with the implied vulnerability of a child over his parent's knee. His arms were deep inside the engine compartment, and he was extending his reach by standing on his toes and shifting his weight forward. His glasses had slid to a precarious position on the tip of his nose, and a low chorus of ragged grunts rose and fell with the fluctuating pressure on his diaphragm.

"What's he trying to do, Dad?" Everything Mister Hansborough did was somehow mysterious, if meaningless, and Thomas had forgotten shots for the moment.

The Colonel was watching the proceedings with a light detachment. "Frank's installing new battery cables, son. He's attaching the positive lead to the starter right now. It's a pretty good stretch from up here."

Thomas spotted a large hydraulic jack sitting beside a gutted axle housing and pointed it out to his father. "Why doesn't he just use that and crawl under?"

"Well, Tom, that just wouldn't be Frank's way of—"

The Colonel was cut off by a deep fart forced out of Mister Hansborough as he hung across the fender, and Mister Hansborough, apparently having overheard Thomas's question, spat his smoldering cigarette against the radiator. "Well, I should be able to get it from up here, but this goddamned nut tries to cross-thread every *fuckin' time* I get lucky enough to get the eye of this shit-eating cable on the stud. But then I have to suck in some more air, and that brings the whole fuckin' mess back out of reach." With that, he gave a hard yank on the cable, jolting loose another fart.

"Goddamn the motherfucker anyway!"

Thomas reveled in being bathed in language that he was so stridently forbidden to use, language that caused his father to nervously shuffle his feet.

"Why don't you stand on one of those soft drink cartons like the boy's doing here, Frank? That should eliminate the reach problem."

Mister Hansborough paused and looked first to the Colonel and then to Thomas, as if a tacit approval by one of something suggested by the other was an unassailable endorsement that even he could not ignore. He drew out from under the hood, then stepped over to the stack of soft drink cartons and pulled the top one off the stack. It hit the concrete with a loud clatter, then shrieked with each shove of Mister Hansborough's boot as he returned to the front of the car. He pushed the carton against the tire, stepped up, lit a fresh Pall Mall, and leaned back under the hood.

It took thirty seconds of whining and cursing for Mister Hansborough to locate a misplaced nut, which eventually revealed itself by falling out of his shirt pocket as he thrashed about in frustration. The disposition of one problem spawned another, as the nut then fell through the open engine bay and rolled rearward to a spot only accessible from the opposite side of the car, prompting the Colonel to order his son to retrieve it in an attempt to forestall further profanity. Finally, with nut and cable in hand, Mister Hansborough pushed his glasses firmly in place with a filthy finger that left partial smears on both lenses, then wormed his way back into the pinched space between the motor and frame.

"Can you reach it all right now, Frank? I'd like to think that every once in a while I offer a man some advice that does him some good."

"Yeah, Colonel, I can reach it fine now . . ." —Mister Hansborough was now fumbling with unlocked elbows— ". . . only now, goddammit, I'm blocking what little light I got! If I could just see the son of a bitch well enough to get this goddamn little nut started without cross-threadin' . . . *SHIT! THIS GODDAMNED HOLE'S HARDER TO HIT THAN MOTHER SUPERIOR'S PUSSY!*"

"I really wish you wouldn't talk like that around the boy, Frank. That's not the kind of language we use—"

"*Motherfucker!* I thought I had the son of a bitch that time. Colonel, do me a favor, would you?" —Mister Hansborough reached into his hip pocket and produced a small flashlight— "Come 'round here and hold this light for me. If I could see it, I think I can get it."

The Colonel stepped around the front of the car and took the flashlight, and Thomas slid his carton over to where his father had been standing as the two men leaned to their work. Thomas's position opposite Mister Hansborough was now optimum, perfect for viewing the addictive theater that was probably what kept drawing his father back to Frank Hansborough's dingy Gulf station like a moth to a flame.

Mister Hansborough bent to his work, his lips drawn back and the Pall Mall clenched in his teeth, and seemed to settle into a subdued, if unproductive, rhythm. He tinkered for several minutes under the light as the Colonel cooed optimistically at anything that could be construed as progress, and eventually Thomas's attention was drawn to the beads of sweat accumulating on Mister Hansborough's brow. They would swell, each in its turn, until stasis was overcome, then traverse the deep furrows to the center of his brow and merge with a quivering welt building behind the plastic bridge of the glasses frame. Thomas registered a silent prediction and was vindicated when here also, surface tension was defeated and the large globule broke over the bridge into a pair of rivulets that dribbled down the spine of his nose, over the flares of the nostrils, and converged at the tip, fueling a drip that fell on the cigarette held in his lips, transforming it from white to a mottled brown. Then the glasses, falling victim to the lubricating properties of the perspiration, began to descend the nose as well, allowing the smoke from the Pall Mall, which had heretofore been deflected from Mister Hansborough's eyes by the glasses, to climb his cheeks and pool in the deep hollows of his eye sockets, precipitating a bout of blinking and squinting. During this course of events, Mister Hansborough's grunts and snarls increased commensurately until, inevitably, the line of leached tobacco and the glowing tip merged to produce a smoke so dense and rich that it shrouded his face like wadded cotton.

The finale came suddenly, setting both the Colonel and Thomas back on their heels. Mister Hansborough spat the Pall Mall into the engine bay and rose up with a howl of rage that was given a symphonic quality midway through by the percussion of his head against the underside of the Buick's hood.

The Colonel acted quickly and preemptively. He placed a hand on Mister Hansborough's shoulder and pulled him down from the carton before he could restore his breath and continue. "Here, Frank. Let me have a look. You hold the flashlight."

The Colonel plucked the nut from Mister Hansborough's trembling, greasy fingers, then stepped onto the carton and bent over the fender with boring competence, thus eliminating any further distraction, and as Thomas turned back toward the Chevy and climbed inside, he felt the dread returning. He picked up the Army, desperately hoping The General's story would flow out of its hammered steel and deflect his anxiety until his father returned and they could get past this horrid morning.

After a few minutes, the hollow clatter of the floor jack being deployed told Thomas that their departure would probably be indefinitely delayed, and he began to consider other diversions out of the sweltering heat.

The layout of Mister Hansborough's station was the same as the Texaco station back in Charlotte where Thomas used to buy Uncle Ray's Raleighs, and every other gas station Thomas had ever seen, for that matter: a square building trisected into a garage, restrooms, and an office, with the public sections set on a raised pad, isolating them from the garage and the apron of pavement that covered the remainder of the property. Some stations had a garage that housed more than one service bay. Mister Hansborough's had two.

Thomas laid the pistol back on the seat and stepped out of the car, then walked toward the office, toward the door of cracked glass holding the faded image of a penguin offering up a cigarette from a green and white pack and inviting you to "Come on in! It's KOOL inside!" from a balloon festooned with icicles. He stepped up on the concrete walk and peered through the grease-smeared plate glass window.

Six chairs of bent metal and lacerated vinyl were pushed haphazardly along the walls, and a Coke machine sat in the corner opposite the cash register—actually no more than an adding machine set atop a small table with a cigar box that served as the till—which occupied the short section of wall that held the entrance to the garage. Two oscillating fans in opposite corners of the bare concrete floor stirred the air unevenly, chattering arcs that fluttered and snapped the wrinkled pages of dozens of dated automotive magazines scattered along the baseboards. The fans were there because a square of plywood, held in place with duct tape, now sealed the opening in the east wall that had once held an air conditioner, making a liar out of the penguin.

If the torn magazines along the floor represented the culture of the establishment, then hanging on a nail beside the entrance to the service bays was its sexual soul, a rendition in tempera of a bare-breasted blonde clad in faded bubblegum-pink shorts that had been a bright scarlet when the month of December under her coyly crossed ankles transpired over a decade before. The nail also served to anchor a ballpoint pen at the end of a piece of dirty twine, and the presence of the peeling chrome payphone on the wall under the calendar dictated that every available surface within reach of the tethered pen—the door frame, the breasts of the blonde, the thirty-one days of a long-past December—would bear hastily scribbled names, phone numbers, and addresses. Thomas walked around the office to the open garage doors. The northern orientation of the building chopped the sunlight off cleanly at the entrance to the service bays, and as he stepped inside, a damp, half-darkness embraced him.

The garage was still except for the slow, drunken arcs of two mud daubers circulating under a ceiling built to a considerable height to accommodate a loft extending up the back wall and a pair of motorized hoists mounted on tracks over the two service bays. A six-cylinder motor encrusted with grease and road grit dangled over the open engine compartment of a blue Ford sedan in the bay farthest from the office. The missing weight had caused the front of the car to rise, as if in a pathetic attempt to reclaim its heart.

There were no windows in the garage, only an opening high along the south wall that held a slowly revolving exhaust fan. A willow had taken root in the narrow strip of earth behind the garage, and its malnourished leaves could be seen resisting the spinning vanes in a stuttering pantomime.

The Colonel frequently nagged Thomas about the workshop in his bedroom closet, often likening it to a trash bin, but if that were true, then Mister Hansborough's garage was the city dump. Tools, parts, cans, and empty cardboard containers lay everywhere: on the floor, along the fenders of the Ford, on the tops of several workbenches, on every other reasonably horizontal surface exceeding a square foot in area. Vertical wall space was just as cluttered, although more organized, and with the exception of the area encroached upon by the loft, the east wall was hung entirely with a tangle of preformed exhaust pipes. Each was collared with baling wire and suspended from a metal hook. They looked like tormented eels, frozen in agony under a patina of soft rust. A sheet of plywood mounted on the same wall held a large inventory of fan belts, each girdled in cardboard and not categorized in any apparent way. The fan belts, like the exhaust pipes, had been stripped of their chastity, the print on their white cardboard sleeves obscured by oil and grease.

Thomas heard a faint buzz and turned toward it. Another mud dauber had floated through the door and was rising toward the ceiling with a gout of brown clay locked in its legs. He watched as it made a wide circle around the Ford before alighting on a clod adhering to the block and tackle in the empty bay. It was then he noticed a brown sheen around a bolt anchoring the hoist to the ceiling, which in turn fed a rivulet that ran down the pulleys before disappearing into several feet of chain. It reappeared on the final link as a trembling drop of gritty water, and Thomas watched it swell, then break free and spatter against the cracked grate over the grease pit.

The raised portion of the foundation that elevated the office and restrooms extended across the rear of the garage, ostensibly isolating the storage area from the contamination of the service bays, and an open cabinet containing motor oils, lubricants, filters, and ignition parts needed for tune-ups was set against the wall under the exhaust fan. A stained sheet of notebook paper was taped to the edge of the bottom shelf. *"Reorder these"* was written at the top in large lowercase letters, and a dozen entries were penciled underneath. The loft was accessed by a makeshift ladder of pine two-by-fours and used exclusively for the storage of tires, some lined up against the back wall and curbed by a two-by-four running the length of the platform, others stacked in piles up to the very edge of the loft.

Thomas was reminded of a particularly cold day the previous January. He had been along when his father had stopped by, and the service bay doors were closed against the north wind, and a kerosene stove lit and fired high under the loft. While Mister Hansborough chatted with the Colonel, Thomas noticed that the interior surfaces of the service bay doors were covered with what appeared to be black tread marks, and an unbidden image came to his mind of Mister Hansborough crouching in the shadows of the loft, pushing tires blindly over the curb of pine. Just enough room for one good bounce, and then the tires would slam into the closed doors and roll God-knows-where before finally settling onto the angled floor with a staccato drumming.

But the ruined garage spoke to him in other ways as well, ways that seemed somehow otherworldly, like the shell of the bombed-out building Thomas and his father had visited in Germany. They were in downtown Wiesbaden, and the Colonel had taken his hand and led him through a breach in the rubble to a clearing within the blasted, softly lit walls. His father had spoken gently and generally of what had taken place there, and about how that was what men like him had to do during war, and Thomas likened war to a season. War would be a bad season, like winter, and as the light started to sink behind the jagged line of the western wall, it was as if the shattered bricks and fire were falling all around them.

Standing there in the empty service bay was like that, only here the black walls reflected no glow of a lowering sun—only the drops of filthy water quivering over the shattered grate held a glint of light—and the Colonel's voice wasn't droning in his ears. Whatever evil the darkness and disorder held would have to be of his own invention.

buzz-click buzz-click

The noise was muffled and indistinct. Thomas stepped deeper into the garage, toward the noise. If some exotic species of cave cricket had evolved in Mister Hansborough's garage, Thomas wanted to be the first to claim it.

buzz-click buzz-click buzz-click

This time the sound was distinct and clearly metallic, and Thomas recognized it to be the sound of a ratchet wrench coming from the cramped nook behind the office wall. He stepped onto the raised concrete pad and into the deeper shadows beneath the loft.

There was a long, narrow storage area behind the office wall, and tool chests and machinery occupied all but a narrow corridor of floor space. A rectangular fluorescent fixture was suspended at the far end, not more than six feet from the floor, its faux Tiffany shade emblazoned with Jax Beer emblems and Old Hickory—the New Orleans brewery's namesake—astride his rearing steed, Napoleonic hat held high. The fixture held three long tubes, and two quivered weakly with a low, erratic hum on either side of the blackened third, framing the lower half of the room with a frantic collusion of shadow, lapping and overlapping in endless combinations.

Under the pool of frantic light was a huge, formless mass. Thomas thought he saw movement, but the animation of light and shadow gave a sense of motion to everything it touched.

buzz-click buzz-click buzz-click

"Ira?"

The sound of the ratchet stopped and the upper half of the large mound warped to the left, and Ira's thick profile embedded itself in the wash of dirty light.

"Yeah. Who's there?" The voice was infinitely deep and warm.

"Thomas."

"Who?"

"Thomas Kessler. Colonel Kessler's son."

"Oh. Well, grab a bucket and step around here where I can see you, Lil Colonel. My neck don't allow my head to turn no further."

Thomas stepped over to a stack of empty lube buckets and picked one up by the rim, then tiptoed cautiously through the tools and parts and set the bucket upside down across from Ira. He sat down and noticed another humming; the voices of his father and Mister Hansborough were droning incoherently through the drywall behind him.

Thomas had never seen anyone as massive as Ira. Although well under six feet in height, his frame was so broad and physically imposing that he seemed compressed, as if when allowed the natural extensions of neck and torso and leg he could easily rise to seven feet or beyond. His uniform was always the same dark blue coveralls, heavily starched and still showing a sharp crease along the upper edge of the shirt sleeves and the final foot of pants leg, but everywhere else the fit was like that of a sausage casing. Despite his work and surroundings, he somehow managed to stay relatively clean, and the white name patch on his right breast pocket was always pristine.

"Don't sit down on that bucket like that, Lil Colonel. Not with them clean clothes on. Grab a clean rag off of the bench there."

Thomas followed Ira's finger to a stack of neatly folded shop towels. He picked one off the top and spread it over the upturned bottom of the lube bucket before taking his seat.

Ira was dismantling a cylinder head resting on his thighs. Thomas counted the spark plug holes in the head. There were six.

"That a Chevy head, Ira?" Thomas was almost sure it was; most other six-cylinder motors still had their valves in the block.

"Sure is, Lil Colonel. It come out of that two-tone '53 parked out there by the restrooms. Belongs to one of the boss's friends, and he just wants me to get it running good enough to sell. The compression was down on every cylinder, so I'm just gonna install new springs and grind the valves. If that don't do it, well, I guess I'll have to ask the boss if his friend wants to ante up for new rings. But the compression test said it was valves."

Thomas watched as Ira set the socket over the head of one torqued bolt after another, breaking each loose with what appeared to be no more than a flick of the wrist. The expression on Ira's face was paternal and endearing, as if he were baiting a hook for a child. Thomas watched silently until the last bolt was out.

"How come your sign wasn't in the window, Ira?" Mister Hansborough was uncharacteristically meticulous about keeping the panel of cardboard reading MECHANIC ON DUTY displayed when Ira was on the premises, laboring in the shadows and wreckage of the garage.

"Well, I think the boss just wants this job done and gone before he starts me on another. He always hurries me along when the money comes outta his pocket."

Ira dropped the last of the lifters and springs into a tray filled with kerosene on the floor to his right, the last two valves into a pair of coffee cans on his left. Then he rose and stepped toe-to-heel past Thomas, along the cramped path to the workbench, the stripped head held in his enormous hands.

Once, on another trip to the station a year or so earlier, they were waiting for Mister Hansborough to pump the fuel when a flatbed truck pulled in and halted in front of the service bays. The driver honked once, and Ira lumbered out of the garage in his shifting gait and walked to the rear of the truck. The bed was loaded with rebuilt automotive parts, some swaddled in burlap, all tagged and strapped to pine skids, and after a thoughtful inspection of half a dozen tags, Ira reached in with both hands and dragged two identical chunks of iron and wood out of the truck by their wire bindings. The loads swung lazily down in synchronized arcs, barely clearing the pavement, and when they stabilized at his sides, Ira gave the driver a departing nod and returned to the garage.

"Did you see that?" the Colonel had said.

Thomas was seated on the edge of the back seat, leaning forward and resting his crossed arms along the front seat between his parents. He glanced to the left, to his father, on hearing his words. The Colonel's eyes were on the spot where Ira had disappeared into the open service bays, lost in quiet disbelief.

"See what?" his mother asked.

Before Thomas's father could respond, Mister Hansborough arrived at his window with a raucous demand for payment on goods and services that brought everyone to laughter, and the matter was forgotten until a month or so later, when some anonymous stimuli in the garage brought the incident back.

"Yes, I remember that day," the Colonel said as he adjusted the chain on Thomas's English racer. "Those parts Ira pulled off the back of that rig were engine heads. *Big* engine heads. I was killing time over at the station when Bull's Machine Shop came and picked them up a couple of days earlier. Frank had bought a '58 Ford at state auction for resale, but the engine was in pretty bad shape—it had been an old highway patrol car with an Interceptor engine—and he was doing an overhaul on it. Ira had more work than he could handle, so Frank decided to let Bull do the head work. Ira was out to lunch when the runner showed up, so I helped Frank get them out to the truck. The things must have weighed ninety pounds apiece, but the fact that Ira was able to get both of them back into the garage in one trip wasn't what astounded me—I've long since dismissed the idea that there are limitations to the man's strength. The thing is, Bull straps everything to wooden skids with baling wire as thick as heavy twine. If I'd tried that, those heads would have hit the ground with eight of my fingers along with them..." —the Colonel paused to check the tension on the chain one last time, then bore down on the rear spindle bolt, rose to his feet, and stood the bike for delivery to its owner—"...and Ira wasn't even wearing gloves."

A new light fell over Thomas's shoulders with the sharp hiccup of a socket switch, and he pivoted on his bucket to face Ira's back. A bare bulb suspended by a cord hung over the workbench and painted the pinched work area with a discordant dance of light and shadow. Ira was shuffling through old paint buckets and coffee cans lining the shelves over the workbench, reading labels.

"Why doesn't Mister Hansborough put better lights back here, Ira? And in the rest of the garage too? I don't see how y'all find anything, as dark as it always is in here."

"Well, it really don't matter none to me," Ira said. "I kind of inherited this place and got to make do, but I 'spose I'm used to it 'cause I can pretty much go straight to whatever I'm lookin' for."

Ira paused in the dim light to read the label on a can he had pulled down, then placed it on the bench with a heavy clunk. Then he picked up a screwdriver, and Thomas could tell by the bobbing of an elbow that he was jimmying the lid. "'Course, I guess it was kind of hard to get around right after the boss mortared the windows shut."

Thomas glanced around the tiny shop at cinder block walls. "You mean there used to be windows in this place?"

Ira turned and leaned with his elbows resting against the workbench, holding the heavy can as easily as the Colonel would hold a beer. His left arm came up with the screwdriver, and he pointed down the narrow passageway, back toward the service bays. "Not back here. They was in the garage, high up on the side and back walls, right up against the ceiling. We had a long stick with a hook on one end that we used to open and close 'em with. They was good during the summertime because the air stayed stirred up in here better, and the hot air had a way of getting out besides. And they let in a lot of light all year round, except when it was real cloudy. The ones on the east side would heat up my little shop back here something awful in the mornings though, for the couple of hours the sun came straight through."

"So what happened? Why did y'all take 'em out?"

"I didn't have no say-so. It was the boss. I liked 'em." "Then why did Mister Hansborough take them out?"

"Well, about ten years ago somebody put a ladder up against the wall outside and slipped through one of them windows, which was easy to do because we never took the trouble to lock 'em. They made off with a bunch of power tools and some tires, and of course there wasn't any insurance. We all figured it was kids 'cause it would have took somebody even lankier than the boss to slip through one of them windows. They was real wide—maybe four feet—but only about a foot and a half high. Anyways, after that we always took the time to shut and lock 'em. And then six months later, same thing, only this time they broke a window out, opened the garage doors, and really cleaned house. There was chicken wire embedded in the glass, but it didn't do much good, other than to make it easier to pick up the pieces the next day. Man! If they didn't make off with it the first trip, then they got it the second time around. Made off with some tools of mine I'd had since I was your age that an uncle had given to me. Even took a bottle of the boss's whiskey. We'd got insurance by then, but the insurance man said the boss would have to put in burglar bars or bulletproof glass if he didn't want to lose his coverage or see it go way up. But you know the boss. He said all that would cost too much money and ended up hiring a cheap crew to come in and pull out the windows and fill in the holes with the same cinder blocks the rest of the walls are made of. You used to be able to see where the windows was. The blocks was lighter, and the fresh mortar round them too. All looks the same now, though. Like I said, must have been ten years ago. Maybe more."

While Thomas mulled this over, Ira hooked the toe of a boot on the handle of a drawer mounted beneath the workbench and drew it open. He stepped aside to let the light from the naked bulb fall on the contents, then reached down and pulled out a hand drill. He lifted it to shoulder level, letting the cord unravel by its own weight.

"But like I said, I'm used to it now, and ain't nobody ever back here but me. I always keep a flashlight handy though, just in case."

Ira noticed Thomas looking up at the Jax lamp. "In case you was wondering, that come out of a bar the boss was partners in that didn't turn out too good. It hung over the pool table." Ira connected the drill to an extension cord plugged into an outlet beside the workbench and started back to his seat. Once again, Thomas leaned clear as Ira negotiated the narrow gap, paying out the extension cord with his free hand as he went. He set the can and the drill on the overturned bucket, then turned and headed back to the workbench. Ira must have gotten tired of passing Thomas toe- to-heel; this time, he took one long stride toward the bench with one leg, then swung the other over Thomas's head.

Ira secured a wire brush from the open drawer and began to scrub the stripped head, his massive body rocking gently to the rhythm of the strokes. Every thirty seconds or so, he would lift the head into the weak glow of the hanging bulb and turn it slowly, at one point bringing it close to his lips to blow a small nest of loosened carbon free from a valve seat. Five minutes later, he returned the wire brush to the drawer and once again brought one leg past Thomas, one over, on his way back to his bucket. He settled in with the head once more across his thighs, his face warm with gentle amusement.

"What really made the boss mad though, was that the insurance company wouldn't pay for his bottle of whiskey." Ira laughed at this, deeply and with a joy that brought Thomas along with him, and then went back to work in the cheerful silence that followed.

He wiped the head down with a kerosene-soaked rag, then scooped a gray glob out of the can with a finger as thick as one of Thomas's wrists and swirled it against his thumb. "This valve grinding grease is a little too pasty, but it'll do okay."

Ira set the head end-up on the floor and locked it between his knees, then plucked a valve from one of the coffee cans on his left, coated it with the grease, and fed it into the valve guide.

"You know anything about head work, Lil Colonel?"

Thomas had received unsolicited instruction on the basics of valve operation one day as the Colonel replaced the head gasket on the lawnmower. He vaguely recalled how the flared base of the valve opened and closed on the round holes called seats, allowing the gases to move in and out of the combustion chambers. "Yeah. I know all about it."

"Good. You can keep an eye on me and make sure I'm doin' everything right. Now, this part's kinda tricky. You got to lift the drill and tighten the chuck on the valve stem at the same time with the same hand—"

Thomas watched Ira feed the valve stem into the drill balanced atop his huge forearm, then somehow twist his hand to grasp and tighten the chuck. When he brought the head back up and laid it across his thighs, the drill dangled just off the floor next to his right shoe.

"Here's another tricky part. The drill's gonna wobble like crazy if you don't feather it just right."

Ira leaned over and fed his left hand between his thighs and seized the cord extending from the grip of the drill, then reached down and locked the trigger with his right. The drill started with a jump and chattered violently before settling into a whirring monotone as Ira adjusted the tension on the cord to even out the pressure, and this process was repeated each time the drill was paused to gauge progress or add grinding compound.

An inspection after five minutes of grinding was concluded with a grunt of approval, and Ira twisted the chuck and the drill fell away. Then the polished valve was wiped clean and set daintily on the concrete floor.

"—and that's all there is to it." Thomas smiled.

Ira moved on to the next valve, and then another, and the operation smoothed and gained the rhythm of a stationary waltz as the row of rejuvenated valves, sporting shining silver rings against the blackened concrete, lengthened along Ira's left flank.

Thomas sat complacent and mesmerized, lulled by the harmony of the droning and the dull heat.

During the moments of silence between valves, the voices of the two men outside continued to play against the drywall, their voices transformed and yet distinct—one a benumbed rasp, the sound of a panicked cricket trapped in a wall, the other resonant and controlled. Other sounds came through the wall as well, some metallic, some rounded and heavy, all lacking a continuity or composition that would give them relevance.

Then the rasp and the drone began to recede, Thomas noticed, and then faded away, leaving only the hum and stutter of the Jax Beer light to fill the void left by the drill.

It was the sound of clicking heels reverberating off the service bay walls that came first, at Ira's back. Then came one of the voices, the rasp, cast in a harsh ring off stone and concrete:

"Ira! IRA! Goddammit! Where is that nigger when I need him—"

The eyes of the man and the boy crashed together. Ira's gentle expression hadn't changed, but Thomas was looking into jaundiced pools of dark rage. He froze, caught somewhere between fear and surprise.

Ira turned at the waist and threw his voice back along the narrow corridor to the service bays.

"I'm back here, Boss, doing head work. Need somethin'?"

"Mister Hathaway here says he may have found a sucker— *oops!—buyer* for that '53 Chevy you're working on. Any chance of you getting it back on the road before we settle into retirement?" Behind the voice, laughter.

Ira turned and started taking inventory of the parts spread out around him, and Thomas could see a man, also middle-aged and wearing shop clothes, standing behind Mister Hansborough where the passageway opened out into the garage.

Ira spun back toward him:

"Tell you what, Boss. This is Friday, but if I come in after church on Sunday, I can have it ready by closin' time on Monday, for sure."

Mister Hansborough glanced back at Mister Hathaway, who nodded in the affirmative.

"Chicken's in the pot then," said Mister Hansborough, and their voices and footsteps trailed away.

Ira returned to his valve grinding, and Thomas sat paralyzed, his face flushed and burning, aware only of the beads of sweat trickling down his chest under the billow of his shirt as he leaned forward, his forearms resting on his knees. His eyes, having found the floor too late, now seemed unable to leave it.

Ira had only been back at his work a few minutes before the whirring stopped, the drill left to dangle. Thomas felt a heavy hand on his shoulder, and he looked up.

"Five, maybe six years ago, when the wife had her bad female problem, I didn't know what I was gonna do. Somehow the boss found out about my trouble—I still don't know how—and said he'd pay for the operation. And then he gives me the day off with pay when she had it done. I'm payin' him back a little bit at a time, like finishing up this job here come the weekend. And there ain't no interest to pay or bill collectors knockin' on the door when I have a bad month. 'Sides, that's just Mister Hansborough's way. To the boss, there ain't no bad words, ain't no good words. Just words."

Ira looked down. His forearms were resting on the iron slab in his lap, and the sight of his idle hands brought them back to the drill. He continued his work as before, but with preoccupation and faded purpose, and the finishing of this valve seemed to Thomas to come sooner and with less enthusiasm.

Ira loosened the chuck, set the finished valve on the floor, then reached into the coffee can for the next one. When he brought his hand back out, it was empty.

He laid the drill on the head, then set the head on the floor at his feet. His focus was no longer on work.

"I went to a funeral once over by the Louisiana border. I was about nineteen, maybe twenty. The summer after I turned nineteen, I think. Anyway, an aunt had died, my momma's youngest sister. She'd got her neck broke when she was throwed by a mule. Momma was due to have a baby, and the doctor was worried about her leavin' town and all, and Daddy had to work, so they decided I should go, me being the oldest.

"Daddy put me on a train the day before the funeral. First I had to ride to Houston, then up to San Augustine. A cousin picked me up at the depot on a mule, and I spent the next two hours looking at nothing but pine trees. I only *thought* I knew country till I met these folks.

"I spent the night fighting mosquitoes, and the next morning they had a nice service, then everybody goes out back to the little cemetery behind the church, and just as they get the coffin lowered into the grave, the first white man I seen since leaving San Augustine rides up on a big swaybacked bay. He rides right up to the foot of the grave with a stick on a string. The preacher was leading a prayer, and everybody had his head bowed except maybe me, 'cause I wasn't used to that kind of disrespect for any kind of church service.

"Anyway, this white man leans over on his horse and drops this stick down into the grave, then pulls it back up by the string till it's tight and just touching the coffin lid. Then he sits there and waits till the prayer is over, then tells the preacher that the coffin is about a foot and a half short of being six feet under, and according to the law that meant we'd have to do some more diggin'.

"I got maybe two words out of my mouth before the cousins on either side of me each grabbed an arm and drug me back over to the edge of the woods. Shut up, they said, you ain't from around here. And that's where I stayed, too. Right there under them pine trees while they pulled that coffin back out and the men all got down in that hole wearing the same good clothes the women spent the whole night before boilin' and ironin', and by the time that man rode off with his stick, the whole bunch looked like they'd just come in from a day of choppin' cotton.

"Soon as they got that last shovelful of dirt piled on, I told 'em I wanted to go on back to the train station, and they all nodded real agreeable-like. I guess they figured it was for the best, that I'd probably just get myself lynched if I hung out in those parts any longer. But I do think of that funeral every time the boss calls me that. I just can't help it."

Ira straightened on the bucket and took a deep breath. "The thing is, I guess that was the only time I ever really felt like one."

"Well, you'll never hear it from me," Thomas said. "That was one of those words I'd get my mouth washed out with soap for when I was a little kid."

"That right?" Ira said. He reached down and retrieved the head.

"Yeah. One time when I was about five I cussed in front of my dad—not that word, one of the others—just to see if he'd really do it."

Ira chuckled. "Well, how did it taste?"

"Not all that bad, but it was just mild hand soap. He said if I did it again he'd use some of Momma's shampoo."

"Ya know, later on I asked our preacher over in Griffintown about that six-feet-deep rule. He said accordin' to Texas law, the top of the coffin has got to be down at least two feet under, and that's it." A wry smile crossed Ira's face. "But I'll say one thing for those folks of my momma's—they don't hold no grudges. That mule my cousin used to haul me back and forth to San Augustine with was the same one what throwed the deceased. Anyway, after that my folks told me that's the reason they settled where they did. Most anywhere in Barrett County, you got left alone. That's why there's so many freedman's colonies in these parts. And my daddy's people never did pick any cotton. For as long as he could remember, they were cowboys. Anyway, being called a nigger doesn't cut as deep as long as they leave you alone. In all my years, nobody in my family ever had any trouble, 'cept maybe for my daddy's uncle. That was a long time ago, though."

"Your daddy's uncle?"

"Yeah. But like I said, it was a long time ago. Nobody knows for sure what happened." Thomas stared eagerly back at Ira, saying nothing.

"Well, Lil Colonel, I—"

Ira glanced down at the head on his lap, then at the cans at his feet, and Thomas felt sure he had lost. He was about to shift his gaze down to his feet when Ira began again.

"Everybody called him Uncle Samson. Said he was bigger than anyone in the family before I come along, so I guess that's where I gets it. Him and my daddy's daddy was renegade Seminoles from the Indian territories up north. They told me I also got his hair"—Ira dropped his chin. Black hair, parted down the middle and swept to the sides, with a gentle wave and an upward flip on the ends—"Betty Boop hair, my wife calls it. Anyway, Uncle Samson left first. Got as far as San Antone, then heared about the buffalo soldiers and joined up. He wore out two enlistments fighting Comanches with the 10th Cavalry outta Fort Stockton, then come back to these parts, married a local woman, and started a three-hundred-acre ranch over in a freedman's colony named Jordan. That's east of here about thirty, forty miles. Flatter than Fuller. Rolling hills with lots of mesquites and elms and oaks.

"Now, this ranch of his was cut off from a white man's along one border by a pretty good-sized creek, and their shared property line ran right down the middle of it. Both men watered their stock at the creek, so for either one to put up a fence would keep their cattle from getting to the water, and of course nobody back in those days ever heard of a way to dig a post hole in a bedrock creek bottom under two feet of water. There wasn't no more to eat on one side of the creek than there was on the other, so the stock didn't have much reason to be changin' sides anyway.

"Everybody branded their cattle back then, but brands didn't mean nothing to this other rancher. Far as he was concerned, any stock what wandered onto his property was his, and if anybody had a problem with that, they could just take it up with his brother-in-law, the sheriff. Well, Uncle Samson starts losin' cattle, and it don't take long before he catches Butcher—that was this other rancher's name, Butcher—tossin' a rope across the creek and onto one of Uncle Samson's steers that come down for water, then draggin' him across to his side. When Uncle Samson rode down and accused Butcher of rustlin', Butcher said he was just claimin' a stray, and when Uncle Samson says he saw him rope the steer and drag him across, Butcher says you can't charge a rope with trespassin'.

"A week later Butcher disappeared. That's all anybody knows for sure; he was never seen or heard of again. The local law and then the Texas Rangers came and questioned Uncle Samson and his wife, and his kids, too, and everybody else in the area, since it was well known that Butcher had a way of riling his neighbors. The only thing the Rangers found out was what the family told 'em, that Uncle Samson had headed for the feed store over on the Camino Real about the same time Butcher's wife said he left their place, headed the same way, so that put them on the same road at the same time. Uncle Samson showed up at the store an hour later. Butcher ain't showed up yet.

"Most everybody, white and colored, figured the men fought and Uncle Samson covered it up, since there never was any body. It shook Saint James Colony up pretty good. Most all of the folks in the community were freed slaves from east Texas where the Klan was strong, and they didn't trust the law any more than they would the Klan, since where they come from it was all the same.

"But that was the end of it, thanks to Uncle Samson's army record, the family figured. They figured nobody could believe a man who spent eight years facing down Comanche war parties would just murder a man in cold blood, that if he did kill him, it would have been in a fair fight. If that was what happened."

"I can't believe they never found the body," Thomas said. He didn't like stories that left him hanging. "Somebody must have told somebody *something*."

Ira smiled at Thomas's frustration. "Well, that was another funeral I remember going to. I was about fifteen, I guess. He lived to be pert near ninety, Uncle Samson did. And whatever he knew, if anything, went right down in that grave with him."

"So we'll never know what happened, then?" Thomas said. He was looking back down at his boots, fighting against thoughts of cold steel slivers entering clenched muscle. It seemed like he had been in the garage forever. Time had to be running out.

"Well, not for sure, I guess. But Uncle Samson's wife died about five years later, and on her deathbed she told their oldest son that his daddy told her, while he was on his deathbed, that the most useful thing he learned in his years out there on the plains, fighting Indians, was how to bury a body fast. That was all, but maybe that's enough."

Ira straightened on the bucket and shifted his attention back to the head resting on his thighs. "Anyway, I got to get back to work, Lil Colonel. And do I like being called a nigger? Hell no, I don't. But what am I gonna do when it's coming from somebody who don't mean no harm by it? And Mister Hansborough always shoots straight with me."

Ira leaned forward conspiratorially. "You know what he done the other day?"

Thomas leaned in as well. "What?"

"A customer come in with a blowout, and the boss went up into the loft and fired a tire off over the edge with the door wide open—"

Footsteps were beginning to ring off the cinder block walls, and Thomas knew instantly whose they were. Ira turned just as the Colonel's head appeared over Ira's right shoulder.

"He's not in your way here, is he, Ira?"

"No sir. Just keepin' me company, and doin' a fine job of it too."

"Well, Son, it's almost time to leave. As soon as Frank is finished negotiating with Mister Hathaway, he's going to fill us up and we'll be on our way."

"Okay, Dad. I'll be back here."

The Colonel nodded and his footsteps faded back through the garage.

"I better make this fast," Ira said. "Well, as I was saying, the boss forgot to shut the door and the tire bounced all the way into the street and slammed into the side of a police car drivin' by. When I told the boss he'd hit a cop, at first he said he wasn't goin' to come down, like I'm supposed to handle it. And then when he does come down, he makes the policeman mad 'cause he tries to blame it all on the tire, like it was the tire that took a notion to run off into the street. The policeman brung out his ticket book but ended up putting it back in his hip pocket since it didn't really hurt the car none, just left a black smudge that I wiped off with my shop rag. I guess the only thing he could think of to charge him with was bein' stupid, and there ain't no law against that."

Once again, Ira seemed to discover the unfinished head laying across his thighs and picked up the drill. "Well, I'd better get back to work if I'm gonna have a workin' motor in that Hathaway fella's car on Monday. Where you and your daddy goin' this fine summer day, anyways?" With that, the gloom rushed back in, complete. "To the base, I guess, to get shots. *God*, I hate shots."

The head was upright between Ira's thighs again, and he was threading the drill back between his legs to receive another valve stem. "Well, I don't know nothin' about no shots, Lil Colonel, but you ain't going to the base. I guarantee ya that." Ira dipped his finger into the can of valve-grinding compound. His remark had rendered Thomas dumbstruck. "No, you ain't goin' to the base, leastwise not today." Now he was leaning over the head, his left hand slung down like a ham in a butcher shop window, finessing the drill while he applied the abrasive to the exposed valve face with his right. "And I can tell by the way you're gawkin' at me that you're wonderin' how I know, so I'll tell ya. Do you remember the last thing your daddy said when he stuck his head in here?"

"Sure. He said we'd be leaving soon."

"Leaving after what?"

"Leaving after Mister Hansborough finishes talking to that guy about the car he's buying."

"No. He said you'd be leaving after the boss filled your tank." "Oh. Okay. So?"

"So that means y'all ain't goin' to the base. Not anybody that's worked here since your daddy started comin' in don't know that your daddy never buys gas here if he's on his way out to the base 'cause the gas is a lot cheaper out there. Lord, you should hear the boss carry on when your daddy rolls outta here, headin' east. 'Well, there he goes,' he says, 'headin' for the base on fumes and a prayer.'"

Ira chuckled, then looked sternly at Thomas: "Promise you won't tell your daddy what I just said. Okay?"

Just then, a woman's scream breached the drywall, and Ira and Thomas came clear of their seats as one. Ira laid the head on the bucket and turned toward the service bays, toward the sharp mutterings of men insinuated in echo within the stained cinder block walls. Thomas followed in the odors of sweat and grease swirling in Ira's wake.

"Ira! Come here quick!"

They broke into the hot sun and walked briskly around the office to the west wall. Mister Hansborough, Mister Hathaway, The Colonel, and a middle-aged woman clad in baggy red shorts were huddled on the walk outside the office, peering back toward the restrooms. The woman was dancing about, flailing at nothing.

"There's a yellowjacket nest right over the ladies' room door, Ira," Mister Hansborough hollered. "Get rid of it quick, would you? They almost got Miz Gillespie here."

Thomas slowed, anticipating a quick return to the service bays for a bug bomb or kerosene, but Ira mounted the walkway instead and moved quickly toward the restrooms. The three men and the woman stepped obediently down onto the drive to allow for his enormous girth, and Thomas followed at his heels.

The nest was large and teeming, an orange-sized cancer wedged into the corner of the eave. Thomas balked at the sight of the churning yellow jackets, but Ira continued toward the rear of the building, then stood patiently under the nest until the last disturbed wasp alighted amid the flickering wings of its comrades. Then, suddenly, the nest vanished behind an intrusion of dark brown, and Ira stepped down to the weed-choked strip of grass and weeds feeding out from behind the garage. There, his hand clenched and churning, Ira completed the redemption of Mister Hansborough's ladies' room in a pose of dignified consecration, and as the shredded pulp and insect parts fluttered from the bottom of his fist, riding the breeze toward the row of broken cars, Thomas stood at Ira's back and once again, in an unbidden abstraction, stared into the malignant eyes.

CHAPTER 9

Pete drew the smirk so tightly that his upper lip rolled up against the base of his nose, and his voice was soaked with sarcasm and insolence.

"What in the hell is this thing, anyway?"

It was just the sort of remark Thomas had grown to expect from Pete these days. After years of sharing the stigma of being the shortest kids in their class—assuming you didn't count the girls, although most of them were taller too—Thomas's latest growth spurt had carried his flaccid flattop a good inch and a half above Pete's pomaded ducks, and Thomas understood that it was just Pete's way of returning the punch. He would have felt the same way if he had been the one left behind. Or, in this case, below. Still, lately it was all Thomas could do to keep from knocking the shit out of him, best friends or not.

Now Thomas wished he had called Pete the morning they brought the car home, before his father had mounted it on cinder blocks behind the limestone walls at the foot of the driveway and removed all four wheels, giving it the appearance of a mothballed war relic. But even that would have been better than what four interminable days of his father's industry had accomplished, four days of Thomas being forced to stand ready and pass the tools that The Colonel used to assail the old Ford with the relish of a fox on a chicken. Begrudgingly, Thomas had to admit that maybe this time Pete's sarcasm was deserved. With the car now missing the grill, both front fenders, the radiator, and most of the suspension as well, it was hard to tell it was a Ford. But he wasn't about to give Pete the benefit of the doubt.

"It's a car, dumb ass."

Pete carried his smirk over to the windshield and peered briefly in, then started slowly around to the rear of the car.

"You sure couldn't tell it by me, Kessler"—he had been addressing Thomas by his last name for several months now, another calculated step back from intimacy—"but if it's really a car, it should have a trunk. If there's a trunk back here, I'll give you that it once was probably a car." Thomas watched as Pete set a boot on the rear bumper and leaned over, his glasses bringing two small discs of sunlight to dance on the faded blue trunk.

"There it is. F-O-R-D. Fix or repair daily. And you will too, from the look of things—for the rest of the summer, at least."

He remained poised on the bumper a moment longer, slowly shaking his head, then stood and faced Thomas. "Why in the hell didn't you call or come by and pick me up? I could have helped you talk your old man into something better than this. Where'd you get it, anyway?" Thomas had anticipated this as well. Had he known in advance where they were going, he would have made sure Pete was along, but Thomas certainly wasn't going to let Pete or anybody else know that he was expecting a round of booster shots instead of a car. "I didn't call because you probably would have spent the whole time arguing with the old man about whose dick was bigger, Lee's or Grant's, and I would have ended up with squat."

Pete stared back in silence, demanding a coherent alibi.

"Besides, picking you up would have been out of the way 'cause we got it way up north 'cause there was an ad in the paper," Thomas lied.

#

"I wonder if that's for sale?" The Colonel had said with a nodding glance to the side of the road, bringing Thomas's attention to the Ford with his first spoken words after their departure from Mister Hansborough's Gulf station. It had been easy to tell it was a Ford then, sitting alongside a small, peeling shotgun house on South First Avenue about a half mile from Pete's old homestead, moldering away under a fluffy shroud of spent mimosa blooms.

The query struck Thomas as irrelevant, if peculiar. Despite Ira's logic and the fact that they had just turned off Arroyo Blanco, which was the standard route to the base, his fatalistic pessimism still left him resigned to shots. Besides, unannounced peripheral errands were routine with The Colonel, and they continued on with The Colonel's comment unanswered.

A quarter mile up the road, they pulled onto the gravel drive of the first of several junkyards commanding much of the real estate along the west side of South First, and Thomas, still locked in his state of sweaty-handed anxiety, assumed a quick stop to pick up a part for the Chevy, or maybe one of Mister Hansborough's cars. It wasn't until his father pointed toward the half dozen cars lined up along the section of chain-link fence with infirmities that had been diagnosed as less than terminal, and said, "Well, this looks like as good a place as any to start," that the knotted dread infesting Thomas's brain began to ebb.

I'm not getting shots. I'm getting a car.

They spent the rest of the day in rare camaraderie like a pair of bar- hopping sailors, haggling over the merits and deficiencies of a wide range of debilitated hulks reposing in the wrecking yards that blossomed with fecundity in the south and east quadrants of the town. Thomas had no actual, realized preferences, since the idea of owning a car had never really taken seed, and it was probably just as well. His father would look only at overall condition, availability of parts, and of course, basic cost. Thomas had voiced a strong preference for an engine with eight cylinders, however, and to this his father—a man whose memory of yanking B-25 throttles back hard and fast was voiced with exhilaration—acceded.

Of course, The Colonel had a flight plan. Most of the Fuller junkyards were positioned in a crescent that originated south of the river, then widened with a northerly sweep across Nebraska before tapering off short of the northern suburbs and fading into farmland. They would begin their search at the southern tip of the crescent, and from there work their way north to East Main, where the bulk of the junkyards competed directly against each other in deep east Fuller.

Finally, they would cross the river for the largest yards that bordered the interstate north of the city. The neighborhoods surrounding these coarse enterprises were enclaves of humble, worn houses along narrow side streets, with an occasional corner given to a laundry, grocery, gas station, or other business of necessity. The residents themselves, whether arcing water onto their lawns, rocking on ivied porches fanning, or engaging The Colonel over the splintered, greasy counters in the junkyard offices, held the only clue to change in community. They were hued brown along South First, paled to white as they neared the interstate, then back to brown along the north shore of the river, and finally to black in the final third of the crescent as it veered northwest and tapered away into the fertile prairie that brought the cotton rows clear up to the Fuller city limit.

At five o'clock that afternoon, The Colonel backed out of the last oil- soaked, bolt-strewn driveway and pulled onto the interstate that would take them south, back over the river. They had seen nothing overtly desirable, although they lingered over a rusted '32 Ford hot rod with an enormous Mercury V-8 that was finally taken out of contention by the lack of a heater and a maximum seating capacity of two (although Thomas secretly calculated). Anyway, it was dinner time, and The Colonel said they could get a fresh start in the morning and head out farther east to the yards that skirted the old cotton gin towns.

They had crossed back over the Nebraska and were sitting at the stoplight at South First and Arroyo Blanco, verbally spent and disconnected, and when the light went green, The Colonel suddenly hit the turn signal and abruptly wheeled the Chevy southward, back up the long, level hill where their search had begun six hours before. "Let's just take a look—" was all he got out before his thoughts stole his voice, and once again Thomas sat quietly while the old houses and tiny fenced yards, now abandoned under the afternoon heat, flew past.

The Colonel slowed toward the crest of the hill, then took a left against the oncoming traffic and pulled into the drive where the old Ford that had caught his attention that morning was parked. It was a light blue four-door sedan with a dark blue roof and looked to be in passable condition, despite being mounted on cinder blocks to take the weight off the four worn tires.

The Colonel climbed out of the Chevy and mounted the plank steps to the porch. Thomas could hear the low babble of a TV behind the sharp raps of his father's knuckles on the screen door, and almost immediately an elderly man holding a can of beer and wearing nothing but suspendered trousers stepped out on the porch. They spoke quietly for a moment, then the man became quite animated—Thomas could hear him speaking rapidly in guttural Tex-Mex—and when they passed the Chevy on their way to the side of the house, The Colonel gave Thomas a come-along glance through the windshield.

Thomas joined the two men as they rounded the corner of the house and halted in the carpet of spent mimosa. "Tom, this is Mister Samudio. I asked him if the car was for sale, but there's a language barrier here. I believe he said that it was, or might be. I'm really not sure."

Mister Samudio was standing behind The Colonel in stained khaki trousers and house slippers, sipping on his beer and wearing the insincere amiability of an eager negotiator. He was about the same size as The Colonel and probably close to the same age as well, although Mister Samudio had a thick mat of dark hair which easily trumped The Colonel's gray sides and exiled widow's peak, trimmed down to invisibility beyond ten feet. Nor could The Colonel possibly compete with Mister Samudio's smile, which was defined by a missing front incisor that transformed his oral cavity into a tiny chamber, and Thomas found himself peeking ridiculously into the intimate, darkened abyss for evidence of life.

"I know he said it's a '53 and has a V-8 in it. At any rate, I think he's willing to let us take a look at it. Do you know how to ask him if it's for sale?"

"*El carro par venta, Señor?*" Thomas said with a forced confidence, not knowing for sure what he was saying. Mister Samudio looked at Thomas for the first time, and then relaxed his grin, which seemed to lift his veil of idiocy. He put a hand to his stubbly face and after a staged consideration of appropriate duration, said directly to Thomas, and quite sincerely: "*Sí, mi pequeño amigo. Por el dinero correcto.*"

"Did you understand that, Dad?"

"I believe I did, Son. Now, would you ask him if he'd mind if we took a good look at the car? And ask him for the keys as well."

Thomas might have been able to put something together about looking at the car, but he didn't know the Spanish word for "key" and was about to confess such when Mister Samudio suppressed a belch, pulled a ring holding two keys out of his pants, and unlocked the driver's side door. "*Sí, señors!* Tek a luke. Tek a luke. *Está muy bueno, señor,* yes? No deents! *Nada!*" Thomas and his father worked their way around the car, sweeping the soft cloak of mimosa blooms to the ground with their hands. Mister Samudio appeared to be shooting straight—the car held up. A careful inspection of the body revealed no dents, an apparent crack in the windshield turned out to be an errant spider's web, and all the discolorations in the chalky paint were nothing more than streaks of dirt or grease. The taillight lenses weren't cracked, the tires still had some tread, and the chrome on the bumpers was dull but intact.

After satisfying himself with the condition of the body, The Colonel returned to the front of the Ford, fumbled briefly for the latch, and raised the hood to a chorus of metallic howls.

Thomas peered into the engine compartment and confirmed what the small chrome emblems affixed to each front fender had declared: the motor was a V-8, a flathead like the one mounted in the hot rod, though not nearly as large. It was coated with grease and sludge, and one of the heads had been removed and sat wedged between the exhaust header and the frame rail.

"Eese eh head gasket, I theek," Mister Samudio intoned. "Oil es een *la agua*—the water." The exposed deck and the pistons and valves were coated with a patina of rust, but the cylinder walls looked smooth and silvery—a good sign, Thomas hoped.

"What do you think, Dad? Do you think it can be fixed? There's sure a lot of rust"—a gentle breeze came up and pulled the dank, heavy air out of the engine bay, and the smell of Ira's shop flared and faded—"but I really kind of like this one, Dad."

The Colonel stood motionless, his forearms crossed atop the fenders, his eyes wandering over the engine in an indecipherable, deliberate pattern. Then he leaned to his right until his shoulder rested gently against that of his son. "Well, the rust is nothing to worry about," The Colonel said, his voice just above a whisper. "The thing that bothers me is why he didn't just put another head gasket in it instead of letting it sit here for what must be the better part of a year or more, judging from the license plates. Do you think you could ask him that?"

Mister Samudio, who was feigning disinterest by sipping his beer and belching in the shade of a live oak at the edge of the driveway, stepped into the conversation. "Thees wuss my wife's car. It is good, but she no need now. She take the bus. Much chipper."

Thomas and The Colonel leaned against the car, silently taking in their thoughts, and after a moment Mister Samudio broke the silence, his face ablaze with sincerity.

"*Es verdad!*"

#

"Okay, Kessler, don't bullshit me. How much did your old man pay for this piece of shit? A week's allowance? Two weeks?"

Pete had taken a seat atop a pile of firewood stacked against one of the stone walls. The logs had laid undisturbed through two warm winters and provided stable housing for a healthy crop of scorpions and centipedes. Had it been anyone but Pete, Thomas would have recommended he sit elsewhere.

"Dad haggled with the guy for a while. The body's good and the paint's not too bad. And the tires still have some tread on 'em, but Dad says the rubber's dried out. Anyway, Dad finally told the guy a car that doesn't run isn't worth more than a hundred bucks—take it or leave it." Actually, there had been no negotiating at all. His father had just thrown out a reasonable figure that he thought Mister Samudio would comprehend and accept, and he proved to be right. But the disclosure of a language barrier would be in conflict with Thomas's assertion that the car had been purchased in North Fuller. Only white people lived in North Fuller, and Pete would have used the discrepancy to fuel further interrogation.

Pete remained perched on the woodpile, picking at a pimple high on his left cheek and composing his next barb. Pete had got pimples first, like everything else. His voice had changed two years before Thomas's, and while Thomas was still scraping the fuzz off his cheeks with his father's razor once a week just so he could say he shaved, Pete's beard had inspired his mother to force him to start shaving while they were in the eighth grade. And the glasses Pete had been wearing since elementary school always made him look older as well. Thomas didn't want glasses any more than he wanted pimples, but somehow that didn't stop him from resenting Pete for them.

"A hundred bucks, huh? How come y'all had to tear it down like this?

And how come it didn't run? And what year is it anyway?"

"It's a '53," Thomas said, disposing of the easy part first. "And as far as running is concerned, just take a look."

Pete rose from the woodpile and swaggered over to the front of the Ford. The narrow heels of his boots sank up to the instep in the deep sand The Colonel had spread over the bare earth, costing him a good inch and a half in height.

"Come around to this side," Thomas said. "That's where the trouble is."

With the car up on blocks, Pete would have needed a ladder to inspect the engine had the fenders not been removed. Now, it sat perched on the frame rails like a meatball on a fork.

"The missing head's in the garage, soaking in kerosene," Thomas said.

Pete ran a thumbnail over a spot of rust on an exposed piston, then examined the residue with feigned expertise. "Why did y'all take the head off? The cylinders are getting all rusted."

"It looked like that when we got it. We thought it was just a blown head gasket, then we got it home"—Thomas leaned over and ran the tip of his index finger along a polished portion of the deck between the first cylinder and a water port, and the nail caught with a sharp click—"and found this. It's easier to feel than it is to see, but you can see it now too, pretty good, since Dad ran steel wool over it. The goddamned block's cracked. So what if it's rusty? We're gonna need a whole new engine anyway."

The Corvair Pete had been driving for a year was a '60 model in good running order, but that didn't seem to inspire any sympathy. "Shit, man. I drove over here thinking I was going to get a ride in your new car. School starts in two months—y'all gonna have it going by then?"

"Yeah, we're gonna put a rebuilt engine in it. But Dad says since we've got the whole summer, we might as well rebuild the suspension and brakes and clean and paint everything and save the motor for last. Besides, he says I have to know how to fix a car if I'm going to own one, since I can't afford to pay someone to fix it for me."

Pete stood quietly in the irrepressible heat, looking as adapted as a penguin on an ice shelf. Both sides of his family had been living, reproducing, and dying in Fuller for longer than anyone could remember, and he wore his faded jeans and cowboy boots without a trace of pretension. Thomas envied his implacable sense of place, his cache of folksy colloquialisms, his ignorance of fleeting friendships and vaguely recalled rentals and military housing, of still, dead slices of the past that come and go like the colorless photos in one of his father's slide shows.

Even after eight continuous years in Texas, Thomas still battled the sense that he was a rootless visitor, that he might, at any moment, fall from the face of the earth.

"Maybe you could get another motor cheap in one of the junkyards over by my house," Pete said with surprising empathy.

"And why did y'all take these off? They look okay to me." Pete was referring to the detached fenders leaning against the limestone walls The Colonel had built to support the climbing roses planted in the flowerbeds at the foot of the driveway. They were separated by a walkway and topped by twin columns that were eventually to be joined to form a portico. Thomas called the structure the Alamo.

"The fenders are off 'cause my old man banged his head on them three times while he was taking the brakes and spindles off. And we don't want a junkyard engine, since Monkey Ward's has good prices on rebuilt engines, plus a guarantee. We're gonna tow it to them when we get everything else fixed."

Pete pulled a pack of Marlboros out of his shirt pocket. "Is your old man around? I ain't scared of him catching me smoking—I just don't wanna listen to his bullshit."

"You don't see his car, do you? I think he went out to the base. Anyway, he's not here."

Pete shook out a cigarette and fired it up with a kitchen match. "Come on," Thomas said. "Let's get out of here. I could use a smoke too right now."

"I'm getting tired of carting you and Bennett around all the damn time." Pete sucked in a mouthful and blew it out between his teeth. "I hope at least one of you turds has a car before the end of the summer." He took another puff off the Marlboro, then leaned slightly forward and expelled it into a breeze that carried it teasingly into Thomas's face. "What's the bottom line here? How long is getting all this shit done gonna take?"

The Colonel had written Mister Samudio a check, and the next morning they returned with a rented tow bar and brought the Ford home. Thomas had been giddy as a schoolgirl when airing up the tires with a bicycle pump in the shade of the mimosa, convinced that he would be on the road as soon as they bolted the head back on with a new gasket. Instead, he found himself picking sullenly at his food at dinner that evening, almost wishing it *had* been shots as his father recited the list of needed repairs to his mother, a list that grew steadily with each passing day.

Once again Pete glared in silence, demanding an answer. "I just don't know. Okay?"

Pete turned back to the Ford, shaking his head as if he were mulling over the charred remains of a burned-out building. "Well, it's a good thing we don't have executions anymore. This thing would be right in our line of fire."

Thomas shook his head, grinning. The executions. They were carried out for two summers before he and Pete outgrew them. "Where in the world did we come up with that shit, anyway?" Thomas said. "Oh yeah—now I remember. It was because me and the old man started calling these walls the Alamo."

"That was it!" Pete said. "And we decided to get even with the Mexicans."

It was fun building the Mexicans, and they got pretty good at it. Carefully fashioned organs were molded from modeling clay— red for the heart, brown for the spaghetti-like coil of guts, purple for everything else— and assembled in the correct anatomical sequence, from the windpipe to the bladder, on a thin sheet of blue clay to be folded over as a torso and left unsealed at the top to accommodate a dollop of ketchup retrieved from the kitchen. Then the finishing touches of a brown head, blue legs and arms, and a twig or sliver of firewood bearing some resemblance to a musket. Pete's boot heels had been resting in the execution chamber while he was seated on the woodpile, a recess into which the doomed would be placed, splinted with a Popsicle stick. Then a coin toss would determine whose pistol would blow the Mexican back into his basic elements of clay and ketchup.

"Remember when Pontius Pilate chickenshitted out?" Thomas asked.

Halfway through the second summer, boredom necessitated a change of theme, and a Passion Play of sorts was decided on, with the figure swaddled in toilet paper to resemble Our Lord with his limbs lashed to crossed Popsicle sticks with fishing line pirated from The Colonel's tackle box. When Thomas demurred under concerns of Eternal Damnation and refused to mount The Lord in the woodpile or participate any further, Pete mocked him and insisted that he held no such fears. Nonetheless, he dallied long enough for the July heat to allow the fishing line to cut through the softened clay, and The Lord's arms fell to his sides, sans hands, creating an imbalance that caused the head to topple forward and hit the toe of Pete's right boot. Fearing this as a tacit message from above, they reassembled the figure minus the toilet paper and the second Popsicle stick and merrily blasted it into an indistinguishable mess as a white-woman rapin' Comanche.

Pete nodded. "Yeah, I remember. I don't know what we both were so worried about—we're going to hell anyway. Listen, let's go. I told Bennett I'd give him a ride over to see his grandmother this morning. His old lady's been pissed 'cause he hadn't been over to pay her a birthday visit yet. I told him I'd be there by ten."

"Sure. Hang on a sec—gotta go get my smokes."

Thomas had just started for the entrance to the kitchen through the open garage door when he heard Pete say: "Oh fuck, your old man's home. He's holding out in the street, waiting for me to move my car."

Pete's impeccably clean white Corvair was parked in the driveway, opposite the kitchen window. It was nothing fancy—a two-door coupe with cloth seats, rubber mats instead of carpet, and a stick shift with just three speeds—but it was low and sporty, fairly new, and didn't have many miles on it. Pete was trying to find ways to soup it up, but all he'd done so far was to have a loud muffler installed. Thomas could hear him coming as soon as he passed the bus stop on Kensington Road, a quarter mile away.

Pete backed the Corvair out of the drive and pulled onto the rough shoulder at the edge of the yard. As soon as the drive was clear, The Colonel pulled in and stopped the Chevy where Pete had been parked, and Thomas walked over to the driver's side window.

"Dad, me and Pete are gonna go pick up Bennett and take him over to see his grandmother," Thomas announced cheerfully. He hadn't left the yard since they brought the Ford home and was giddy with the prospect of escape. "I probably won't be back till later this afternoon."

The Colonel's face fell and he turned his gaze back into the windshield, saying nothing, his right thumb stroking the steering wheel. He spoke just as Thomas was about to repeat himself. "You're forgetting something, aren't you, Son? Maybe you'd better rethink your priorities." Thomas was stunned. "What do you mean, Dad? I know I've been around to pass you tools and stuff for the last few days, but you can work on it without me here, can't you?"

The Colonel got out of the car and closed the door, his eyes opaque under the lowered brim of the fedora. He plucked his pack of Pall Malls from his shirt pocket, shook one out, and brought the tip down sharply three times on the Zippo in his palm. Then the lighter clacked open, the cigarette was brought up and lit, and smoke danced out to the rhythm of the words: "Son, the day we began this project I asked you if you wanted a car, and you said yes. I asked you if you realized that we were on a budget and whatever we got would probably require a lot of work, and you said yes. I asked if you were sure you were ready to accept the responsibilities of owning and maintaining a car, and again you said yes. Is all that not correct?"

Thomas nodded.

"Now, let me ask you something—who paid for the car?" "You did, Dad."

"And who's going to be paying for the engine we'll be putting into the car?"

"You will, Dad."

"And who's going to be paying for new brake shoes and wheel bearings and Lord knows what else before it's all over?"

"You are."

"And who is going to be paying the insurance after we get it going? Who will be providing you with an allowance that will put gas in the tank to get you back and forth to school?"

"You."

"We'll get it running and back on the road, but I'll be doggoned if I'm going to lift a finger unless you're here working with me and showing some interest. It's an old car, Thomas, and I don't mind fixing it up for you, but the next time you need new brake shoes or a new water pump or just need to change your oil, you'd better know how to do it yourself. It's not like you can afford to take it down to Ira and pay Mister Hansborough's prices to get it fixed. Not on a five dollar weekly allowance."

Thomas felt light-headed, detached, as if he were awakening from a plunge in a dream. Did he actually agree to all that while they meandered through the town, rummaging through junkyards and climbing in and out of old jalopies? He could hardly believe that such a nightmare could have befallen him. His chariot to freedom had become his ball and chain.

"But Dad, I haven't done anything but work on the car since we brought it home. Are you saying that I can't leave the yard until it's fixed? That could be the rest of the summer. Please, just this one afternoon. What's—"

"I know what you're driving at, Tom, and believe me, I understand. If you think about it, I haven't done much else either.

But I know you, and I know how quickly you can lose interest if allowed to, and this time I'm not letting you off the hook. Now, if you think you've bitten off more than you can chew, then I need to know right now, before I invest any more time and money. So what will it be? Do we finish it up and get it back on the road, or do you just want to throw it back together and put an ad in the paper, or maybe haul it down to Frank's and see if he can sell it?"

YES! SELL IT! Sell the goddamned thing or just throw all the pieces in the goddamned trunk and roll it into the goddamned Nebraska for all I care!

"Well, Son, what's it going to be?"

"Please, Dad, just this once. I already told Pete I'd go, and I haven't seen him or Bennett in over a week. I'll work on it every day after that. Promise."

The Colonel started to speak, then shook his head with a sputter of exasperation. Thomas stood limply, drained and silent, waiting for something more concrete. Then, finally: "Be home by four. I'll let your mother know."

#

Thomas walked toward the waiting Corvair. Pete was standing outside his open door, crossed arms resting on the roof. "It's about time, fuck- bubble. You ready to go?"

Thomas snapped the passenger door open and was about to tumble in when he remembered his smokes. "Get in and park your ass a minute, Peety-Weety"—a name Pete's mother had used when he was small that she still let slip out from time to time, and Pete hated it—"I'll be right back."

"Okay. I'll wait, asshole. Your old man torqued your jaws, didn't he? Well, don't take it out on me. You know I'm on your side"—Thomas reached behind his back and shot Pete the finger as he walked back toward the house—"*and that Peety-Weety crap's gonna cost you some gas money, asshole. If you think I'm gonna haul—*"

Thomas's mother turned to him with a smile as he closed the door. She was watering the row of miniature cactus plants set along the sill of the window over the kitchen sink, her eyes soft and brighter than usual. Blue eyes. Carolina blue, his father would say.

"Well, Honey, what does Pete think of the car?"

Thomas tried to smile back. "Oh, he likes it okay, I guess. Not much to like right now."

"Well, be patient, Honey. You and your daddy will get it going. I have no doubt about that."

"Yeah, I guess you're right, Momma."

Thomas strode the length of the house to his room and entered the dark closet, then reached up and thrust a flattened hand into the middle fold of the Mackinaw blanket. The Kents were there, as he knew they would be. His final pack, and half-smoked at that. He was sure his mother knew about the Kents, just as surely as she knew about the Playboy magazines under his bed that magically maintained a neat, even stack in spite of his blind groping, or the two packs of rubbers he got from the vending machine in Mister Hansborough's horrid men's room just in case he got up the nerve to see if they'd fit. He was jolted awake the next morning by the realization that he had left them in the pocket of his jeans, which were now gone from the floor, and he anticipated a stern lecture from The Colonel. But he found them back in his closet the following afternoon, washed and neatly hung, the pockets empty. It wasn't until three weeks later that he discovered the two round foil discs under the folded briefs in his top dresser drawer, stacked and aligned as carefully as the magazines under his bed.

The Corvair was still grumbling away as Thomas opened the passenger door and got in.

"Come on, let's get the fuck out of here. And give me a light, would you?"

"How am I supposed to dig in my pockets while I'm backing out of your fuckin' driveway, Kessler? You'll have to wait till we get on open road. Or you can use the one in the dash."

Thomas pushed the dash lighter in for what he thought was a reasonable amount of time, then pulled it back out. The iron-gray coil was barely glowing pink as he pressed the tip of his cigarette into it, and it took several seconds of feverish puffing to bring up a flame. Several strands of smoldering tobacco adhered to the underheated element as Thomas withdrew the cigarette, and he waited for them to burn out before returning the lighter to the socket.

Pete swung north on Ridgewest at the bottom of the hill without checking his speed. Ahead lay the four-way stop at Casey, and beyond that, through the thick stand of cedars that still survived the first one hundred feet of eastern Ridgewest frontage, the scattered outline of the Gregors' red brick ranch-style. Mister

Gregor had two attractive daughters, and the older one often starred in Thomas's nocturnal fantasies, but Thomas wasn't thinking about that now. He was thinking about the shoulder of the road in front of the house, empty at this time of day, but the place where tonight, hopefully, Mister Gregor's company car, a white '57 Ford four-door, would be parked, well away from the house set deep on the lot, away from the glow of the streetlight at the intersection. In all likelihood, the back seat of the car would be stacked with cartons of Kents, the doors unlocked. There would be Salems too, but Thomas hated menthols.

"I gotta make a cigarette run tonight, Pete. You want in on it?"

Pete reached over and plucked the Kent out of Thomas's mouth. "Man, I can't believe you're still smoking these things." He held the cigarette up to the top of the windshield, examining it in the sunlight as he simultaneously ran the stop sign at Ridgewest and Casey and swung a hard left onto the paved portion of the half-paved road. "Hell, this one here's pretty good, Kessler. I can't see but two weevil holes, but then I'm having to drive, too. Is saving thirty cents really worth smoking little bugs? You know that's what you're doing, right? And these are so dry they smell more like newspaper than tobacco when they burn. Hell, if you turn 'em upside down, half the tobacco falls out."

"That's gonna cost you one of yours, unless you wanna give it back. I've never seen a bug yet, and I've looked. I think maybe they just made those little holes, then left. Besides, if they're no good, what would Mister Gregor be doing with them anyway? He's in the business. He should know whether they're good or not."

Pete handed the Kent back. "Yeah, he's in the business, all right, and he knows that if he wants people to keep using his vending machines, they'd better not be stocked with weevil-infested cigarettes. But instead of tossing them out, he just leaves them in plain sight in the back seat of his car so dumb-asses like you can get hooked for free. You'll see. Someday he's gonna cut off your supply, and you'll be picking up pop bottles on the side of the road to earn the money to pull the good shit out of one of his machines. Haven't you ever wondered why he parks it on the street every night, unlocked, and not in his driveway? It's like a bird feeder. A bird feeder for cheap dumb-asses."

Thomas leaned across the seat and spewed a mouthful of hot smoke into Pete's face. "Fuck you. What time is it, anyway?"

Pete glanced at his watch as he positioned his hands on the wheel for the next turn. "About fifteen after ten. He's gonna be pissed."

#

A spare, blue-jeaned figure could be seen undulating in the heat a quarter mile away as Pete whipped the Corvair onto Grady Way. It was Bennett, leaning on the Caldwell mailbox with one leg crossed behind the other and braced by the toe of a penny loafer. His right hand was raised, the middle finger extended, and he was smiling.

"Well, well. It's about time, girls. I was beginning to wonder if I would get to see my dear old granny alive again."

Thomas opened his door and leaned forward, pulling the back of the seat with him, and Bennett folded in behind him. "So what took you guys so damn long? Did the old man lose the keys to your cage, Tom?"

"Yeah, and it's big and blue and sitting behind the Alamo, and if you'd like a car I've got one I'll sell cheap. We got here as soon as we could— okay?"

Pete tweezed a Marlboro out of the pack in his shirt pocket and clamped it between his teeth, and as he reached to push in the dash lighter, Bennett's arm shot over the seat and a Zippo popped to life under Pete's nose. "Don't mind Tommy-boy too much"—Pete sucked the flame into his cigarette and the Zippo retreated with a loud clack—"I think him and the old man kinda had it out back there."

Pete steered onto the Caldwells' circular driveway, maneuvered the Corvair through the empty carport adjacent to the front door, then launched the right rear wheel off the curb as he cut the corner back onto Grady Way. The engine burst into a roar while the tire was airborne, and when it hit asphalt, the Corvair squalled back toward the half-paved road trailing smoke.

"So the old man finally got you some wheels, huh?" Bennett said. He was wedged sideways onto the back seat, smoking a Parliament. "Well, from the way y'all are talking, I have absolutely no doubt it's a piece of shit, but you're still closer than I am. And get this—my old lady gives the good car to my asshole sister this morning 'cause the bug is in the shop, then chews my ass out when I wake up for not driving over to pay my grandmother a birthday visit! What does the old bitch expect me to do? Fly? And what's the hurry, anyway? Her birthday was last week—"

At the end of Brady Way, Pete spun the wheel a hard left onto the unpaved portion of Casey Lane, and Bennett's voice died under the drone and rattle of limestone gravel churning under the Corvair's tires.

"Goddammit, Pete, get this thing back on the road!" Bennett snapped from the back seat, once again declaring his long-held contention that no one should drive on gravel when a paved alternative was available. Neither Pete nor Thomas had ever ridden with Bennett when he didn't negotiate the eastbound portion of the half-paved road on the wrong side, and every time, Pete and Thomas, unbeknownst to each other, would say an unspoken prayer that would place Lowry at the intersection, his gray face baking in the Texas heat like carrion on the road. "This piss ant back seat is hard enough without you driving over a goddamn washboard."

"You gonna pay my ticket, Bennett?" Pete had to raise his voice to compensate for the road noise. "You gonna pay my old man the hike in my insurance? Right now all I need from you is some directions. Where to from here? Straight ahead through the park and across the river at Mirabeau, or right and through Granite Heights to the low-water bridge?"

"Turn right. We're not going over to my grandmother's right now. She's been waiting a week—a few more hours won't kill her. In the meantime, I think I might have found something you'd be interested in, Petey, my boy. Just keep going straight. After you cross Kensington Road, take the next left."

#

Bennett directed Pete to a modest split-level with pine siding and a brick facade set against a steep hill along Timberidge Drive in one of the older, less pretentious sections of Kensington Oaks. Thomas knew this to be the home of Marty Bastrop, the only child of a beautician and an electrician, and he and Pete waited in the car while Bennett climbed the concrete steps and rang the doorbell. Soon Marty's mother appeared, and after a few words from Bennett, she gestured to the east side of the house, toward the rutted caliche drive running up the hill to the back of the property. Bennett nodded and turned back toward the road, and the door swung shut.

"Come on. He's behind the house, working on his car."

Thomas and Pete climbed out, and the three boys started up the steep trail leading to the back of the house. Thomas and Bennett had footwear with rubber soles that gave them reasonable traction, but twice they had to stop and wait for Pete. He refused to wear anything on his feet not made entirely from cowhide, and the crushed limestone was skittering out from under the hard leather soles of his cowboy boots like ball bearings on a hardwood floor.

"Don't you know you're supposed to have a horse under you when you're wearing those things?" Bennett said. "Move out of the ruts. That part in the middle has some grass and not nearly as many loose rocks. If that doesn't work, well, there's always your hands and knees."

Pete moved to the center of the trail and gingerly crept up the hill. "Okay, now get in front of us," Bennett said. "We'll push your ass up the rest of the way if we have to."

All three boys were breathing heavily when they reached the top of the drive and the leveled expanse of barren yard that separated the upper floor of the house from the raw cedar brake girding the property line. There was no fence, but the thick woods and unadorned wall of the house lent a sense of isolation. Toward the back of the clearing, under the only substantial tree on the whole property, a live oak, sat Marty's rust-brown '55 Chevy. The car was mounted atop three piers of scrap lumber and a floor jack, and, like Thomas's Ford, lacked wheels; they had been removed and stacked under the tree at the edge of the woods.

Thomas was the first to spot Marty, hunkered down beside the live oak tree on an overturned lube bucket. He wore greasy, split-kneed jeans and a red flannel shirt, and his forearms were resting heavily on his thighs, a brake drum in his hands.

He's gonna do it. Sooner or later he's gonna do it just like he does at the bus stop when we're sitting on the stone wall waiting for the school bus. He's already halfway there now, with his shirt stretched out and his fat hairy belly hanging out.

Marty looked up as the three heads bobbed into view from the drive. "Well, I'll be damned. If it ain't a herd of virgins."

Thomas had known Marty, or at least known of him, ever since arriving in Kensington Oaks. He was notorious for obscene behavior, and local legend placed his seed outside the bedroom window of virtually every attractive female residing west of the river. They were in the same class at school, but it was quietly assumed that Marty was considerably older.

Physically, he was rife with contradictions—large and stout but not particularly muscular; blue eyes in contrast to brown skin and black hair; a handsome face set between a pair of jug ears.

Thomas had become acquainted with Marty on the school bus about a year before, and Marty didn't waste any time living up to his reputation. During their first meeting, he had casually invited Thomas along on one of his nocturnal forays—"You ever been window-peeping?" he had said—and when Thomas expressed apprehension, tried to draw him in with lewd depictions of the haughty girls chirping away in the front of the bus. Thomas ultimately declined—on grounds of cowardice rather than moral principle—but found Marty's vile anecdotes memorable and exciting, and during rides to school, he still enjoyed transferring the smug profiles conversing in the front of the bus onto svelte bare bodies dancing behind parted window shades.

"Well, Pete, I guess you're the reason y'all are here," Marty said. "I think I've got something you might be interested in over there on the workbench. You other guys can sit your asses down anywhere except on my car. It's got enough scratches on it already. Besides, those two-by-fours ain't set too straight. If it falls over, I'm fucked."

Thomas looked around and finally settled onto one of several railroad ties defining what appeared to be a trash bin, although the discarded Coke bottles, oil cans, and crumpled cigarette packs were clustered in shallow, parallel depressions that insinuated an earlier attempt at gardening.

Pete followed Marty's gaze to the workbench along the back wall of the house and started toward it. Bennett stood in place a moment longer, looking uninitiated and miscast, then noticed an upturned flower pot sitting beside the drive not far from Marty. He walked over and took a couple of swipes at the coat of dirt on the base with a flattened hand, then folded into an ungainly squat. He was up again almost instantly, looking for another seat, and finally settled for leaning against one of the Chevy's fenders.

"I didn't even know they made something like this for my car." Pete was holding what appeared to be a pair of bicycle handlebars with a huge carburetor mounted where the headlight would normally be. "Did you talk to whoever had it before?"

"Look, a lowlife who works for my old man when he's not dealing in midnight auto parts pulled it outta his trunk one day and said he was having a hard time moving it, and let me have it at a good price. I hadn't been able to find a serious buyer either and was about to try and dump it off on somebody else myself when I ran into studmuffin here at the Stop-N-Go— he was buying a Playboy and a jar of Vaseline, if I recall rightly—and he mentioned that you had a Corvair."

Thomas was quietly observing Marty. Dirty brake parts were stacked on the ground to his left, and on his right, neatly arranged on a towel, lay several clean ones, still glistening with whatever Marty was now vigorously applying to a brake drum with a frayed paintbrush. A smoldering cigarette butt dangled from his lips, and on the ground between his feet lay a large baking pan full of greasy solvent. Thomas recognized the smell; he'd been sniffing it every day since they brought the Ford home.

"Marty, do you think it's a good idea to smoke while you're using kerosene? That stuff burns, you know."

Marty rolled his eyes up from the brake drum and onto Thomas, then dropped his head and spat the burning cigarette sharply into the pan. It died with a barely discernible hiss.

"What's this thing gonna do to my gas mileage, Marty?" Pete said. "This is a four-barrel. I have enough trouble getting enough gas money out of these cheapskates as it is."

"Well, just keep your foot out of it, then. It only runs on two barrels unless you floor it and kick in the other two. What's your car got on it now? A two-barrel?"

"Naw, two one-barrels."

"Well, there you go! Unless you get on it, you'll still be running on two barrels, just like now."

"It looks like you just take the stock carburetors off and bolt this thing on in their place," Pete said, the furrows in his brows fading. "It looks simple enough. How much do you want for this thing?"

"Tell you what—twenty bucks and it's yours. The carburetor alone is worth that much. It's a good Rochester. I can get twenty bucks for it any day of the week."

"I don't know, Marty. Mind if I think about it? I'll let you know in a day or two. Okay?"

"I'll give you a week. After that, the carburetor goes on the block and that pipe on the scrap pile. Now, come on over here and find a seat and let's get caught up. What have you little peckers been doing with yourselves since school let out? You still the only one with wheels, Pete?"

"Well, Tom's got him some wheels now, and some fenders and a whole bunch of other parts besides. But if you mean a complete car capable of rolling down the road under its own power, well—yeah, I guess I'm still the only one."

Thomas didn't take offense to Pete's remark. He was free from his father's indenture and among his own for the first time in weeks, and the Ford just seemed like a bad dream. And how long would it take to fix the car, anyway? They might have it knocked out in a month, maybe even less.

"It's a '53 Ford," Thomas volunteered. "Two-tone blue. A four-door. Needs a motor. You don't know where I could pick up a good flathead V-8 cheap, do you?"

"I'll see if that scumbag who works for my old man has anything you can use, but I think a whole motor is out of his league, but you never know. He might be able to yank one out so fast, you wouldn't notice anything was wrong till the light turned green."

Bennett's Zippo clacked open and, as if on cue, Pete and Thomas reached for a cigarette.

"My hands are all greasy," Marty said. "One of you guys is gonna have to set me up. My smokes are in my shirt pocket. Come dig one out for me."

Pete had just taken a seat beside Thomas on the railroad tie, so Bennett accepted the task by default. He pulled a second Parliament out of his pack, added it to the one already in his lips, then lit them with the Zippo before walking over and planting one in the corner of Marty's mouth.

"It's on me, Marty."

"Thanks, Bennett. And by the way, what's your first name?"

"That is my first name."

"That's your first name? Well, what in the hell's your last name then? Fred?"

"My last name's Caldwell."

"Caldwell, huh. How'd you end up with two last names, anyway?" "Bennett was my mother's family's name."

"Damn, I'm sure glad my folks didn't do that with me. I'd be Pugh Bastrop."

"Pugh?" Pete asked.

"Yeah, Pugh. P-u-g-h. It's pronounced like 'pew-ee, that sure smells like shit!'"

"Or like a seat in church," noted Thomas. "It's spelled different though." "Hell, that's even worse. Anyway, enough of that"—Marty set the brake

drum down and wiped his hands with an oily rag, then stood and stretched. He plucked the cigarette from his lips and flicked the ash off, and when he stuck it back in his lips, black fingerprints were clearly visible on the paper. Then he sat back down on the bucket and leaned his shoulders against the trunk of the live oak tree. "Well, at least you got a four-door, buddy, and not a two-door like our friend Pete here's got, with that dinky little back seat. That was my first consideration when I bought a car. Eight cylinders would have been nice, but with the cash I had, I settled for six. But with doors, that was different. It had to have four doors."

Marty turned to Bennett. "Now, take that beetle I saw you in the other day, Caldwell—that's your first name, right?"

"I answer to both."

"Well, those bugs are actually all right, 'cause the front seat will fold all the way down. I know a waitress who works the late shift at Galloway's that owns one. Last year her husband moved out for a while, and she'd come pick me up after her shift on Saturday nights. We'd find a quiet place down in the park and she'd feed me a free chicken-fried steak, then fuck my eyes out in those laid-back seats. She always felt bad about not taking me back to her apartment, 'cause she was afraid her husband would show up. I never had any complaints, though. Anyway, whose bug is that? Is it yours?"

"It's supposed to be mine and my sister's both, but I never get to use it 'cause she gets first dibs. If I drive anything, it's usually my mother's car, a Chevy like Tom's dad's got. Ours is just a two-door, though. The Kessler's is a four-door."

"Well, just remember to try and get your sister's car if you think you might have a chance at getting your cherry popped. There ain't nothing worse than trying to knock off a piece with your knees and head wedged between a couple of armrests. It's either that or doing it in the front seat and choosing between a steering wheel in your crack or one knocking against your head."

Bennett leaned his head back and launched a smoke ring into the leaves of the live oak. Suddenly, he seemed more relaxed, even prepossessing. "There are lots of places to do it besides the back seat of a car. Anyway, there's nothing wrong with Pete's car. At least it's clean and new. Girls like that." A second smoke ring rose into the leaves and melted into the remnants of the first. "And it is running. And if Pete really needs a back seat, he can always drive over here and use yours. It doesn't look like it's going anywhere anytime soon."

Thomas and Pete were spectators now, muted and impartial. The conversation had moved far beyond their level of expertise.

Marty crushed the Parliament out and flicked the butt at Bennett's penny loaders, his brown face open and smiling. "Well, well, mister studmuffin, I do believe you're the most uppity virgin I ever ran across."

Bennett sent a third smoke ring into the live oak. "Well, I don't see any point in arguing with someone who doesn't know a virgin when he sees one. Kind of makes me think he might even be a virgin himself. Anyway, that's all I got to say."

"So you're saying you're not a virgin, huh? Well, I said and still say you're a virgin, unless you can pass along a few names. There ain't nothing goes on in this neighborhood that doesn't get back to me, or doesn't come if I go asking. I ain't saying you're lying, but you gotta be able to back up a claim like that. Besides, what's the point of getting a piece of tail if you don't talk it around? 'Course, if you picked up a cheap piece of poontang down in Laredo or managed to save up enough for a ride across town to Hattie's or over to the chicken ranch, I wouldn't know about that. That's it, ain't it? You paid to have your cherry popped."

"I told you I'm not gonna talk about it anymore."

"Then keep your comments to yourself, if you ain't willing to back 'em up."

Bennett looked upward and sent a final smoke ring into the leaves, then flipped his cigarette into the pan of kerosene. Marty leaned forward and picked up the brake drum, examined it, then nodded approvingly and placed it on the towel to his right. "Anyway, Pete, the Corvair is probably okay for you, being as how you're so short and all"—his left hand groped briefly in the filthy kerosene, then reappeared with the brush—"but just stick to spinners. Anything else would likely get stuck, and I ain't just talking about your dick."

Thomas and Pete exchanged glances, and at the end of a long silence, it was Pete who finally spoke up. "What do you mean by 'spinners,' Marty?"

Marty reached over and pulled a brake cylinder from the pile of parts on his left, then directed his response to Bennett: "Hell, I'll bet old Caldwell's had a spinner or two in his time. Go ahead, Caldwell, tell him. Tell him what a spinner is."

The Zippo clacked again. "It's not anything I've ever heard of, unless you're talking about hubcaps."

"Or fishing tackle," Thomas blurted out. "My dad's got some spinners in his tackle box. Real shiny. Good for bass."

Marty rolled his eyes, and Thomas shrank back into silence. "A spinner is a little gal; it's as simple as that," Marty said. "Now I'm gonna let Caldwell here explain to you why a little gal is called a spinner. Go ahead, stud-hoss, we're listening."

Marty turned his attention to the brake cylinder in his hands, waiting for a response that never came. Bennett was watching his latest batch of smoke rings fall apart in the leaves when Marty finally looked up.

"You know, I'm surprised, Caldwell. It seems like a cocksman like you woulda earned his spinning badge a long time ago. I've known about it ever since I was five or six, when my cousins down around Port Aransas filled me in. And you seem to be pretty much a highfalutin city boy, so you sure as shit don't have any excuse." Marty pointed up, into the boughs of the live oak. "You see that rope hanging from that big limb there?" A thick rope was draped over a stout limb about ten feet up the trunk, with one end anchored to a short gnarl and the other knotted into a large loop and dangling a foot off the ground. "That's where I do my spinning, boys. Just hitch 'em up, lower 'em down, and let her rip! Now y'all getting the idea?"

"Sounds like kid stuff to me," Bennett said. "Wouldn't it just be easier to take 'em to the playground over at the grade school?"

"Sounds like you still got kid stuff on the brain, asshole. Look, it's simple. You just sit the gal in the loop—preferably buck naked, but panties off with her dress hiked up will do—then hoist her up. Then—and this is the tricky part—you get down on your back, slide under, and just lower her down on your pecker. When she's juiced up good, you grab an ankle or knee and spin her like a top. After you get her wound up in one direction and the rope's about to pull her off of your pecker, you just let go and let the rope unwind. God-*HAWD-damn!* I'm tellin' ya, there ain't nothing like it. They get to going so fucking fast that it don't matter if they're good-looking or ugly, 'cause when you get your nuts off she's nothing but a blur anyway."

Marty looked the brake cylinder over approvingly, then set it back in the pile and picked up another drum. "So that's a spinner. She's gotta be small enough for you to hoist her up and hold her. And they can't be too tall neither, or you might get cold-cocked by a heel. I don't think you or Pete should try it yet, Tom. Most of the girls around here weigh more than you, and you probably couldn't get them off the ground anyway."

What followed was a silence so total that the buzzing of the flies and gnats swirling about the four glistening faces filled the stagnant air like the shriek of a dozen band saws. As for Thomas, he was transfixed not so much by the mental image provoked by Marty's surreal tableau as by the unimaginable discourse that would be requisite for such an activity to occur. Thomas found it difficult to ask a girl to scoot over so he could take a seat on the school bus.

Bennett was the first to speak. "That's the stupidest thing I've ever heard of. You can feed this shit to Pete and Tom if you want, but don't expect me to swallow it. How come the end of that rope you claim you use for this 'spinning' bullshit is so grimy? You lube your ladies up with axle grease before you hoist 'em up? If I didn't know any better, I'd say some grease monkey had been using that rope for pulling engines rather than twirling women. But then that can't be right, can it, Marty? I mean, I don't see any grease monkeys around here. Do you?"

Marty dropped the brake drum and the brush into the kerosene and wiped his hands on the tops of his thighs, then swiveled on the bucket, his demeanor calm but a hot blush seeping into the dull bronze of his cheeks. "Okay, shithead, let's see if you can back up that smart mouth of yours." He glanced at Thomas and Pete to bring them into the conversation. "Let's forget about spinning for now. First things first. Who can be back over here tomorrow night, say around seven? I can't guarantee you'll lose your cherries, but I swear you'll at least get a shot. Any takers?"

"Sure, Marty," Pete said without hesitation, much to Thomas's disgust.

Easy for you to say, asshole. Your car's in one piece.

"I'll come too," said Thomas, with little enthusiasm, since he wasn't sure he could escape his father's clutches before nightfall.

"Are you kidding?" Bennett said. "I wouldn't miss it for the world!

What's it gonna cost us? Do we have to put the brakes back in your car?" "Just be here, city boy. As for what it's all about—"

Here it comes, just like at the bus stop—

Marty looked down and laid his hands along the sides of his exposed belly, then began to squeeze. A pair of plump, hairy swells formed and grew until they met and swallowed his navel, and he delicately adjusted the pressure until a small breach appeared. A few more minor adjustments, and then, satisfied that his hands held a faithful reproduction of an image that might have been quarried from the dark side of a window on a moonless night, he looked up at the three boys with a grin that hung on his jug ears like a hammock.

CHAPTER 10

The drive out of Granite Heights and across the Nebraska was monotonous and muted, given the mission, and Thomas and Pete had been over to the Caldwell house in West Fuller several times before on lesser errands, so no direction was required. Thomas had met Bennett's grandmother once before; like Bennett's mother, she exuded a benign tyranny that fomented chaos rather than order. She was the sole family member living there now, Bennett said, attended to by a live-in nurse for the past two years.

One block past the stone-columned arch announcing Confederate Home in wrought-iron letters, Pete steered the Corvair left. Halfway up the hill, commanding an undiminished view of the quarter-mile of gentrified floodplain that stretched to the Nebraska River, sat the Bennett homestead. A postbellum Victorian of two stories, it dominated the hillside and loomed well above the small bungalows and cottages set against the narrow oak- lined streets. Sharpening the distinction further was a wall of limestone blocks that held the terraced and neglected yard and grew as the street descended, achieving a height of six feet along the facade, where the sharp climb from the street to the columned front porch exceeded twenty feet. Newer by half a century, yet almost a half century old on its own, the neighborhood that had been carved into the former estate grounds left the old Bennett place looking like the final tier on a fantastic wedding cake.

They had just begun the short ascent when Bennett leaned forward and yelled over the roaring exhaust: "Hey! I'm almost outta smokes. Go on up to the top of the hill and take a left, then the next right. You know, to the grocery across from Griffintown."

Pete followed Bennett's directions and pulled into an empty parking slot in front of Griffintown Grocery, a small whitewashed brick building with a single glass door set into the corner that faced the intersecting roads. Three large squares of sharper, smoother brick were clearly noticeable in the worn facade, shadows of former windows lost to needed shelf space. Two large glass windows framing the door still remained and served as bulletin boards; taped notices announcing church socials, yard sales, missing pets, and the daily and weekly specials covered the panes, with items of interest to children affixed below a height of three feet.

Thomas bent at the waist, and Bennett shoved the seat back forward and stepped out. "I'll be right back. Y'all gonna stay or go?"

"Aw, what the hell. I'll go," Pete said. "If I don't buy some too, I'll have to bum pretty soon."

"Not off me, you won't," Bennett mumbled.

"Yeah, I know," Pete said. "So what then, one of Kessler's Kents?" He shut off the engine, got out, and he and Bennett stepped up onto the curb.

The midday sun was directly overhead and a steady southern breeze flowed through the open windows. Thomas pulled a Kent from the pack in his jeans, inspected it for weevil holes, then lit up. The foot traffic through the grocery's single door was so heavy that it took Pete and Thomas several tries before they managed to slip inside, presaging a long wait, so Thomas made himself comfortable by sliding the seat back against the stops and stretching out with his boots in the driver's seat.

He smoked his cigarette and mindlessly watched the shoppers churning through the glass door—in with nothing but a purse or pocketed list or small shopping cart, out with at least one loaded paper bag, usually more. White customers invariably fed in from the west, in cars, and the blacks on foot, crossing over through busy traffic with Griffintown dust covering their shoes and bare feet.

Griffintown. Ira gave him the history one day while he changed the spark plugs in a brand new Riviera. The community was named after the founder, a freedman who was able to buy land west of Fuller during Reconstruction only because no white man wanted it. Eventually, other families were invited in, and Griffintown thrived as Fuller expanded westward until, with the arrival of automobiles and graded roads, the city completely overtook and engulfed the colony, which had grown into an efficient, if isolated, community of domestic workers and skilled laborers situated atop some forty acres of rapidly appreciating suburban real estate. The city had utilized all available means to uproot Griffintown—the withholding of annexation and the city services that would come with it; generous offers of relocation assistance to the officially recognized colored side of town, as East Fuller was now known—but the residents of Griffintown held firm. The result was a bucolic village of dirt roads and small clapboard houses nestled cleanly into the pavement, cleared lots, and brick homes of white Fuller like a black tile in a pristine white floor.

The scant Griffintown business district ran along the community's eastern border on the only road that accessed the outside world, and eventually growth required the city to zone their side of the road commercial as well. Offered up along a three-block stretch were a gas station, a liquor store, a pharmacy, two barbershops, and a grocery store. As inconceivable as it was, the businesses on both sides of the road, black and white, had integrated quietly, almost unconsciously, as time and intimate proximity eroded the social precepts that cleaved the communities as a whole. Only the barbershops, bastions of male bluster and biased humor, remained racially exclusive.

Thomas lay slumped with his back against the door, watching as the customers, black and white, entered and left in a constant stream, only occasionally nodding or speaking as they held the door for one another or politely stepped aside, sharing the same language and carrying in their sacks the same purchases to satisfy the same needs.

Just the opposite of Cheruskerweg Street, the final stop on a trip that began with a long drive for a round of shots, then continued with a flight to New York and a seemingly endless voyage across the Atlantic that ended with the sight of his father waving from the dock at Le Havre.

The '49 Lincoln sedan was waiting too—The Colonel had shipped it over as well—and the back seat swallowed Thomas up as it always had. Then the long drive to Wiesbaden and two years of struggling to comprehend it all.

#

What happened to all those houses, Dad? They were bombed in the war, Son.

Who bombed them, Dad? Well, we did, Son.

They settled into a two-story stone house on Cheruskerweg Street and hired a live-in maid, the widow of a German soldier, who brought with her a son. She was Katie, and he was Wolfgang, but everybody called him Wolfie, and they moved into the basement and slept on cots distanced from the furnace according to season. And there was Katie's boyfriend, Fritz, a jocular baker who prepared wonderfully decorated birthday cakes for Thomas's birthdays and Christmas. Like Katie and Wolfie, he spoke little English, but it didn't matter because humor was his language of choice. At their first meeting, he held his hand up in front of Thomas's face and teasingly wiggled the stump of a missing finger—lost to shrapnel during the war, according to Katie—and framed it with a wide, silly grin, so Thomas would have to grin too. A wound of war turned tool for laughter.

The house sat at an intersection where five arteries converged, and a traffic lane cut between two adjoining streets created a wedge of wooded lawn that served as a playground where the neighborhood children would gather. Katie told Thomas's parents that several of the children on the block, like Wolfie, had been left fatherless by the war, and The Colonel instructed him to report any bullying or abuse, should it happen.

Mostly, it was marbles that they played, and at first Thomas could only observe and try to interpret rules and strategy. Occasionally he would be addressed in a querulous manner, usually by one of the older boys, and always in German, and he quickly learned that just saying "American" was usually enough to deflect their attention back to their game. For the most part, they would ignore him—the noncomprehending, mute spectator—and except for an occasional bike ride, Thomas came to spend increasingly more of his time behind the stone columns and iron pickets that encircled their home.

There was a green apple tree in the backyard with large, accessible branches, and The Colonel constructed a tree house in it over the course of a single weekend. Not a house, really—there was no roof, nor were there walls—but an open platform of planks and heavy beams wedged into the angle of the four major branches. A low bench was built along one edge and a railing all around for safety, except where the trail of sturdy board steps affixed to the trunk led in. One day, as Thomas was climbing to the tree house, he noticed that one of the limbs stretched to a deck fronting his parents' bedroom on the second floor, and the deck extended under one of his windows as well; the deck and the tree could provide anonymous passage. He was not given to mischief, but the idea of a secret passage gave him a sense of empowerment, and he learned to ignore the furtive glances of the two women that would occasionally float to the kitchen window, then quickly fall away.

Eventually, Thomas started first grade at the school on the Air Force base and began lessons in German, and this, along with his daily interactions with Katie and Wolfie, granted a fluency that would enable an occasional inclusion in the marble games on the traffic island, at which he proved to be remarkably inept. His playmates generally fell into three categories— disinterested, amused, and grudgingly tolerant—and more and more of his time went to stretching out on the planks high in the green apple tree, his back resting against the bench on which he never sat, eating fruit plucked from the swaying boughs. He loved the taste of the green apples and would eat them even though he knew they would bring a bellyache; eat them as the sun and the laughter of the children faded from the traffic island; eat them down to the core and spit the seeds into the air over his American- made sneakers until his tummy was hard and sore. Then his mother would call, and as if in defeat, he would force himself onto the limb that would deliver him to the deck and his room and his bed, there to continue his desperate struggle to understand how he should feel as the son of a man who would have widowed a maid, taken the fathers from marble-playing boys on a traffic island, and removed the finger of a baker.

#

The blade of sunlight was leaving the dashboard and moving uncomfortably close when Pete and Bennett emerged from the crowded doorway. Thomas jerked his knees to his chest and swiveled in the seat when he saw them coming; his feet were firmly back on the floorboard by the time Pete got in the car.

"About time. It's starting to get hot in here."

Pete backed into the street, and in the time it took Bennett to tear open his cigarette pack and light two smokes with his Zippo, Pete was pulling the Corvair up to the curb opposite the Caldwell homestead.

"What are you doing, Pete?" Bennett motioned over his left shoulder to the steep, rutted driveway leading to a small parking lot behind the house.

"Back up and pull into the yard, dumbass. Tom and me can't get out with the damned car parked like this."

Bennett was right. The steep street was deeply guttered, and the passenger door arced into the curb as soon as Thomas pushed it open.

"Y'all can both get out on my side. This car is too low-slung for that cow path you call a drive, Bennett. Unless you don't mind buying me a new undercarriage."

"Okay, okay, but we gotta finish our smokes first. Odessa don't allow it."

They finished their cigarettes, then got out of the Corvair and crossed to the opposite curb, where a flight of concrete steps breached an overgrown hedge of crepe myrtle and delivered them to a flagstone walk leading to an obscure door on the west side of the house. Bennett tried the knob, found it unlocked, and pushed the door ajar.

"Hello! Odessa? Grandmother? It's just me, Bennett, and a couple of buddies. Anybody home?"

When they were met with silence, Bennett looked back at his friends, shrugged, and they all stepped inside. Soon a large black woman in a green uniform leaned into view through a door at the far end of the foyer, a finger pressed to her lips.

"Shhh. Y'all be quiet. Miz Caldwell might still be asleep. Bennett, I hadn't seen you in ages. What brings you over here?"

"I just came by to wish Gran a happy birthday, Odessa. These guys gave me a ride."

"A happy birthday? It's a little late for that, ain't it? When your momma and sister was over here last week with presents and cake, you were nowhere to be found. 'Course, that's not what she told your granny—she told her you wasn't feeling well. But somebody as old as your granny is, and in bad health too, even a day late could be too late. And this time it took you a good week to get over here."

"Okay, okay. I feel bad—all right? Now, could you see if she's awake? Please."

Odessa kept her disapproving look on Bennett for a moment longer, then shook her head and turned away and left them standing in the foyer. Once again Bennett looked back at Thomas and Pete, and the smiles they were wearing at his expense had barely faded when Odessa returned and bade them follow with a wave of her hand. "Y'all come on in. She's in the garden room, awake and resting easy."

They stepped out of the long foyer, leaving the deeply patinaed oak floor for the soft nap of the Persian carpet running the length of the study. Oak wainscoting and plaster the color of old piano keys shared the walls with fully stocked bookcases with sliding ladders that extended to the high ceiling, and the delicate glow of lamps with shades of stained glass fell gently onto furniture—a roll-top desk, a bureau, a writing table—of a bulk that inferred permanence. Under the arched doorway in the wall opposite the foyer, Odessa stopped and halted the boys with a raised hand.

Despite Odessa's considerable girth, Thomas was able to see much of the large room beyond. The long wall opposite was dominated by tall casement windows that revealed a garden lush with calla lilies, and climbing roses and bougainvillea entwined and trellised to form a wall of brilliant privacy. There was no air-conditioning, but the sashes of the windows were open and the shades drawn, and pages in the opened magazines lying on the table next to a hospital bed rose and fell rhythmically as ceiling fans cast garden- scented breezes through the room. Several vases were arranged on the table as well, all bearing notes or cards. Only one still held flowers—a spray of yellow mums with wilted stems evenly draped around the rim, their withered petals encircling the base.

Odessa stepped to the side and motioned Bennett through, and Thomas could see Bennett's grandmother seated in a wheelchair beside the bed, her hands perched on the armrests like lifeless birds, an oxygen mask strapped over her mouth and nose. Behind lids barely open and only then by a quivering exertion, her eyes seemed to be searching.

"Okay, y'all, who all is going in?" Odessa whispered.

"Just me, Odessa. I'm not sure Gran would even know these guys." "Okay, then. Now, she doesn't have much to say these days and she wears down quick, so don't stay too long . . . although I don't know why I'm even saying that, seeing as how it took a week for you to get yourself over here. As for you other two, come with me—"

Thomas and Pete turned and dutifully followed her back through the study and into the foyer, then through a doorway to the right of the entryway and down another hall to the kitchen. Odessa was an ample woman, but moved with the graceful efficiency of unfettered purpose. Her pea green uniform was spotless and severely starched, with ironed creases held as sharp, tiny ridges that made a low rustle as she walked, but the sterility of her appearance was contradicted by the aroma of baking biscuits, frying chicken and bacon, and hot pancakes under melting butter and warm syrup trailing in her wake.

A breakfast nook was set into an alcove opposite the kitchen's work space, and Pete and Thomas took positions across from one another. "Okay, what'll y'all have while you're waiting? Don't have too much to offer, I'm afraid. I just cleaned up all the lunch and hadn't started dinner yet. There's apples and bananas, and I think we still got some birthday cake in the icebox. Don't know how good it is, though. Got tea. Can I offer y'all some iced tea?"

"Tea sounds pretty good right now, ma'am. With sugar, please," Pete said.

"Honey, 'round here sweet is all we do." She turned to Thomas. "How about you?"

"Nothing, thanks."

"All right, then. Y'all make yourselves comfy."

Odessa removed a large pitcher from the refrigerator, stocked two glasses with ice, then poured the tea. She left one glass on the counter and brought the other to the nook and set it in front of Pete. For the first time, Thomas noticed a slight trace of perfume, hardly discernible through the blended aromas of the kitchen.

"So, y'all are buddies of Bennett's from across the river, huh? I don't recall ever meeting you before, but then I don't think I've seen Bennett more than once or twice since Miz Ernestine moved about a year ago."

Pete spoke up first: "Yes ma'am. Actually, I met Bennett through Thomas here. I don't live in the same neighborhood as they do."

"Me and Bennett knew each other a little bit from school, but we started hanging out together after he moved," Thomas said. "I think we first ran into each other on the school bus. Or maybe it was on the way to the bus stop. Bennett cuts through the woods behind my house like I do, 'cause if you stuck to the roads it would take twice as long."

"I don't ride the school bus," Pete said. "I have a car. That's how we got over here." Odessa smiled as Thomas bit his lip and shifted in his seat, and Pete quickly attempted to redeem himself. "Anyway, if it wasn't for the car, these guys probably wouldn't give me the time of day."

This brought a shared chuckle. Odessa walked back to the kitchen counter, picked up her glass, and drank it halfway down. "Well then, you should be thankful. Not many kids your age got their own wheels, at least not wheels they'd trust to get 'em across the river and back." She walked over to the refrigerator and retrieved the pitcher of tea. "How are things going over there? I mean with Bennett. Is he stayin' out of trouble?"

Thomas and Pete looked across the nook at one another. Odessa's back was to them as she refilled her glass, so they couldn't see her face. The lack of humor in her voice gave the seemingly innocuous question an edge. Then a moment more in silence, and Odessa turned and leaned against the counter, tea in hand, a mild smile on her face. "I mean, you know, a new place and all is probably a good thing. We could probably all benefit from a fresh start in one way or another. Anyway, if he's stayin' so busy he can't shake loose on his granny's birthday, he must not have time to be bad. And maybe bad is the wrong word—and maybe I never shoulda opened my big mouth in the first place. Bennett was never a bad boy, just real rash and reckless sometimes. Let's just say he had a tendency to go against the grain."

"Bennett hadn't been in any trouble that I know of," said Thomas. Bennett might have a smart mouth from time to time, but it wasn't like he went around tossing bombs in people's backyards. "At least, not while he's away from his house. He gets into it with his mom and sister a lot while he's home, though."

Odessa threw her head back and shook with laughter. "Lawdy, lawdy! You're tellin' me! One time when those three was livin' here, the preacher at my church dropped by to discuss some church business with me while they was going at it about somethin', only God knows what, and I had to keep 'im outside on the stoop, in the terrible heat, till we got done. He kept looking toward the door—I could tell he was wonderin' why I didn't invite 'im in—and I felt real bad and all, but there was just no way. Good folks, but they sure talk salty, and that's puttin' it mildly. Bennett's granny don't talk that way, but she never did pay 'em no mind. 'Course, she don't hear too good, so that might be part of it too. Anyway"—Odessa raised her glass in a toast—"life goes on, no matter what side of the river you're on. So here's to fresh starts."

Pete raised his glass, and Thomas nodded his assent. He was rethinking the offer of tea when Bennett walked into the kitchen.

"Well, you guys ready to go?"

"What's the rush, Bennett?" Odessa held up her glass. "Don't you at least want a glass of iced tea before you leave? How did it go with your granny?"

"Okay, I guess. She was tired and didn't say too much, but she smiled a couple of times. At least I think she did. It was hard to tell with that mask on." Bennett was gazing blankly through the arched doorway, down the foyer. "We used to talk a lot, and now when I visit her, it just makes me miss her even more. All it does is remind me of how things used to be. Maybe she feels the same way—who knows?"

"Well, don't feel too guilty about missin' her birthday. For all we know, she might think it's still her birthday. Anyway, sounds like you made 'er smile, and that's what counts. But let this be a lesson to you"—Odessa swept Thomas and Pete in with a glance—"and you two as well. There ain't no stoppin' the march of time. Appreciate who and what you got while you got 'em." Odessa raised her glass. "You want some tea before you go, Bennett? There's really no need to rush off."

Thomas had been nervously monitoring his Timex and decided to speak for Bennett. "Ma'am, if it's all the same to you and these guys, I need to be heading home. My father wants me home by four o'clock."

Odessa looked genuinely disappointed. "Well, y'all scat then. Obey thy father and thy mother. I need to go check on Miz Bennett anyway. Just leave your glass on the table there, young fella. I'll pick it up later. And as for you"—Odessa stepped over and engulfed Bennett with a prolonged hug, then held him at arm's length, her hands on his shoulders—"remember now, there ain't but one reason to cross that river and come back 'round here, and that's to come see your granny. And me. You hear?"

Bennett said nothing as he shuffled his feet and fidgeted with the belt loops on his jeans, but Odessa stood firm, her gaze planted firmly behind unblinking eyes. Finally, he said, "Yeah, yeah, Odessa. Quit worrying so much. I'm a big boy now."

Odessa released his shoulders. "Yeah, I know. I guess that's what I'm worried about. Anyway, behave yourself. Y'all all behave, for that matter. I gotta go now—"

Odessa left the kitchen for the garden room and her charge. The click of her heels echoed down the hall, then died in the Persian rug as she entered the study.

"Holy shit, Bennett. What was that all about?" Pete said. "From the way she talked, you didn't move out—you got thrown out!"

Bennett pulled his cigarette pack out of his pocket and started for the exit, and Thomas and Pete followed. When he pushed the back door open and stepped down onto the walk leading to the street, "shotgun" was all he said, and they were pulling back onto Sixth Street before Pete thought to give it another try. "Come on, Bennett, she really got me curious, man. Why did y'all move out to Kensington Oaks, anyway?"

"Do I really have to answer that? Come on, man, with my grandmother lying in a hospital bed in the middle of the house like a mummy and Odessa prying into every little thing I do, what do you think? Besides, dumb-ass, I'm not the one who made the decision to move; my mother did. Why don't you ask her?"

A soft rain had begun to fall. Pete switched his wipers on, and they drove back across the river in silence.

#

"The General's Army's ready, Son," the Colonel declared as Thomas slipped out of the Corvair well ahead of his assigned deadline. The rain had eased to a slow drizzle, and his father was pruning the rose bushes in the flower beds at the base of the Alamo. "I put a second coat of varnish on the grips right after you left this morning. They should be dry by now."

Pete had already backed halfway down the driveway when Thomas spun, hollered, and motioned him back. As the Corvair pulled abreast of Thomas and his father, Pete angled his head out the open window.

"Dad says The General's Army is ready to go. You wanna go shoot it tomorrow?"

"Now just hold up a minute, Son," the Colonel interrupted. "Aren't you forgetting something?"

Thomas's focus shifted slightly from his father's face to the rose-laden wall beyond his shoulder, and the lurking, detestable mass of blue sheet metal it partially obscured.

"You just went a whole day without so much as touching a tool. And now you're shopping for two in a row?"

Thomas had genuinely not taken that fact into account, and now regretted even calling Pete back. It wasn't like The General wouldn't let them take it to the range some other time. If a gun still shoots, go ahead and shoot it, he had told Thomas more than once. It helps keep 'em alive.

"I'm sorry, Dad. You're right. I wasn't thinking."

"Give me a call in a little while, and we'll try and set something up," Pete said as he slipped the stick into reverse. "I'm gonna drop Bennett off, then head home. Gimme about an hour."

What happened next was the last thing Thomas would have expected. "Hold on a minute, Pete," the Colonel said. "Look, Tom, you worked hard on that pistol and I know how much it means to you, and if you want to shoot it, you might as well do it now. I'm all for a test fire, and I'm sure General O'Grady would be interested in the results. Look, I'll tell you what"—the Colonel glanced at his watch—"I'll ask your mother to push dinner back a couple of hours. If we start now, we can put four or five hours in on your car before it gets too dark, assuming the rain doesn't start back up. If you agree to that, and Pete can make it back over here in the morning, then I'll give you until noon to be back to work on the car. That will give you the whole morning on the range. Deal?"

Pete and Thomas eagerly agreed, and as the Corvair made a final run down the driveway and roared way down the cul-de-sac, Thomas looked up into the clearing sky and started toward his whitewashed cabinet in the garage, to his oil-stained overalls that he would remove from the bottom shelf with a long, joyless pull.

#

The next morning, Thomas was seriously considering not only the possibility that there was a God, but that God was good. He and his father had been working on the Ford less than an hour when the sky erupted with pounding rain, suspending their efforts, and by the time the storm abated, they had already cleaned up and sat down to dinner. After the meal, Thomas called Bennett and invited him along on the trip to the range, and then called Pete to update logistics, not thinking to stipulate who should be picked up first. When the Corvair pulled into the driveway, Bennett was already sitting shotgun. Thomas got in, thinking "asshole," if not actually saying it.

Thomas settled into the backseat with the Army laying across a clean rag in his lap, and Pete and Bennett turned in their seats to get a better look. There was still the heavy dimpling left by countless fence staples driven into an endless procession of West Texas fence posts—nothing could or should ever be done about that. But a brisk application of steel wool had exposed gray, worn steel beneath the matte of cinnamon rust, and a light coating of gun oil gave it an elegant sheen. As for the missing stocks, the longer grip of the 1860 Model Army was unique among Colt pistols, and fabrication was the only alternative. The Colonel had gone through his scrap bin and found just enough black walnut for the job and fashioned a perfect set of stocks that looked incongruous on the battered Colt, but they fit as if they had been removed a century before, when the pistol was new, and were just now being put into service.

Thomas thumbed the hammer back to full cock, then squeezed the trigger and gently lowered it back down. He and his father had assumed that the broken mainspring would probably challenge them the most—finding parts for a pistol that had been out of production for a hundred years seemed daunting—and Thomas felt uneasy about the prospect of having to ask The General to pay to have one fabricated by a gunsmith. Then, on a whim, he removed the spring from his .45 Peacemaker and found that it fit the Army perfectly. They picked up a replacement at Buster's Gun Shop on the next trip to downtown Fuller.

"So, are y'all really gonna shoot that thing?" Bennett said. He was looking at the pistol as if it were a coiled snake.

"Shit, no," Pete quipped, "you think we're crazy or something? That's why we brought you along."

"Yeah, right. When was the last time anybody shot this thing, anyway?"

Thomas knew that Bennett's question was rhetorical, and the unexpected realization that he had the answer gave his reply an air of astonishment: "The Civil War."

"The Civil War?" Pete had started backing down the driveway, but braked sharply and brought his eyes back between the seats, back down to the Colt in Thomas's lap. "No shit?"

"You can ask The General if you don't believe me. It was taken off a Yankee officer, and the guy who ended up with it just used it for a hammer."

The General's Army wasn't the only pistol Thomas had brought along. Before he got in the back seat, he had passed two gun belts holding Colt single actions—a .45 and a .22—through the window, along with a can of black powder, a ball-peen hammer, and a paper bag containing a small tin of percussion caps and a dozen lead balls The Colonel had picked up at Buster's. Pete brought an old pistol as well, a .41 Colt Thunderer that had been handed down through his family "by one of my dad's uncles, or somebody." It was the only revolver in their arsenal that was a double action: the hammer could be cocked manually, with the shooter's thumb, or by simply taking a long pull on the trigger. Pete's other contributions included a box of .22 shells and a thick scroll of target resting on the shelf behind the back seat.

There were only two cars at the police pistol range when they arrived, and neither was a black Oldsmobile, meaning the range master had the day off. Pete pulled under one of the large live oaks shading the gravel parking lot, and as the boys climbed out, a sporadic popping of gunfire could be heard just beyond the west wall. They gathered their guns and gear, and Thomas led the way through an opening in the low wall that bordered the length of the firing line.

There were fourteen firing positions under the narrow pine roof running the length of the firing line, and downrange from each were two metal target racks. The first was mounted behind a berm at twenty-five yards, the second against the base of the broad, steep hill that encompassed the entire northern edge of the property fifty yards from the firing line. The first two shooting stands were in use, so Thomas headed for the far end and for no discernible reason stopped at the eleventh firing lane and set the Army, the can of black powder, and the paper bag atop the shooting stand.

"Don't put all that shit there, Kessler," Pete said. "Let's stack everything over here on the wall so it won't get in the way. Besides, let's not shoot The General's gun first. You know, save the best for last."

Thomas retrieved his load from the shooting stand and placed it on the wall. "Okay, Bennett, here's how we're gonna do this.

Since you've never shot a pistol before, why don't you just watch me and Pete for a while? Then we'll give you some pointers and you can give it a try. Okay?"

Bennett backed up to the wall, placed his palms on the edge, and hopped up, facing downrange. "Boy-oh-boy, I can hardly wait for the show to begin. I got five bucks for the first guy to shoot himself in the foot."

Following range procedure, Pete and Thomas held behind the firing line until the two shooters at the opposite end signaled a cessation of fire with a laying down of arms and a wave of the hand. As the two men walked out to check their targets, Thomas strode out to the twenty-five yard berm and tacked a paper target onto the riddled sheet of plywood held in a metal frame.

As he stepped back into the shade of the long, low roof, Pete was turning the .45 over in his hands. "Let me give your old Peacemaker a try, Kessler. The only time I've ever shot it was at beer cans in the caliche pit."

"Yeah, what a waste of ammo that was. Go ahead, but every time you miss the target, you owe me a quarter."

Pete picked up the gun belt holding the Peacemaker and walked over to the shooting stand. He pulled the pistol out of the holster, coaxed five rounds out of the loops on the gun belt with his thumb, then loaded up. Using the shooting stand for a rest, he squeezed off each shot with slow deliberation, then waited for the thick cloud of white smoke to clear before bringing the barrel of the Peacemaker back down to level for the next shot.

"That's one thing about a .45," Thomas said, "the damn holes are so big you don't need binoculars. You got 'em all in the circles, Pete, and you can thank me for that, you cheap sonofabitch."

There was a break in the shooting at the other end of the range just as Pete finished the second five rounds, and Thomas walked out and tacked a new target onto the plywood. He handed Pete the perforated sheet of paper upon returning. "Not bad. You just shot up about fifty cents worth of powder and lead, and nine holes means you only owe me a quarter. Try it without your glasses next time."

Now it was Thomas's turn. He pushed the remaining .45 rounds out of the belt loops and fired five shots from a rest, then five more offhand, managing to keep all ten holes within the concentric circles. While Pete walked out to switch targets, Thomas stepped back to the wall and swapped gun belts.

"Damn! That thing sure makes a lot of noise," Bennett said. His palms had stayed on the wall only until Pete had fired the first shot. After that, they covered his ears. "It's a miracle y'all aren't deaf. And that smoke stinks like shit."

"Your ears ring for a while, but you get used to it. Store-bought rounds are a lot tamer and don't smell, but loading my own with cheap black powder is the only way I can afford to shoot it. A box from Buster's would cost me two weeks' allowance, and I can shoot my .22 for a year on that. I hope you don't mind that I didn't save any shots for you, what with you sitting back here with your eyes shut and your hands over your ears and all."

Thomas picked up the gun belt holding his Colt Frontier Scout and the box of .22 shells Pete had brought along and returned to the shooting stand. As soon as Pete was back behind the firing line, Thomas drew the pistol and fed in five rounds from the belt, then waited for the two shooters at the opposite end of the range to indicate they were clear.

Pete went first again, firing ten rounds from a rest and ten more offhand; then targets were swapped, and Thomas did the same. The report of the smaller pistol was no more disruptive than the pop of a small firecracker, and Bennett's palms were once again resting along the rough edge of the limestone wall.

Thomas's last volley depleted the store of rounds in the gun belt. "What now, Pete?" Thomas asked. "You wanna keep going with your ammo, or you wanna shoot your .41?"

"Hell, I don't know. I don't see much point in having to clean it tonight for just ten shots, which is all the ammo I've got. And shells for that thing cost a frigging fortune. You know how cheap I am, Kessler. Why don't we just go ahead and shoot The General's gun?"

"Harr-umph!"

Thomas and Pete looked back at Bennett.

"I'm not interested in shooting any cannons, but that last one looked like fun. Don't tell me you used up all those bullets, too."

"Sorry, city boy," Pete said. "I guess I'm so used to hearing you run your mouth, it was like you weren't even here. We got a whole box left. Come on."

Bennett walked over and reached for the pistol in Thomas's hand, but Thomas pulled it away. "Hold on there. Not so fast.

You're on a pistol range now, and there are rules you gotta follow. First, keep the muzzle pointed downrange or at the ground at all times; second, don't fire until you've got the all-clear from not just us, but those other shooters down there too."

"And third," Pete volunteered, "after you're through, set the gun on the stand and wait for the all-clear before going out to check your target. And make sure there are no live rounds left in the cylinder. No loaded guns allowed if anybody is downrange."

"Now watch." Thomas pulled the hammer back to full cock and lowered it back down. "Both my Colts and The General's Army are single-actions. You gotta pull the hammer back for each shot. Pete's .41 over there is a double-action, which means you can shoot it by thumbing the hammer back like I just did with this one, or you can shoot it by just pulling the trigger, but that's only for rapid fire at close range 'cause it's hard to hit anything like that. Now watch me load it, and you can do it next time."

Thomas pulled the hammer back to half-cock, flipped open the loading gate, and picked up a cartridge. "All these pistols fire six shots, but we only load 'em with five 'cause that way the hammer never sits on a live round. If you drop it, it won't go off."

Thomas fed five rounds into the cylinder, then closed the loading gate and lowered the hammer down onto the empty sixth chamber. As he held the loaded gun over the shooting stand, the muzzle pointed downrange, he motioned for Bennett to step forward and take it. "Just crank the hammer back, line up the sights just like on a rifle, and squeeze off your shot. You can use the stand for a rest or just shoot it offhand, with one or both hands."

Thomas took a seat beside Pete on the wall, and they watched Bennett take two shots from a rest, then straighten and fire the three remaining shots with a two-handed hold. After the last shot, he gently laid the Colt on the stand and looked back at Thomas. "This thing's fun to shoot. Do we wait for those other guys so we can check the target?"

"Naw, it could be a while before the other end quiets down. Go ahead and keep shooting. Reload like I showed you. And remember—only five rounds."

"Okay, but how do you get the old ones out?"

Thomas dropped down from the wall, strode over to the shooting stand, and picked up the pistol. "I guess it would help if I showed you how to unload it, huh." He picked up the gun, brought the hammer back to half-cock, and flipped open the loading gate. "This thing mounted on the barrel is the ejector rod. Just knock the empties out like this"—Thomas turned the cylinder five clicks, manipulating the spring-loaded rod each time, and the five spent rounds clinked into the gravel at their feet—"then load back up and fire away."

After Bennett's third five-shot string, a mutual cessation of fire was signaled and all three boys walked out to check the target. Damn, not bad for the first time, and a city boy at that, said Pete. Bennett had managed to hit the target twelve times out of fifteen shots, and eight of those were within the concentric circles.

"Are you gonna shoot some more?" asked Thomas. "If so, I'll put up a new target. If not, then we'll just use this one for the Army. It'll be a miracle if we even hit it anyway."

"Naw, I'm through. Besides, I'm ready for a show. If you need me for anything, I'll be ducked down behind the wall."

The boys returned to the shade of the firing line, and Thomas retrieved The General's Army, the can of black powder, and the paper bag from atop the wall and returned them to the shooting stand. Pete and Bennett stood opposite each other, watching as Thomas picked up the ball-peen hammer and cradled the pistol in his left hand. After knocking out a small wedge, the barrel fell away from the frame and the cylinder slid into his palm.

"Why are you pulling it apart?" Pete asked. "I thought it was ready to shoot."

"It is, but the front of the cylinder on this thing is so beat up that you can't put enough force on a ball with the loading lever to push it into the chamber. Believe me, Dad and I tried. So I'm just gonna beat 'em all in with the hammer."

Thomas set the cylinder on the stand with the chambers facing up, then picked up the can of black powder, oblivious to the shaking heads of his companions. He unscrewed the cap and filled all six chambers to the brim, then fished six balls out of the paper bag and set one atop each chamber.

"Are you sure that's not too much powder?" Thomas might have expected a question like that from Bennett, but not from Pete. "I mean, I know if you're loading a black powder Colt, a standard load is to the brim, but why not just use half? You're just shooting at paper, not a grizzly."

Thomas picked up the ball-peen hammer and started tapping on the first ball. The force of the blows increased until it was fully seated in the cylinder, and his first blow to the second ball was devoid of restraint. "You're right. This is the standard load, and that's the load I'm using. Look, there's nothing wrong with this pistol. It's old and it's dented up, but it's just as tough as it was when that Yankee was blasting away with it. If you wanna shoot it after me, I'll load it just halfway up, if that's what you want."

"Naw. I think I'll pass."

"How come six?" Bennett asked. "Whadaya mean, how come six?"

"You're loading up all six holes. How come not five? You both said you only load five shots, not six."

"Look, Bennett, if I'm gonna have to go to this much trouble, I might as well just load 'em all. Let's just say I'm making an exception in this case— okay?" Thomas had tapped the balls into the chambers with the flat side of a ball-peen hammer and was now using the round end to seat them firmly on the packed powder. "*Man!* And I thought my old man was a pain in the ass."

By the time Thomas had reassembled the pistol and pulled the tin of percussion caps from the paper bag, he was conspicuously alone. Bennett was standing behind the wall, having dropped to his knees to be certain his blast shield was of sufficient height. Pete showed considerably more mettle and boldly seated himself atop the wall, albeit in a position that placed one of the heavy timbers supporting the canopy between himself and the end of Thomas's outstretched arm.

Thomas slipped percussion caps onto each of the six nipples at the back of the cylinder, rested the gun on the stand, and took a deep breath. He set the tip of his thumb on the hammer spur and slowly pulled it back, noting approvingly that the cylinder spun smoothly and locked securely in place with a sharp clack. Everything felt right. He brought his right arm up, and the Army balanced naturally, settling on the target with hardly a quiver. The Colonel's grips filled his sweating palms perfectly. The sights settled onto the target, and he began to squeeze.

Later, Thomas would recall nothing of what immediately followed—it was as if all his senses had shut down—and when consciousness returned he was standing dazed in a thick cloud of sulfurous gray smoke with a sharp pain running through his hand and wrist, a shrill, almost deafening ringing in his ears. He could still feel the heft of the Army in his aching hand, but it was reversed and behind him now, his right arm having been brought up and over his shoulder by the recoil. He brought his arm back and felt the pistol's weight shift in his hand. As he laid it on the shooting stand, something sharp pushed into his palm and the barrel seemed to sag.

He turned a dazed look to his left, to the first sound discernible from the ringing. It turned out to be gravel grinding under the feet of the two shooters from the opposite end of the firing line; they were moving expeditiously in his direction, and he watched them emerge from the thick cloud of smoke with mindless amusement, as if they were mantis-headed aliens.

"Tom, are you okay?"

Thomas felt a hand on his shoulder and turned around. It was Pete's. The ringing in his ears was abating, and other sounds were beginning to come through. He shook his right hand, then held it up and clenched his fist. Everything worked, and the pain was easing.

"Is everything all right here?"

The shooters from the other side of the range had arrived and were standing beside them. They were probably in their thirties and dressed in jeans and boots, with police badges clipped to their belts. The older-looking of the two had graying hair and spoke first, addressing Thomas: "You were the one shooting, weren't you? Are you okay?"

Thomas nodded. His mind was starting to clear. "Yeah, it was me. I'm all right. My hand kind of hurts though."

"Let me see you make a fist."

Thomas held his right hand out and clenched. It hurt, but everything worked.

"You're okay. It's probably just bruised."

The other man had reached over and picked up the Army and was turning it over in his hands. "Well, it looks like you loaded this thing full up. What kind of grease did you use to seal the chambers with?"

Thomas looked at Pete for help but only received a befuddled look in return. "I don't know anything about using grease. I just loaded it up like I do the shells for my .45. You know, pour the powder in and seat the lead on top."

The man lifted one corner of his mouth into a smile and shook his head. "Here's your problem. Whenever you shoot one of these old cap-and-ball Colts—especially one as beat up as this one is—you always have to seal the chambers with some sort of grease. It doesn't matter what kind—lard, petroleum jelly, axle grease, whatever. If you don't, the flash from the first shot will bleed into the rest of the cylinders, and this is what you get"—he held the Army barrel-up and pointed to the six empty chambers—"multiple detonation. You just shot off a three-pound elephant gun one-handed, son."

#

The Corvair pulled up to the curb at Bennett's house shortly after eleven in the morning. Bennett climbed out of the front seat and turned to close the door.

"Hey, Bennett!" Pete yelled, "don't forget about tonight. We're supposed to be over at Marty's about eight o'clock. Want me to pick you up?"

Bennett bent at the waist and brought his head level with the open window. "Shit, no. Marty's nothing but a fuckin' waste of time. I just said I'd go tonight 'cause I didn't want to put up with all his bullshit if I'd said otherwise. Anyway, I've got better things to do." Bennett peered into the back seat. "What about you, Tom? Are you going?"

Thomas was sitting with The General's Army once again laying on the cloth across his lap, and he continued to stare down at the pistol, saying nothing. The steel backstrap of the handle had snapped under the heavy recoil, and a ragged shard of steel now angled out from between The Colonel's walnut grips. The General had entrusted the gun to his care, and Thomas betrayed that trust. He wished he was dead.

"Okay, then. Well, I hope y'all have fun, but I wouldn't count on it.

Anyway, stay outta trouble. I'll try and do the same."

With that, Bennett turned and walked across the gravel drive. By the time he twisted the knob and pushed the front door open, the Corvair was passing Miz Grove's house, already halfway to the half-paved road.

#

Over the years, in endless revisions of this moment, Thomas would pull himself from the impenetrable, myopic gloom consuming him as he stared down at the broken Army in his lap. He would bring his head up and watch Bennett—his shirt color random, meaningless, but always in jeans and penny loafers—stride down the gravel drive to the front door stoop. As Pete drove away, Thomas would have himself look over his shoulder through the rear window. Sometimes he would have Bennett look to his left, to the departing Corvair, before stepping inside, and they would exchange waves; other times he would just watch Bennett pass through the door and vanish.

#

After Pete dropped him off, Thomas walked the length of the house to his room with the Army concealed in the cloth. His father had been in the den, lounging in his recliner and smoking a cigarette. Everything had gone fine, Thomas had said in passing, fearing the truth would eclipse his trip over to Marty's, although even that didn't seem to matter anymore.

But he needn't have worried. The next day, after Thomas's wrenching confession, The Colonel would be thankful—not mad—thankful that no one had been hurt, and guilt-ridden that his own ignorance had placed his son and others in peril. They took the Army down to Buster's that afternoon and waited while the backstrap was brazed, then returned it to The General with another scar, another story added to it. Thomas would even take it to the range one more time, joined by his father and a glob of Mister Hansborough's axle grease.

But Thomas Kessler would never see Bennett Caldwell again.

EPILOGUE

Thomas drew his eyes out of the mirror and onto the Coors clock. Four forty-five, real time, and the reflection of the brunette seated to his left was edging toward a six, so he had to be careful. Since his divorce was finalized almost a year ago, he tended to be overly generous, and if she were to glance at him through the mirror, even fleetingly, his objectivity might collapse.

Surely Pete wouldn't be much longer.

Behind him, the gray wall of shifting smoke soaking up the glow of the fluorescent lighting running along the top of the mirror had thickened as the bar filled, and scattered tips of cigarettes danced in tight, erratic circles like tethered fireflies.

Thomas had intended to spend a free hour or two touring their old stomping grounds, but subsequently scrapped the idea after Pete delivered a depressing update over a lunch of barbecued ribs after the funeral. Thomas had known that Kensington Oaks and Granite Heights were annexed by the City of Fuller not long after he packed the family off to pursue his airline job, but never stopped to consider the cultural impact, the utter transformation of his hallowed hills into high-end suburbs with wide streets, curbs and gutters, subterranean utility lines, and some of the steepest tax rates in Barrett County. Pete spoke of lawn sprinklers that ran constantly, allowing the indigenous forest of rangy elms and live oaks, stunted by years of competing with cedar and juniper in the harsh environment, to bloom into a luxuriant and meticulously pruned canopy. The meandering swaths of dense cedar brake where they once hunted rabbits and squirrels were now elegant landscapes framing spacious brick homes; the craggy arroyos that had bruised their shins and callused their hands had been lined with conduit, then filled and graded into oblivion.

Pete told of driving by the Kesslers' old house on James Place only because Thomas had inquired, and related his findings in the same voice he had used when phoning with the news of The General's passing. The Colonel's flagpole was gone, and a latticed redwood deck stood at the end of the drive where the Alamo used to be. "What's the point in having a hot tub in Texas, anyway?" he had said, consolingly.

#

Pete's father had been a salesman, in practice and temperament, but more than a few lawyers had sprung from every generation of Barrett County Campbells, and Pete had gone that route as well, planting his deep Fuller roots in the county attorney's office straight out of law school, where a flare for contentious courtroom litigation lent his career buoyancy and notoriety. Eventually, his roots would steer his curiosity as well, sending him down the creaking staircase that led to the dusty archives in the old courthouse in pursuit of cases long gone cold. It was a passion that would grow to consume his leisure time until his bachelorhood was deemed unassailable.

Pete's side of the conversation during their occasional phone calls was invariably fixated on his work, but as the years passed, his enthusiastic discussions of criminal investigations gave way to rants about unnecessarily heavy workloads and administrative incompetence, so Thomas registered little surprise at the funeral when Pete informed him that he would be running for district attorney in the next election cycle.

Thomas felt Pete's odds were good. He had built a reputation as an able prosecutor, having spent the last fifteen years strutting the oak floors of the Barrett County courthouse like a banty rooster in archaic broadcloth with a frontier style, twirling a watch fob while firing off questions in a sharp staccato. He was already raising campaign money, he had said, then in the same sentence:

". . . and you won't find it on a campaign poster, but one of the main reasons I'm running is I'm sick and tired of these damn depositions taking up so much of my time. As DA, I can just tell some other poor bastard to do it."

Thomas again registered no surprise—indeed, he had almost expected it—when Pete said one of the first things he would do if elected was assign a task force to go back and take another look at what happened along Riverside Drive in 1963, before The Drop-off had been bulldozed and sold off like every patch of raw acreage south of the Nebraska. It would probably never come to pass—nothing was left over from those days but the balmy air wafting up from the southern bank of the Nebraska River— but if something new in the Riverside Drive murders did point toward the river, he'd have to go to court and get a goddamned warrant, since The Drop-off was now just the abrupt terminus of some rich bastard's backyard.

#

For Thomas, the case began about twenty-four hours after Pete and Bennett pulled into the driveway for their trip to the range with The General's Army. Once again, it was Lowry's dogs that woke him, but this time the reason for their barking was evident—no less than six patrol cars of various hues and liveries were parked in the Lowry driveway or along the road in front of the property, and none of them was Lowry's. A large crowd, comprised primarily of James Place residents, was milling in the heart of the cul-de-sac, his parents included, their heads held close in intimate chatter.

Within an hour, the police presence had diminished to one custodial vehicle, and the residents quietly dispersed, knowing no more than when they had gathered. No one had been approached and questioned, his parents told Thomas; Mrs. Lowry was seen being escorted in tears to an unmarked car and spirited away, and that was all.

It was the lead story that night on the six o'clock news. At approximately fifteen minutes after midnight, a nurse who lived on Ridgewest Drive was on her way to her job on the night shift at Fuller General when she came across a scene involving a patrol car parked against traffic along the northern shoulder of the undeveloped western end of Riverside Drive. Two members of the Granite Heights Police Department (Thomas knew this had to be Lowry and Upshaw, since they were the Granite Heights Police Department) were found in the car, dead of gunshot wounds. There had been no arrests, and no further information was available. The victims' names were being withheld pending notification of next of kin.

Days passed, and no information was forthcoming. After the funerals, several neighbors dropped by the Lowry house with gift baskets and flowers, but civility preempted any mention of the investigation, and in each case, Mrs. Lowry merely voiced her gratitude and sealed the door without further comment. In the weeks that followed, little emerged beyond victim identification, and Mrs. Lowry could once again be seen in the front yard tending her flower beds. By the time cold weather set in, the case had faded from the media and left the public consciousness.

Pete was still in law school the first time he dug into the Riverside Drive murders file. The case had been assigned to the Texas Rangers due to legal irregularities—the victims were peace officers operating outside their jurisdiction—and although professional and thorough, their report offered little beyond a ruling of homicide, and the case quickly went cold for lack of new evidence. Pete had shared what he knew from the file with Thomas at the time, and subsequent telephone conversations almost always included some discussion of the case.

The Rangers' report began with one of the few indisputable conclusions drawn: Mike Lowry and Lewis Upshaw had no business masquerading as peace officers and were primary contributors to their own demise. Neither had a record of previous law enforcement experience or accredited training, and their *pro bono* employment by a mayoral authority granted them the approximate legitimacy of a deputized posse. Furthermore, unlike other cases involving peace officers, there was no record of radio contact on the night in question due to the simple fact that their car had no radio. The *de facto* police chief, the mayor of Granite Heights and uncle to one of the slain officers, claimed to have demurred on this expenditure due to the fact that the two men constituted the entire force and usually patrolled in a single vehicle, so there would have been no one else to call.

Lowry and Upshaw had apparently attempted to detain someone in the City of Fuller, a half-mile from their legal jurisdiction. The time of the crime had to be approximated. The stop had taken place on the undeveloped west end of Riverside Drive, well away from any existing structures. A canvassing of the nearest houses proved fruitless, but a local resident had contacted authorities after seeing news reports and volunteered that he had driven by the location cited at about ten forty-five that night, and the road was clear, a time which didn't contradict blood clot analysis.

Mike Lowry's Plymouth was found parked against traffic on the shoulder of the north side of the road, about ten feet from the entrance of a path feeding into the cedar brake that led to a bluff overlooking the Nebraska River. The engine was idling, the headlights on, and the flashing dome light on the roof was deployed. Lowry's body was found in a sitting position in the driver's seat, his back against the closed door, his Stetson dislodged by the force of a bullet that entered his right eye. His hat was wedged upside down between his head and the window frame, slowly filling with blood from the exit wound in the back of his head. The bullet was found buried just under the bark of a juniper tree sixteen feet to the left and slightly uphill from the body.

The rear passenger's side door was fully open and still holding at the stops, in spite of the uphill position of the vehicle. Lewis Upshaw's body was lying face up on the rear seat, his legs bent at the knees and his feet flat on the ground. He had been shot once through the chest at point-blank range—the hole in his shirt and the hair around the point of entry had been singed by the muzzle blast. The weapon, a .38 Smith and Wesson service revolver, was found on the pavement beside the right front tire with two rounds fired out of five. Ballistics matched the pistol to the bullet taken from under the skin in Lewis Upshaw's back and the one dug out of the juniper tree, and fingerprints and wear marks matched the pistol to his empty holster. The geometry of the ballistic evidence suggested both shots were fired from just outside the right rear door.

Other physical evidence was minimal. Given the nature of the wounds and the ownership of the weapon, murder-suicide had to be ruled out first, and it was quickly determined that in no way could the pistol have been placed outside the car and on the ground eight feet up the hill by either victim. The black patent leather shoes both men wore were coated with caliche dust, indicating they had probably mounted the trail leading through the woods to the bluff, but this remained speculative since the path was too coarse and impacted to yield reliable footprints. A thorough scouring of the heavily wooded area surrounding the trail yielded nothing beyond beer cans and cigarette packs in varying states of decomposition, evincing only a high degree of popularity among the local teenagers.

In the end, the report was only able to draw broad conclusions. Due to the activated dome light, it was assumed that the deceased ("deceased" and "victims" had replaced "officers" midway through the report) had made a stop of one or more individuals suspected of an unknown violation; the suspect(s) may have been on foot, although given the remote location and time of day, it could be presumed that at least one other vehicle was involved; the deceased had, in all likelihood, accessed the caliche path leading to the bluff along the southern bank of the Nebraska River prior to their deaths, but the purpose of said action could not be determined, although pursuit was ranked highest in probability, closely followed by a need to urinate, since several empty coffee cups were found in the car; the murders had occurred adjacent to the victims' patrol unit, indicating that at least one individual was being questioned or readied for detention; finally, the deceased did not consider themselves threatened, as no handcuffs were deployed.

Pete had solicited dozens of off-the-record evaluations from veteran criminologists and investigators, and their carefully crafted scenarios bore haunting similarities. It was generally agreed that only one individual had been involved, a person who would have committed an infraction in Granite Heights. Since there had been no complaints or subsequent reports of disturbances or suspicious activity in that area, it could be assumed that the infraction was isolated and minor. The deceased had pursued the perpetrator into the City of Fuller and made an illegal stop, a fact that assisted further inquiry by negating any doubt as to a lack of competence. Some evaluations favored the hypothesis that the dust on the shoes of the victims indicated pursuit; others didn't, but none gave it a high priority. The foregoing of physical restraint suggested the person apprehended was not considered a flight risk, was of non-threatening stature—possibly a juvenile or a female—and displayed no signs of aggression or resistance. The person could also have been injured, disabled, or distraught, although there was no physical evidence to suggest that an injury or accident had occurred. Mike Lowry had gotten into the car first; then Lewis Upshaw would have opened the rear door on the opposite side to seat their detainee. Here, everyone agreed, is where it got deadly.

There were approximately a dozen bloodied periodicals, mostly gun magazines, fanned out like a hand of cards under the body of Lewis Upshaw, and the opinion was universal that these had been stacked on the rear seat and the dead man had turned his back on his charge to clear the obstruction. It would have been then that the perpetrator would have pulled the service revolver from the holster, pushing the victim into the back seat as he did so. A few believed Lowry would have been shot first because he would have been the only one of the two still armed, but that theory was generally discounted on the grounds that such an act would have required premeditation, which was not supported by the evidence. Maybe Lowry was alive when his partner turned and rose from the back seat to take his bullet; maybe not. Either way, his hand never reached his gun. The murderer then would have walked to his vehicle parked farther up the hill, dropping the gun as he went, and driven away. In the end, every evaluation reached the same conclusion—without new evidence or the emergence of a reliable witness, the case was not solvable.

And then something new came up—due primarily to Pete's persistence— and he thought there was a sufficient cause to bring the case out of the shadows. On the eighteenth anniversary of the Riverside Drive murders, a chronic itch had sent Pete back to have another look at the evidence, and he decided on a long shot. Fingerprint techniques had improved; he would take the pistol out of the evidence locker and have it dusted one more time. Initially, the higher-ups were dubious, and he was preparing to cover the costs out of his own pocket when his request was finally approved. The first time the Smith and Wesson was printed, the investigators had failed to dust the hammer, and this was where it was found—a partial thumbprint in the curve of the spur, the shallow valley just forward of the knurled tip. Not that it was an excuse, but Pete could see how it could have been overlooked and why prosecutors would have ignored it. The pistol was a double-action revolver fired at close range under dire circumstances. Why would anyone have taken the time to crank the hammer back?

#

Thomas had planned his day on his predawn flight down. Rent a car, attend the funeral, then a quick lunch with Pete before an afternoon spent revisiting a slice of his past. But not this way, not by sitting in a bar and staring into a mirror, soaking up beer. He had planned for the drive on Arroyo Blanco to take him past the scooter shop, through Live Oak Park, then a right onto Kensington Road, *where he would instinctively scan the gravel parking lot for the range master's Buick as he passed the pistol range. Down Kensington Road, through Kensington Oaks to the eastern edge of Granite Heights, for a circle of the cul-de-sac at James Place to see what color roses festooned the Alamo. Then back down the cul-de-sac, passing Lowry's house on the way, listening for his dogs, then a right on Ridgewest, back onto Kensington Road, and west another half-mile to the base of Crest, to feel his back press into the seat like it did that hot August night twenty-three years ago, as Pete's Corvair labored up the steep grade with Marty sitting shotgun and Thomas staring morosely at the back of his head, still feeling the weight of the broken Army, as if it had never left his lap . . .*

#

Thomas smiled. He hadn't been expecting much from Marty that night— Bennett had seen to that. But Bennett had been wrong. Joyously, incomprehensibly wrong. At the top of the hill, Marty had steered Pete onto the first driveway on the right, a steeply descending strip of asphalt weaving through thick live oaks to the vague outline of a limestone structure buried in shadows toward the back of the property. At the bottom of the hill, they left the Corvair, and Marty led them into the carport of the sprawling single- story ranch-style house, to a door lit by a softly glowing curtain. When he knocked, the door opened almost immediately.

They were three sisters newly arrived in the neighborhood, the daughters of a widower whose work took him out of town for days at a time and who assumed that his charges, all in their teens, had proven their maturity by demonstrating an ability to feed and dress themselves. Their forced isolation and anonymity proved useless against Marty's carnal instincts, and he was discovered kneeling outside the bedroom window of the oldest sister by the youngest, on his third nightly foray to the bottom of the hill. "Would you like to come in?" they had said, in unison.

It was the youngest, Cherie, who drew Thomas's attention when he stepped past the two girls at the door. She was standing next to the refrigerator on the far side of the kitchen in cropped jeans and a T-shirt, looking down at the glistening red polish on her extended right foot. Their eyes met when her soft smile emerged from the shroud of long blonde curls, and The General's Army ceased to exist.

That evening was no less like a dream then than it would be in recollections that seemed to become more fragmented and banal as the years passed. *A can of beer being passed around; Pete knocking an ashtray on the floor; Marty and the oldest sister making a rollicking departure to the rear of the house shortly after their arrival; Pete's clumsy pursuit of the remaining sister.* The only memory to survive truly intact would be the immeasurable ecstasy of Cherie gently taking his hand and leading him to the sofa, where she would curl up beside him and put her head on his shoulder. He could still feel the fingertips of her free hand softly running along his arm, still hear her giggling at his mindless responses to her whispers. Conversely, Pete's advances were met with condescension and forced smiles, and he eventually retreated to a recliner to bear the frustration of having to watch his quarry sit on the carpet in front of the TV set, painting her toenails in the glow of The Twilight Zone.

After two hours, Thomas could take no more, and he rose from the sofa with a startled and stumbling Cherie in tow. He pulled her through the kitchen and out the door into the moonless night, and they were halfway up the dark driveway, toward equally dark Crest Road, before she found her balance.

#

The phone had rung not long after the crowd in the cul-de-sac dispersed, and Thomas's mother called from the kitchen, saying Pete was on the line. He picked up the phone in his room and immediately launched into a description of the unfolding drama taking place on the block, but Pete would have none of it ("Probably no big deal. Just a break-in or something.") The only thing Pete wanted to talk about was what happened the night before, after Thomas and Cherie walked out of the house and disappeared up the driveway.

Thomas had told Pete to hold, then laid the phone down and walked through the house to the kitchen. After affirming that the wall phone was securely cradled and his mother was back at the sink, washing dishes, he grabbed an ostensible apple and returned to his room, sealing the door behind him. Then, in the spirit of crass braggadocio endemic in teenage boys, he picked up the phone and launched into a contrived cliché of lucid debauchery that held no semblance to what had actually occurred the night before, when he and Cherie had stumbled hand in hand, drunk with anticipation, down the dark empty road flanked by houses hushed and somnolent except for the occasional flicker of a television screen behind plate glass. Cherie's head was still on Thomas's shoulder when the dim yellow stain of The General's porch light briefly put them in shadow as he led her across the front lawn, past the old house and the old guns with their sleeping stories, past the carport, and into the shifting darkness of the overgrown trail that led to the north end of the property. Halfway down the path, the sparkling lights of Fuller emerged from beyond the silhouette of the old cedar rails, and they began to run.

At The Overlook, their bodies clenched, and nothing existed but him and Cherie and a boundless, inelegant passion that left them standing naked, their clothes laying first at their feet, then spread hastily across the wooden bench as Cherie pulled Thomas down onto her, and only by some inchoate tendril anchoring reality was he able to stifle his ecstasy, his raging testimony to his first utter deliverance from the inscrutable torment that had come to haunt his idle hours since his voice began to deepen.

A moment of gleeful exhaustion, and then a soft giggle returned him to the sweat and dust of the world as he knew it. He lifted his head from her shoulder and looked down at her soft, moonlit smile. "Mind if I have a cigarette?" was all he could think of to say.

"I was afraid you were going to say that," she had replied, and he still remembered the tone of her voice leaving him feeling selfish. "Go ahead. I'll just lay here and look at the stars," she had said. He kissed her and rose. His jeans were draped over the bench, and he fumbled through the pockets for his Kents and matches. He felt no urge, nor need, to get dressed. He stepped over to the worn railing under the starry sky and popped a match.

It came to him first as engine noise through the thick trees behind him, from the far end of the road they had just walked. Not the roar of Pete's loud pipes but familiar nonetheless, a mellow clatter that rose and fell with the gear changes. A Volkswagen.

Thomas shook the match out, leaving the Kent in his lips unlit. He would strike another after the car rounded the corner and left the pavement of Crest for the dust of Casey Lane. It was almost twenty feet down to the road, and the lights would only sweep the woods on the opposite side as the car negotiated the curve, but he took a precautionary step away from the railing anyway. A tremulous pool of light began to flare in the cedar brake across the road to his left, then moved in an accelerating sweep to the right as the clattering motor crescendoed and the car left pavement and the pop and crunch of gravel began. When the lights straightened out onto Casey Lane and the woods opposite fell back into night, Thomas stepped back up to the railing. He could now see the car was white, with two stripes of barely discernible red running its length, and as it flew past beneath him, the glow of dashboard lights through an open window presented a fleeting image of hands, of fingers, some dark, some fair, entwined and resting in a cleft of floral cotton. A few minutes later, he would feel a soft hand on his shoulder and would be taken aback by the clothes Cherie held out to him, having forgotten he was naked.

#

Pete's reaction had been predictable—a short rant of envy followed by sullen silence—and Thomas terminated the call with the lie that his father was calling him out to work on the Ford. He had sat on the edge of his bed, the phone cradled in his lap, and watched the detached, slowly shifting scene across the street, figures and faces and vehicle liveries incoherent through the matte of the screen. A solitary, silent hour later, he would rise and place the phone back on his desk, then gather his clothes for the day.

And now he was back in real time, and it was fifteen till five in bar time and still no Pete. The last flight to Chicago was leaving in two hours, and the prospect of getting stuck in Fuller overnight made crappy airline food for dinner seem appealing.

He felt like getting drunk.

The jukebox was blaring out *"Once a Day,"* one of his old favorites. Connie Smith. At least in this seedy dive, the music was still the same. And the beer as well, although in name only. Lone Star just seemed to taste better when you could only get it in Texas.

Ever since he left Fuller for the cities up north, it seemed like life was not really living, but merely enduring—enduring the traffic and the snowstorms, enduring the short summers, enduring the hard, dense structures and shuffling crowds that gave up no secrets, told no tales. But then, in a sense, it was Barrett County that held the blame, not New York or Chicago. The feral hills had somehow traveled with him in vivid, meandering abstraction, and almost nightly they were the stage of his dreams—surreal episodes colonized by the dead and living with no regard to chronology, where the past hung in the air like caliche dust swirling over a half-paved road, to be breathed in and cast back out thousands of times, in a thousand different voices. Things were beginning to change, though. This year and for the first time, beginning with the warmer weather of May, he was actually starting to like Chicago. Post-divorce, his only major expenses were rent and child support, and after two years of adjusting to single life and part-time parenthood, he decided it was solitude that mattered most and didn't mind paying the steep price for a condo on the Gold Coast overlooking Lake Michigan to achieve it. He was hesitant at first—he would miss his backyard garden, the therapeutic downtime of the train rides back and forth to work, and he knew living in the city was expensive—but he had grown comfortable with his decision, and even the extra cost of living on one of the highest floors, away from the traffic noise and gawking pedestrians, was worth it.

He had spent that first winter on the lake in virtual hibernation, plodding between his office and his condo, an isolation that took him beyond the hills, back to the house of massive granite blocks under a steep tile roof on Cheruskerweg. He had even considered taking a few days off in the fall to go back to Germany. He could fly into Frankfurt and rent a car, then drive over to Wiesbaden and see if the traffic island was still filled with tow- headed boys, their knees set in the dust, shooting marbles. But not now. His return to Fuller had shattered any illusions about revisiting that or any other part of his past, whether it be fleeing cobblestone streets for a sanctuary wedged high in the branches of a green apple tree or sailing flat rocks out over the dull green water of the Nebraska River.

Anyway, he had another sanctuary now, isolated from his work and his neighbors and the grind of civilization on the street. It was a place where he could sit with his eyes cast out to the top of the lake with his feet resting on the railing, nursing his thoughts and sipping a beer instead of spitting apple seeds into an oblivion beyond a pair of scuffed sneakers; a place where on summer nights, after the city's shadow darkened the water and filled in the void to the horizon, he would be taken back to those evenings when

Cherie would climb through her window and meet him in his blue Ford at the top of her driveway. They would drive down Crest Road, past The General's house, and take the steep, hard right onto the half-paved road, where the grinding gravel would discourage talk until they reached the four-way stop. Then a left turn, and the half-mile ride to Riverside Drive. There, they would leave the car on the shoulder, step over the defeated barbed wire, and walk arm in arm down the winding trail until the trees fell away and the lights of the town would be spread out in front of them as if from the far side of an immense field. It was as if you kept going, you could run all the way to Fuller. Or Griffintown, for that matter.

#

It all came together on a Saturday morning two weeks after the concurrent funerals of the murdered men. Thomas and The Colonel had pulled into Mister Hansborough's Gulf station and found the owner apoplectic. Cars were positioned for refueling at both pumps while others were lined up, waiting, and at least one driver could be seen drumming his fingers impatiently on the dashboard. The lifts in both bays held cars—one was missing front wheels; the other was bleeding a thin black stream into a bucket—and three men and a woman with two small children could be seen through the smudged plate glass window, seated and fanning themselves furiously with grease-stained magazines. Mister Hansborough had been forced to give Ira the day off to attend a funeral and left him alone to contend with a day that, according to Mister Hansborough, turned out to be "the busiest goddamn motherfuckin' day of the whole goddamn motherfuckin' year!" It took fifteen minutes for The Colonel's turn to come up, and Mister Hansborough spat out further incidentals as he squeegeed and pumped. Two weeks earlier, a young niece of Ira's over in Griffintown had gone missing, and Ira was so sick about it that he moped his way through his workdays with hardly a word said. She had told her parents she was taking the bus to east Fuller for a sleepover with friends—something she had done many times before—and was never heard from again. A week later, her body was pulled from the Nebraska River under the Mirabeau Bridge.

Autopsy reports were inconclusive but suggested severe general trauma, possibly from a fall. There was absolutely no evidence beyond the body and what little clothing remained, and suicide, homicide, and death by misadventure were all possibilities. The body had been found entangled in submerged tree branches along the south shore of the river where the currents were strongest, and the point of entry could have been anywhere between the bridge and the dam, two-and-a-half miles upstream to the west. No one believed she ever made it to east Fuller, but this too never moved beyond speculation, and it wasn't long before the case, like the Riverside Drive murders, lapsed into obscurity.

#

The General would be in the ground by now, buried with honors in the Texas State Cemetery in Austin. Thomas regretted not going, not joining the serpentine funeral procession weaving through the neighborhood after the service, threaded through the streets like a suture. He could have had a decent dinner at Scholz's, gotten a good night's sleep, and taken a nonstop back to Chicago the next day instead of having to connect through Dallas or Houston.

Brigadier General Patrick O'Grady would have had his honor guard, his three volleys of seven shots, but what of the tales that were buried with him, the fables he spun out of the old guns turning in his hands? It seemed unthinkable, but could it be that they weren't The General's stories anymore? Since The General was gone, were they Thomas Kessler's now?

No, they weren't, and they didn't belong to anybody else, either. It was so much more than a coffin lid that the hard Texas clods would have drummed down on after the sweating throng departed—it was the closing of the cover of a book that would never be read again. And how much of that book went unread? In his hundred years, to how many stories did The General assert his rights of ownership and leave untold?

Five-thirty, real time. Thomas stood and waved the bartender over. He would call Pete tonight with some bullshit apology and excuse. Sorry, man, I had to get back—you know, goddamn airline business. Pete would probably try to apologize too, for leaving him to sit in a sleazy bar for an entire afternoon, but Thomas wouldn't let him take the rap. It was Thomas, after all, who requested they meet, and he didn't even specify a reason.

There had been an urgency in Thomas when he walked into the bar, but not now, not after spending the afternoon sitting in what had been a scooter shop on the afternoon after the Riverside Drive murders, when he and Pete drove down Grady Way and found the Caldwell's house empty with a For Sale sign in the front yard. Miz Groves had been kneeling in her begonias four houses down, talkative as ever. "Ernestine stopped over bright and early to say goodbye, and she was just crushed," she had said. "She said Bennett decided he wanted to go live with his father, just like that." Bennett had taken the first bus out that morning, and Mrs. Caldwell and Tina began the move back across the river as soon as he left.

Pete had told Thomas of seeing the obituary for Bennett's mother in the newspaper several years ago, and he had gone to the funeral just to see if Bennett would show up. Only Tina was there, and all she said was she hadn't been in contact with Bennett for some time. Then she turned and walked away.

Thomas glanced at the brunette in the mirror one last time. Just an empty vessel, her head aswirl in smoke, her eyes lost in the refuge of the mirror.

He would see how Pete does in the election, see if he can win the muscle to have the case reopened. Besides, maybe Pete could solve it without knowing what happened after Thomas popped his second match as the Volkswagen passed beneath him and the taillights shifted out of the roiling dust just past Grady Way and onto the paved side, the wrong side, of the half-paved road. It stayed there all the way to the stop sign at the four-way intersection before skewing left onto Ridgewest Drive, toward the river.

The memory had a vibrancy that time would never diminish—first, the clattering of the Volkswagen and the glow of the lights flickering through the rooftops and treeline to the north, and then a metallic cranking and a menacing, familiar rumble; then, his pulse quickening as the intersection again flooded with light as Lowry's Plymouth lumbered through, sending a second, faster seam of light hurtling through the tops of the trees that had reflected the first. It had just acquired a pulsing red tint when he felt Cherie's hand on his shoulder.

A racing stripe. Contrasting fingers entwined under a breath of soft light. A shifting over to the paved side of a half-paved road. All circumstantial evidence at best, and even Pete's involvement wouldn't guarantee that they would ever learn what happened that night. But in those unguarded, naive moments between sleep and consciousness, another image began to appear, unprompted, in that same place in his mind where he would be back in Pete's Corvair, The General's Army in his lap, and watching Bennett disappear into the house on Grady Way. But now, Bennett is standing in the dry dust of The Drop-off trail and facing the river where the rage and pain of a fisherman once came back to them from the clapboard of old barracks across the Nebraska. But this tableau is framed in a deathly silence, and Thomas doesn't know if it's because he's incapable of imagining what Bennett must have heard that night, or is simply too terrified to visit it. Then he looks down and his feet are straddling the rusty barbed wire that once blocked a path that led to nowhere, a story left untold.

For five years that surreal image haunted Thomas, until the day he skipped morning classes at Texas College and sought out the autopsy in the county courthouse that suggested if Bennett had heard anything that night, it could well have been the imagined, fading whimper of the child he would never know.

Thomas paid and tipped the bartender, worked his way through the happy-hour crowd, stepped into the heat of the parking lot, and looked east, toward the intersection of Arroyo Blanco and Mirabeau.

The tableau on the southeast corner brought him back to the cruel present. On the approximate spot where an enigmatic giant once sat with an engine head cradled on his thighs, anonymous hands were passing grease- stained paper bags to hands reaching through the windows of one idling car after another. That was also where Ira had been sitting when Thomas offered awkward condolences a week after his niece's funeral. "Her name was Pearl," Ira had said, without emotion, before setting his eyes on the wall in the direction of the river. He quit his job at the Gulf station shortly after that, and Thomas never saw him again.

An old Mercury sedan with bad paint and a growling exhaust was backing away from a convenience store next to the bar and cut Thomas off as he was crossing the parking lot to his rental. Cigarette smoke and music poured from the open windows as the car arced into his path, and the sticker on the rear bumper—*My other car is a piece of shit too*—brought a smile to his face.

Then the Mercury halted, and Thomas found himself staring through the back seat window at a scrawny kid with a crumpled baseball cap engaged in raucous animation with his companions. Then he turned his head toward the window, and silence fell as their eyes met. Thomas nodded and offered a light smile, saying nothing, and the boy responded with a lifted hand, almost as an afterthought, before turning back to his friends, to his world of smoke and exuberant, wasted passions. Then the sound of gnashing gears, and the car jerked forward with a squeal and lurched out of the parking lot and onto Arroyo Blanco Road, toward Live Oak Park.

Thomas walked over to his rental, then crossed his forearms on the roof and squinted into the haze of the coming dusk. He would get in, start the engine, and make it back to the airport in time for his flight to Chicago, but not before watching the Mercury accelerate into the rush hour traffic, then break free and slowly dissolve into the sun-bathed hills along the Nebraska River.

www.ingramcontent.com/pod-product-compliance
Lightning Source LLC
Chambersburg PA
CBHW060349080526
44583CB00012B/240